modern firearms

Yves Cadiou
Alphonse Richard

modern
firearms

translated from the French by Simon Pleasance

WILLIAM MORROW AND COMPANY, INC.
New York

contents

Library of Congress Catalog Card Number 76-8787

ISBN 0-688-03073-4

introduction

Firearms have consistently intrigued even the most peace-loving, ever since man made his first appearance on our planet, combining as they do their impressive and (some would say) evil capacity to kill at long range with a simple mechanical beauty. As a result, long ago they were a luxury restricted to the privileged few. But human nature is so designed that men will profess a deep and even mystical respect for these gadgets which, at the same time, are capable of dealing death and conveying a sense of superiority and power, whether used at the range, for hunting, in war or for self-defence. The two of us are no exception to this rule, and we want to share our attachment and interest with our readers. This is why we set about the task of preparing this book; we have tried to include as much factual information as possible without embroiling ourselves in purely technical detail, which would be of interest to no more than a handful of enthusiasts and cognoscenti. Such details would only have the effect of putting off the layman.

We were at once faced with a particularly difficult problem: what period is covered by so-called contemporary firearms? Were we to limit ourselves merely to a discussion of firearms in current use? If that was the case this book would have turned into a vast catalogue of every specification and every piece of information about every type of firearm being manufactured at the present time. We were not happy to accept such a convenient solution and so we systematically turned our thoughts to other possibilities. By opening up the past a little we could discuss one or two classic models which paved the way for the modern firearm as we know it, though they no longer really influence modern production methods. It was in the discovery of 'smokeless' or 'pyroxiline' powder, which created such an upheaval in the gunsmith's trade, that we saw the perfect starting point.

The term 'firearm', in the proper meaning of the word, covers a very wide field: from the battleship and its armament to the smallest pistol that fits in your pocket, via the tank and the fighter. Here again we have had to define the categories of weapons to be dealt with.

It was not our intention to compile a 'Firearms Encyclopaedia': others have already done this most ably. Our aim was to popularize the subject, and so bring it into everybody's home. Encyclopaedias seldom manage this. As a result we have concentrated on portable arms, such as many of us, at some time in our lives, have handled, occasionally under the scrutiny of an instructor who is often so versed in the art that he can recite army textbooks backwards.

Some readers will perhaps criticize us for having omitted certain categories of weapons which are more often than not excluded from the limelight, such as the modern bazooka or the grenade, but we have tried to limit our frame of reference to its already considerable boundaries. In all probability the bazooka would have led us on into the realm of the recoilless gun and, while on that topic, the Strela rocket with its homing device: both weapons are compact and would thus comply with our portable, personal criterion.

We have tried to present the widest possible survey of the contemporary firearm. But we realize that wittingly or not we are guilty of several omissions, some more glaring than others. We apologize for any such oversight, but it was a virtually impossible task, with the few pages at our disposal, to find a place for the vast array of all firearms, most of which have been written about in specialist books, sometimes running into several volumes.

It is virtually certain that by the time this book is published some weapons will have already been replaced by other more modern ones. Like everything else, the firearm is not exempt from the process of constant development. This is the hallmark of our present-day society, where mechanical beauty is apparently doomed to be sacrificed in favour of the new god: 'productivity'. As model succeeds model, stamped and welded metal replaces forged and machined steel, and that noble material, wood, gives way to plastics . . . This does not mean that modern guns are any less effective than their forebears. But our thoughts cannot help being tinged with nostalgia when we gaze at those masterpieces created by gunsmiths during the Golden Days of the art, which are now to be seen only in museum show-cases, or even at the old revolver belonging to our forefathers.

Things these days seem to have got out of control, so the reader will be good enough to excuse us for not having followed this insane tempo of modern production. Our own ambition is on a smaller scale: we simply hope that with this book our readers will enjoy one of those short-lived moments of relaxation which are so hard to come by in this modern world.

Yves Cadiou and Alphonse Richard

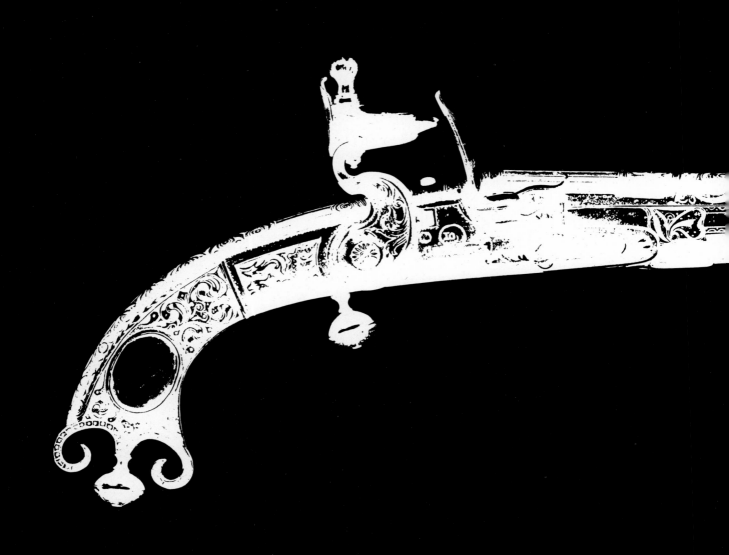

I
a brief
history

The first personal firearms often
came in strange shapes and sizes.
Vegezio, *De Re Militari* (1511).

Bygone ancestors

Gunpowder is a mixture of saltpetre, sulphur and charcoal in proportions which remained almost unchanged until the eighteenth century. One fine day, someone, somewhere, had the bright idea of using the force of the expanding gases produced by its combustion to propel a projectile. History has handed down no precise record of this someone. This is often the case when a discovery is closely allied with the use of the thing concerned rather than the thing itself. Before the year AD 1000 the Chinese seem to have known about the properties of the powder which they used for making fireworks. In 1249 the English philosopher Roger Bacon mentioned it in his work: *De Secretis Operibus Artis et Naturae.* And in the same period a description of it was given by Albertus Magnus of Cologne. The German monk, Schwartz – whose very existence is disputed by numerous historians – is thought by others to be its inventor in Europe.

We do know beyond any doubt that in 1278, at the siege of Trent by the people of Verona, the Count of Tyrol lent Verona devices for and specialists in 'hurling iron missiles and fire'. These devices, known as 'bombarda', originated in Italy. They made their debut in France in 1324, at the siege of La Réole, where Count Charles de Valois used them fast and furiously to force the besieged English to surrender. Although at the time no one could see as much, the appearance of these first firearms rang the irrevocable death-knell of all the other types of missile-slinging devices, whether manual or mechanical. It is fair to say that the introduction of the firearm marked one particular period in our history, just as the invention of the atomic bomb has marked another.

From its first appearance, use of the firearm assumed a dual function: technical and psychological, and the latter was by no means its least significant property, particularly to begin with. The first weapons, known as 'vase-guns' ('vases à feu') used arrows as projectiles. Between 1300 and 1350 these 'vase-guns' became more manageable and their use became widespread; arrows were replaced by stone bullets, and subsequently by similar bullets made of iron. But the art of foundry in those days limited output to small and rudimentary missiles. Their actual firepower did not outdo that of weapons like the crossbow, the ballista, the mangonel and other sorts of catapults. And yet these not very practical, rather unwieldy and virtually ineffectual weapons were used more and more: 'They are feared because of the intolerable noise they make,' in the words of a contemporary document. In addition the powder – one of whose ingredients was sulphur – smelt somewhat of witchcraft. The power to have mastery over lightning had for so long been thought of as a divine prerogative (popular imagery having for centuries included descriptions of fire-spitting monsters), that the noise, smoke and flames produced by these new weapons were for some time their most dreaded aspects.

But even in those early days the wielders of these devices were keen to have a more powerful, manageable and effective weapon. This initially took the form of siege artillery, intended to batter enemy fortifications rather than the men behind them. But in 1346 it was used in the open country at Crécy, where the English, who had had ample time to appreciate its effectiveness – to their detriment twenty-two years earlier – surprised their French foe, who had demonstrated the new weapon on the previous occasion, but now found themselves on the receiving end.

Artillery pieces in those days were made of iron staves assembled to form cylinders and reinforced by bands and straps; between 1350 and 1450 the inadequate size of blast furnaces and their low thermic output did not allow casting or melting techniques to be practised. Canons often exploded; but little by little people learnt how to gauge the charges, and improve the quality, consistency and stability of the powder.

Almost as soon as it came on the market, studies were embarked upon with a view to making the new weapon a 'personal' one. In fact, with this new device, physical strength and luck were no longer the decisive factors they once were: until that moment a strong warrior who could cope with a costly suit of armour was more or less invulnerable. The first portable guns, which appeared in 1370, tolled the knell of the feudal lords. But things advanced at a snail's pace. First, new techniques had to be perfected and the reservations of the warmongers had to be overcome; for the new weapon, too heavy for hunting, would, first and foremost, be a weapon of war.

However, it was not so very long before weapons started to appear which, though not increasing the real effectiveness of such guns, did nevertheless contain the seeds of what was to come: in some light cast iron guns dating to about 1450, the powder chamber and the barrel, were screwed together before firing, were made separately: this was in effect the first breech-loading system; several guns were likewise attached to the same mounting, and this was the original machine-gun. From 1450 onwards iron was replaced by bronze, which was more malleable and easier to cast. This advance meant it was now possible to manufacture less primitive guns with a constant thickness and a uniform texture. It is worth mentioning that from 1380 onwards it was the custom, especially in Germany, to test weapons with larger than normal charges.

But let us now leave artillery on one side. The artillery piece developed in its own way on the basis of the criterion fundamental to its purpose: its power; all its other features – weight, handling, precision and structural strength – were secondary to this criterion. The portable weapon really made an appearance from 1450. To start with it was a smaller version of the first guns. Here the compromise between weight and wieldiness (weight having now become an element in the handling ability of the weapon) gave rise to two sorts of firearms which were destined to co-exist right up to the present day: the long arm and the handgun, the former more powerful, and the latter easier to handle. But the handgun was not to make its real appearance until the technical development of the long arm had paved the way for it sufficiently.

The matchlock

In about 1420, when it appeared, the personal gun was still no more than a small cannon, usually mounted on a staff, and fired by taking this staff in both arms; the barrel rested on a fork driven into the ground. The user was in imminent danger of getting burnt when he ignited the powder with a burning coal which was placed on the open priming-hole on top of the barrel. An early improvement consisted in placing the priming-hole on the right hand side of the barrel and putting a small pan beneath its outlet, so that it would hold a small amount of powder which would make it easier to fire. Later the burning coal was replaced by a match which was fixed to an S, provided at its central point with an axis fixed to the apposite part of the stock, enabling the gunner to ignite the powder in the pan by tipping the S on its axis.

A practical gun had been born. In about 1480 the S was mounted as a serpentine on a lock equipped with a spring and a trigger. All the basic elements of the firearm as we know it today were already there: a barrel, a butt and a lock. Of course there were countless variations as far as the names of these guns were concerned: harquebus, petronel and culverin all had different calibres, weights and shapes, but were basically similar.

From this time on they played an important part on the battlefield, although their use was not without its problems: the most serious was the very long time needed to get them operating. For all this, however, in 1494–5 Charles VIII used 400 harquebusiers in his Italian campaign; these gunners terrified the Italians with their firepower and mobility. Spain, too, developed the use of firearms, and Spanish harquebusiers played a major role in the conquest of the West Indies. In 1492 Christopher Columbus's three caravels carried several dozen pieces of artillery of varying shapes and sizes. Military tactics were now steadily progressing and in battle the army was made up of a framework or core of halbardiers and lansquenets in square formations, around which marched the harquebusiers. In 1515, at the battle of Marignan, François I put 6000 harquebusiers in the field. And, as a passing note, Bayard had all captured harquebusiers hanged: he considered the weapons of these 'beggars' to be unfair.

The wheel-lock and the lead bullet

In about 1550 gunpowder underwent a considerable advance by being produced in granular form, which was how it remained until it was replaced by new types of explosive in the nineteenth century. At the same time the use of lead for bullets permanently replaced other materials, such as stone, iron, copper, bronze and so on. During this period Leonardo da Vinci was showing considerable interest in the new weapon, and offered a partial definition of the basic laws of ballistics. In other respects weaponry was the object of aesthetic concern: heir to the engravers who embellished swords during the Middle Ages, the new breed of gunsmith started to engrave and decorate firearms; some of these firearms which were made for important figures achieved nothing less than artistic perfection.

In the subsequent period, from the sixteenth to the eighteenth century, the gunsmith's art knew its heyday, and firearm decoration, all done entirely by hand, was never to be equalled. With the spread of the wheel-lock the handgun made its appearance. Probably invented by a northern Italian gunsmith, it is dealt with by Leonardo da Vinci in his *Codex Atlanticus*. Firing was no longer

achieved by igniting the powder with a lighted match, but by the sparks obtained by milling a firestone against a serrated wheel. Its construction was complex, but it was relatively simple to use. This lock made it possible to produce a smaller harquebus: and the pistol was born. The name of this weapon derives, according to the various authors, either from the town of Pistoia in Italy, or from the Czech word 'pichtal', or from the French 'pistole'.

The new possibilities created by a small weapon which could be operated with just one hand, and was always ready to fire, was a source of worry to the authorities (the problem is not a new one): in 1517 the Emperor Maximilian I prohibited the manufacture of wheel-locks. But this did not prevent the firearm – wheel-lock harquebuses for the foot-soldier, and pistols for the cavalry – from replacing pikes and bows as the standard armament of fighting forces. At the end of the sixteenth century the increase in portable firearms became a turning-point. Foot soldiers adopted a more flexible battle array and abandoned their closed ranks, initiating the line formation which foreshadowed the extended order for infantry. With the firearm it was no longer a matter of impressing the enemy, but of causing him the greatest possible harm.

Improvements in manufacturing techniques were then introduced, particularly in boring the barrels to obtain more uniform calibres. As from 1600 the curved butt became more widespread and enabled guns to be fired from the shoulder without a rest. In 1630 the musket became the main armament of the armies of King Gustavus Adolphus of Sweden. The wheel-lock continued to be manufactured for two centuries, often in conjunction with other models. In 1829 at Paris the Lepage pistols became a sort of anachronism – the last to use this system. After this, for a period, types of guns and techniques overlapped, but space prevents us from any discussion of them here.

The wheel-lock was also fundamental to the use of the firearm as a sporting weapon for hunting. In fact if earlier huntsmen had already used the matchlock harquebus, an Italian document of the day informs us that the 'noise of the report scares the game in the vicinity and causes it to flee'. The advantages of the firearm in terms of accuracy and power had not yet offset this major disadvantage. The wheel-lock harquebus was to enable huntsmen to kill big game with bullets more effectively.

Chenapans and miquelets

But the new lock was not flawless: it was important not to mislay the small crank used to wind up the lock, the iron pyrite wore out quickly, and dust infiltrated the mechanism. And not least, this complicated and delicate lock was costly.

The next step brought a decisive advance with it: the appearance of the snaphance (early flint-lock) lock, where the spark was produced by a flint striking the frizzen. Using this system, which had probably been known about since 1550, the so-called 'chenapan' system appeared in Holland. From 1630 onwards a lock known as a 'miquelet' appeared in Spain and Italy; based on the same system, it was more complicated but more effective than the 'chenapan'. Some authors maintain that the

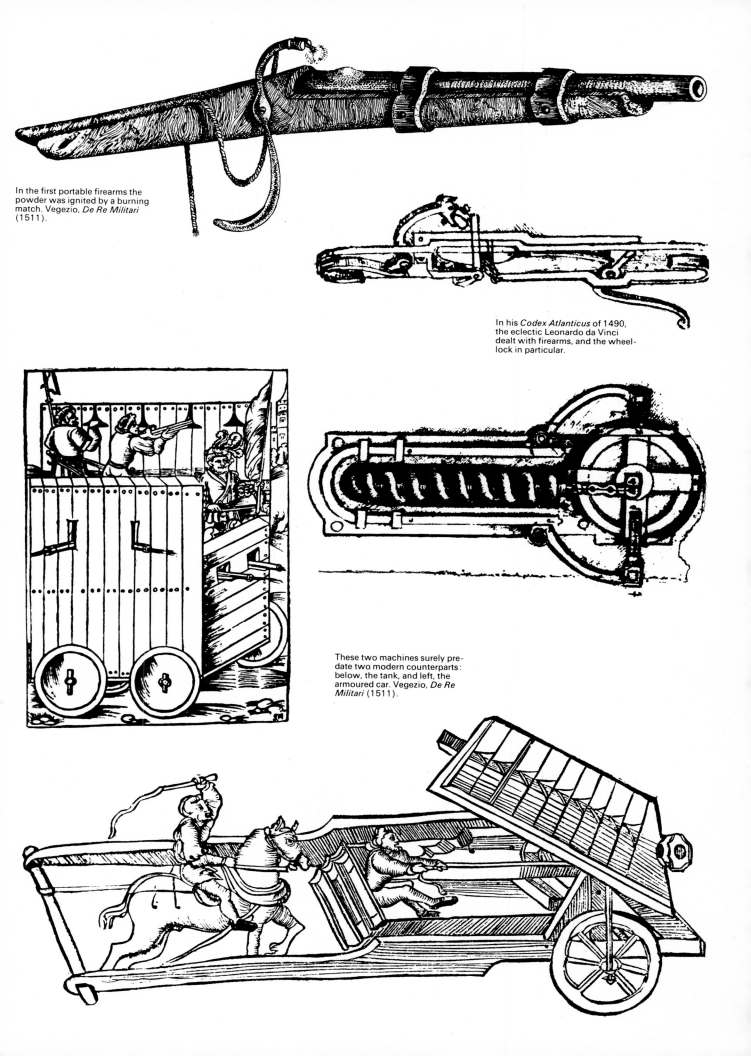

In the first portable firearms the powder was ignited by a burning match. Vegezio, *De Re Militari* (1511).

In his *Codex Atlanticus* of 1490, the eclectic Leonardo da Vinci dealt with firearms, and the wheel-lock in particular.

These two machines surely pre-date two modern counterparts: below, the tank, and left, the armoured car. Vegezio, *De Re Militari* (1511).

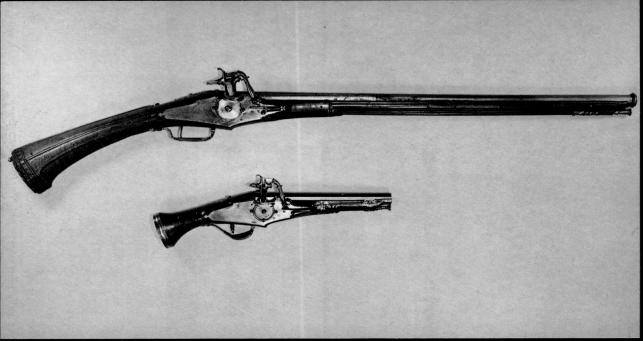

Signed by Lazarino Cominazzo, the master gunsmith from Brescia, these two magnificent wheel-lock guns are currently on display in the National Artillery Museum in Turin.

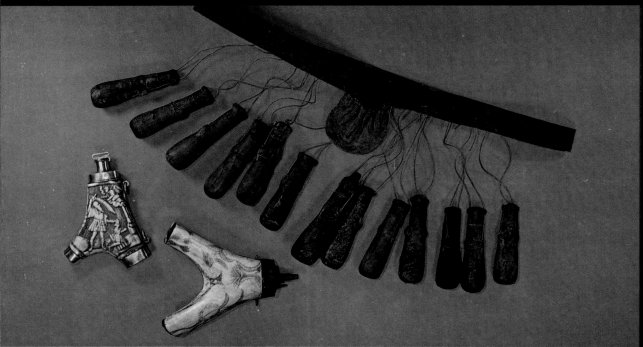

A harquebusier's bandolier and powder-flasks made of carved horn, to be seen in the National Artillery Museum in Turin.

A flint-lock on the standard-issue French Charleville rifle.

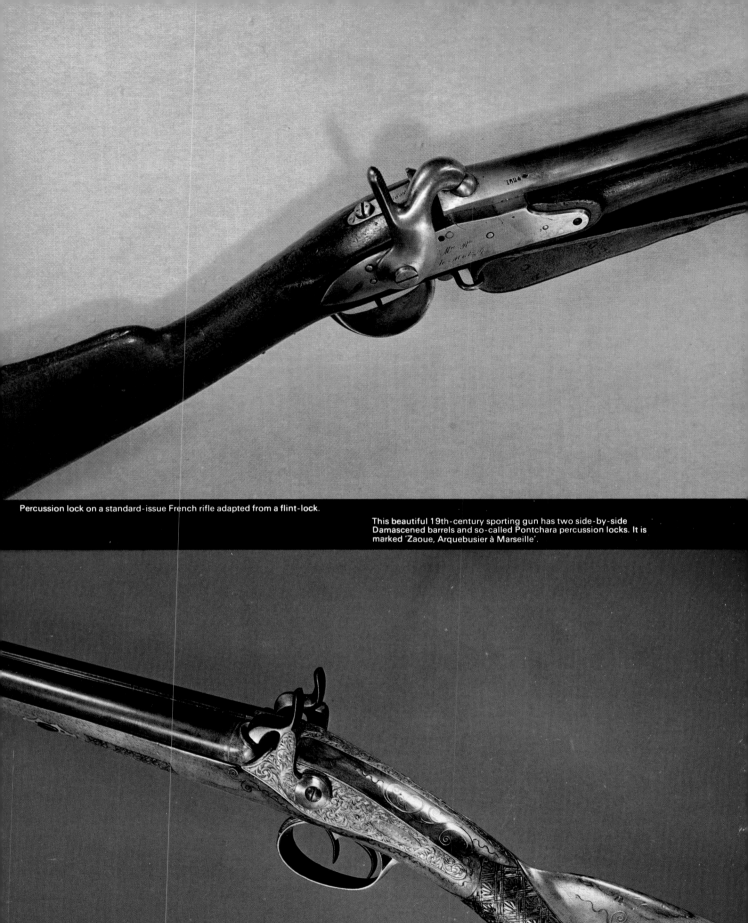

Percussion lock on a standard-issue French rifle adapted from a flint-lock.

This beautiful 19th-century sporting gun has two side-by-side Damascened barrels and so-called Pontchara percussion locks. It is marked 'Zaoue, Arquebusier à Marseille'.

miquelet' was invented by Simon Marquate. Scottish and English gunsmiths subsequently manufactured locks which borrowed heavily from the 'chenapan' system. Both the Dutch and the English were at once clever traders and experienced colonizers, and these models were in brisk demand in territories such as Morocco until 1880. Sweden and the Baltic countries also manufactured weapons working on a nearly identical principle, but with a distinctive hammer, which was almost vertical, and a spring situated on the outside of the gun.

The flint-lock

The flint-lock was almost perfected in France. In its new form it was a mixture of the 'chenapan' and 'miquelet' systems: from the former it borrowed the large inner spring bearing against a tumbler, and from the latter the pan and the frizzen. A gunsmith from Lisieux by the name of Le Bourgeois improved the trigger mechanism and virtually guaranteed that it would function without fail. In 1610 he made the first flint-lock harquebus for Louis XIII. This action gradually ousted all the other types, but its superiority only asserted itself little by little. The new gun, as it became more and more refined and increasingly light, was first and foremost appreciated as a hunting weapon. To be adopted as a weapon of war it first had to erode various conventions, but between 1700 and 1815 it dominated the battlefield. Among numerous other models the historical role of two in particular has made them eagerly sought after by collectors: the English 'Brown Bess', and the French 'Charleville' muzzle-loaders. The latter, lighter than its English counterpart and the subject of several minor modifications, became the best gun of its time. It was used in the French Revolution and the First Empire.

Things had come a long way from the first bombards! The difference in weight, handling quality, robustness, refinement and elegance is vast. The gun had become an extremely safe implement in the hands of those who knew how to use it correctly. People today, who sometimes dabble with gunpowder, tend to have misconceptions about this point, through lack of sufficient knowledge and experience (with some exceptions of course). Shots could be fired in quick succession: the use of a pre-prepared charge contained in a paper cartridge — which came upon the scene in the early eighteenth century — made it possible to achieve a rate of four shots a minute, after considerable training and practice. And handguns naturally benefited from this progress. Thanks to an invention by an English gunsmith, H. Nock, it was found that barrels could be shortened even more. This man perfected a system which improved the combustion of the charge by splitting the chamber into two unequal volumes and shortening the primary hole. Pistols had mechanisms which were surprisingly quick and accurate. Their use in duels led to the development of adjustable trigger mechanisms. They were made in pairs and every collector is well acquainted with the magnificent caskets in which they were kept. The barrels were made lighter, and as a result the manufacture of double-barrelled sporting guns which were easy to handle and safe to use was made possible. In the case of some of them, the use of precious metals, and metal and wood engraving, shifted the emphasis from the technical nature of the gunsmith's trade to its art.

It had taken five centuries to reach this level of production. Most of the men who contributed to these advances are nameless. Among other things we have lost all record of the name of the first man who had the idea of forging barrels by twisting them in a spiral, so that the metal fibres are positioned in such a way as to have the greatest resistance to expansion, thus doing away with the clumsy business of welding together pieces of barrel measuring some 4in. (10cm) each, a technique which was responsible for most of the burstings that occurred. Other ideas were not to enjoy the development they deserved, because they were too far ahead of the technology of the day. Who first thought of rifling a barrel? Some museums house weapons dating back to the time of Maximilian of Austria (the fifteenth century) which have rifled barrels. And we do not know who was the first to use shot in sporting-guns.

Up to this point shoulder-pieces and handguns both followed more or less the same path, with improvements to one affecting the other and vice versa. Sporting weapons and weapons of war were interchangeable because they were all smooth-bored. They used either shot or bullets, and both were made in the Versailles workshops where, between 1793 and 1815, Nicolas-Noël Boutet produced masterpiece after masterpiece, guns which are still the envy of every connoisseur.

The percussion lock

The end of the eighteenth century and the nineteenth century were hallmarked by the advent of steam, which in turn paved the way for new developments in the techniques of machining, an important factor in the manufacture of arms. Sporting guns were the first to make regular use of two decisive steps forward, one more significant than the other: the first, which applied only to this category of guns, was the development of the so-called Damascus barrels, and the second, which was to be essential for the development of all portable arms, was the invention of the percussion lock.

Numerous gunsmiths played a part in the creation of the Damascus, whose actual inventor is not known, and it is the culmination of all these efforts to obtain ever lighter barrels with an ever greater resistance. Doubtless inspired by the manufacturing techniques used in the Middle East to produce high quality swords and the like, an inventor had the idea of sandwiching a strip of welding steel between the strips of soft iron used hitherto. Barrels of equal weight, known as 'strip' barrels, were obtained in this way; they were more resistant, and made it possible to increase both the charge and the calibre. Subsequently, more and finer strips of iron and steel were used which were twisted around each other to obtain a closer bond. Barrels made in this way with a combination of malleable iron allied to the resistance of steel gave excellent ballistic results and showed themselves to be very strong. Even after the appearance of bored, solid steel barrels, the Damascus barrels were still favourably regarded by a good many gun-owners because if an overlarge charge should cause an explosion, the Damascus barrel did not burst like the steel barrel. Technically the heights for these Damascus 'strip' barrels were reached in about 1885 by the gunsmiths Leclerc and Bernard. The appearance of

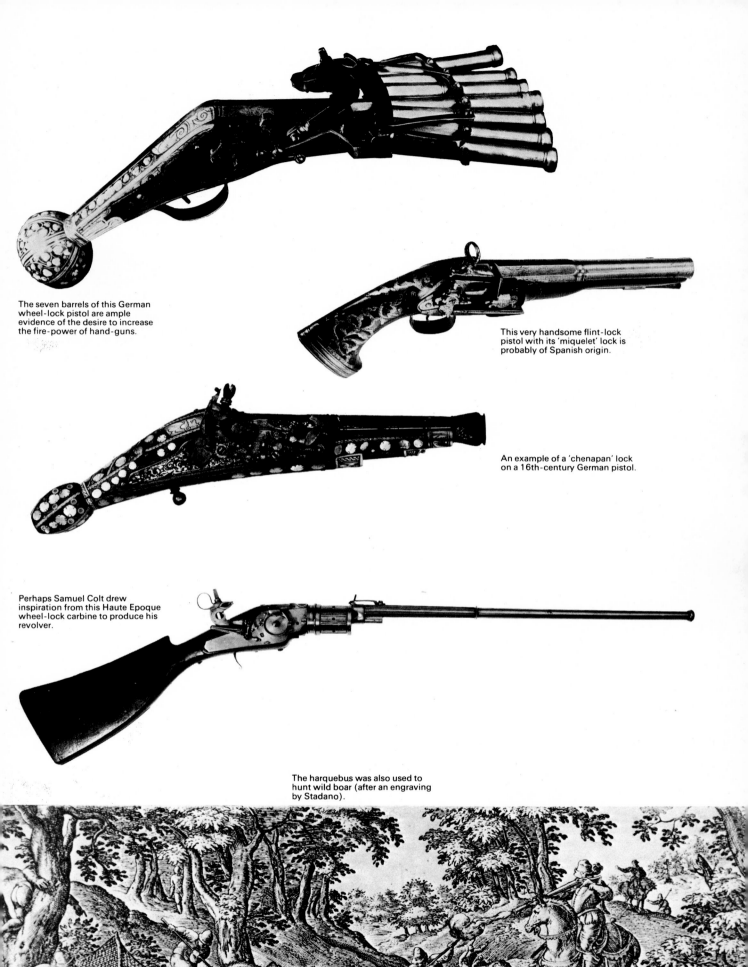

The seven barrels of this German wheel-lock pistol are ample evidence of the desire to increase the fire-power of hand-guns.

This very handsome flint-lock pistol with its 'miquelet' lock is probably of Spanish origin.

An example of a 'chenapan' lock on a 16th-century German pistol.

Perhaps Samuel Colt drew inspiration from this Haute Epoque wheel-lock carbine to produce his revolver.

The harquebus was also used to hunt wild boar (after an engraving by Stadano).

smokeless powder did not instantly stop the manufacture of Damascus models. In 1900 the gunsmith Mallet and the Manufacture d'Armes et Cycles de Saint-Etienne produced a gun called the 'Damas-Eclair', specially designed for smokeless powder. As for the percussion lock it was awaiting the imminent birth of the metal cartridge.

Fulminating compounds, with a chemical make-up which would ignite or detonate when struck, had been known to chemists for some time. At the beginning of the eighteenth century the French chemist, Berthollet, experimented with potassium chlorate, and the Englishman, Edward, with fulminate of mercury. But it was not until the beginning of the nineteenth century, in the figure of the Scottish pastor Forsyth, that this scientific knowledge was actually applied in practical terms to firearms. In the year 1807, after lengthy research, Forsyth took out a patent covering the use of fulminate of mercury for firing powder. His first lock, known as the 'scent bottle', a delicate and costly one, used the fulminate in powder form. Numerous improvements had to be made to it before it assumed the form which was still in use comparatively recently. So in about 1820 the flint-lock disappeared, making room for the new system in which a copper cylindrical cap, containing fulminate or chlorate, was situated over a touch-hole connecting directly with the chamber. The blow struck by a hammer with a recess on its striking face (which covered the touch-hole) detonated the cap which in turn ignited the charge. The discharge was quicker than with the flint-lock, and more reliable in every way; loading was slightly simpler. Hunters were quick to see the advantage of the new system and the first percussion guns fired shot. For almost a century the double-action percussion sporting gun was the most popular model throughout the world.

Pistols followed close on its heels: from 1825 onwards an American gunsmith, Deringer, adopted the percussion system for guns manufactured in his workshops. More compact than the flint-lock pistol, the Deringer models enjoyed an immediate success. In 1840, or thereabouts, once the test of time had established the superiority of the new system, it was adopted for rifles and carbines by every army in the western world.

Rifled guns

The logical nature of the system itself meant that attempts were made immediately to combine detonator and charge. This first happened with the sporting gun, which was then very much ahead of its time, when a certain Lépine invented a method in 1833, subsequently purchased and patented by Lefaucheux, whose name is still as famous as it ever was.

This period also witnessed another decisive step forward. Captain Delvigne was instrumental in popularizing the use of projectiles with a hollow base, which were subcalibre and expanded to fit the bore, and permitted quick loading for rifled guns. The rifled gun, as we mentioned earlier, had existed as far back as the reign of the Emperor Maximilian. Since that time it was known that a rifled barrel with a spiral twist gave more accurate results. But the projectile must interact with the grooves of the rifling if it is instantly to acquire the rotatory movement which improves the trajectory. Despite the use of the

bullet patch – a thin leather or canvas wrapper which was placed round the bullet before it was loaded into the barrel – loading was slow and awkward. Thus the use of rifled barrels had been restricted to the hunt and the range. The so-called Kentucky American rifles were among the best of their kind until 1810. The Baker carbine, which was tried out by the English against the Americans during the War of Independence, was one of the rare European attempts to make military use of the rifled gun before 1840.

The percussion lock on the one hand and the bullet which would alter in shape as a result of the action of the gases on the other brought about a genuine revolution in military guns: smooth-bore military shoulder-pieces disappeared in 1840 and the increased accuracy of the guns once more changed conditions on the battlefield. The Civil War in America was something of a testing-ground for these new tactical conditions. From now on the only smooth-bore weapons were sporting guns.

Repeating arms and the revolver

The percussion system of a fulminating cap swiftly led to the emergence of a revolutionary gun: a light, effective pistol capable of firing several shots which was at once safe, and really portable: the revolver had arrived. Heavy and cumbersome weapons had been produced for a long time, sporting either several barrels or a cylinder with several chambers which rotated in front of a single barrel. But these early models had met almost insuperable problems: the main ones were chain firing and the alignment of the cylinder with the barrel. It was Colt who resolved all such problems in 1835, patenting his own revolver, the Colt Patterson. The Texas Rangers experimented with the gun, and it showed itself to be safe and accurate. In 1847 the United States equipped their troops with the Colt Walker. The single-action Colt had a simple, tough mechanism and, more importantly, for the first time a gun of this type was machine produced with interchangeable parts.

It had one weak point: the barrel was attached by a cotter pin to a spindle screwed into the frame around which the cylinder revolved. The thread was subjected to considerable stress which, with use, caused the screw to work loose and develop play, thus rendering the firearm unusable. Remington solved this problem by developing a revolver whose frame consisted of a closed housing on to which the barrel was screwed, and where the cylinder turned round a removable spindle. The basic structure of the revolver has not changed since. The success of the new gun stimulated manufacturers throughout the world to dodge the Colt patents. Numerous models, some of them odder than others, appeared on the market, giving the impression that their authors had explored more or less every conceivable avenue.

The metal cartridge

The development of the percussion cap gave rise to a new development in the firearm by opening the way to metal,

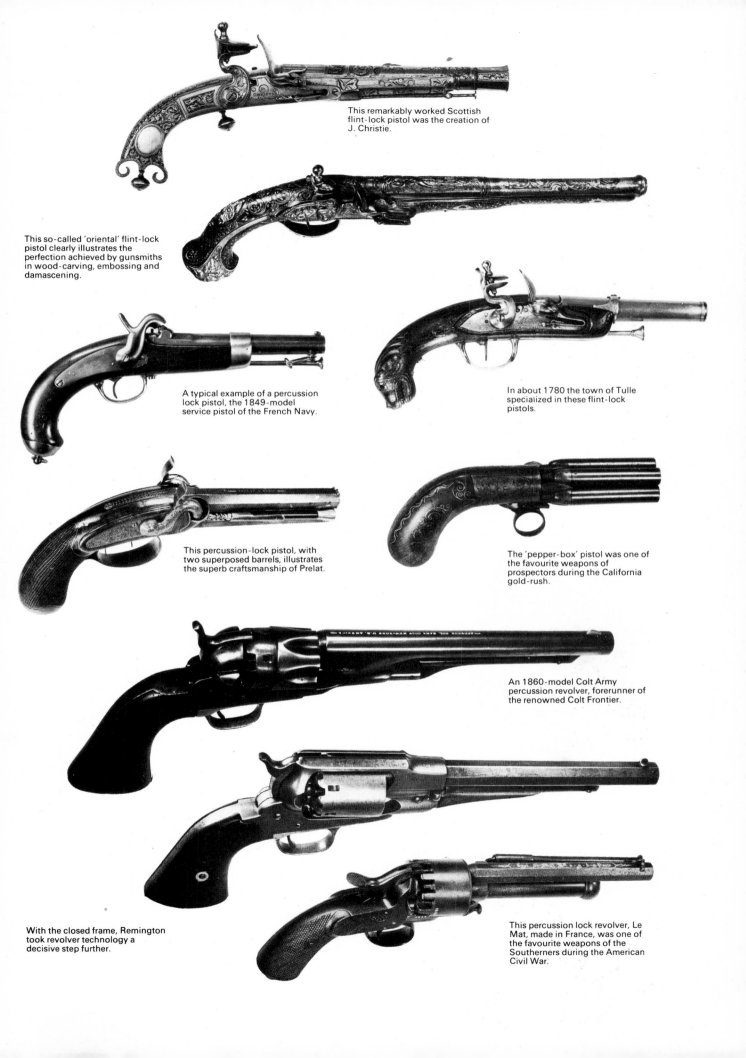

This remarkably worked Scottish flint-lock pistol was the creation of J. Christie.

This so-called 'oriental' flint-lock pistol clearly illustrates the perfection achieved by gunsmiths in wood-carving, embossing and damascening.

A typical example of a percussion lock pistol, the 1849-model service pistol of the French Navy.

In about 1780 the town of Tulle specialized in these flint-lock pistols.

This percussion-lock pistol, with two superposed barrels, illustrates the superb craftsmanship of Prelat.

The 'pepper-box' pistol was one of the favourite weapons of prospectors during the California gold-rush.

An 1860-model Colt Army percussion revolver, forerunner of the renowned Colt Frontier.

With the closed frame, Remington took revolver technology a decisive step further.

This percussion lock revolver, Le Mat, made in France, was one of the favourite weapons of the Southerners during the American Civil War.

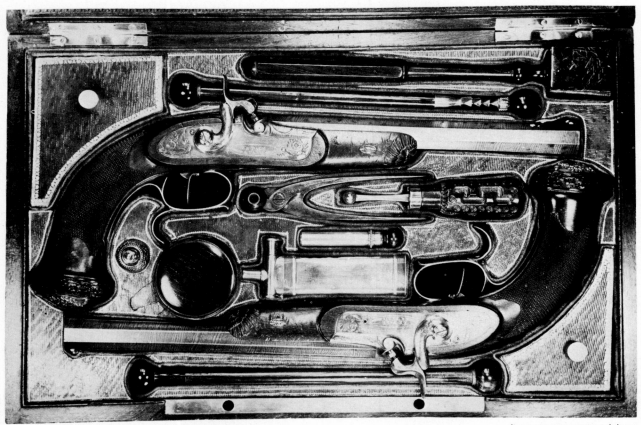

A sumptuous case containing a pair of duelling pistols, signed 'Lepage à Paris'.

The so-called 'Volcanic' Smith and Wesson repeating pistol which led to the famous Winchester carbine.

With its remarkable craftsmanship this centre-fire Perrin revolver is evidence of the expertise of French gunsmiths at the end of the 19th century.

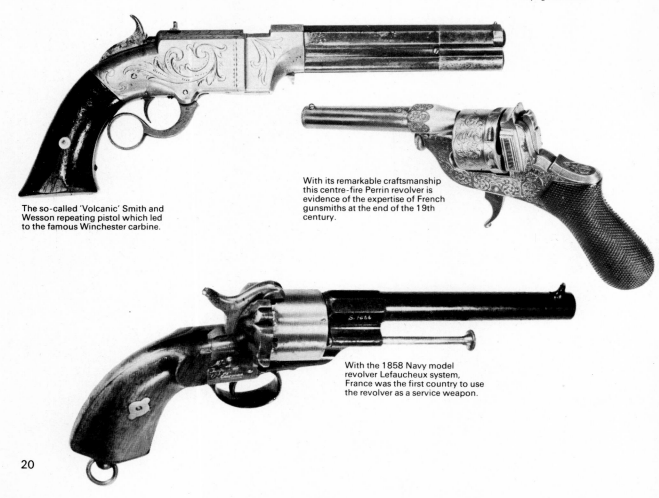

With the 1858 Navy model revolver Lefaucheux system, France was the first country to use the revolver as a service weapon.

pin-fire cartridges, then rim-fire and finally centre-fire cartridges. In about 1867 the new highly resistant Siemens steels appeared on the market. These were immediately used for the production of military weapons and the development of breech-loading systems; in the case of sporting guns they led to the manufacture of stronger barrels and the development of break-open drop-down systems. It is worth noting, however, that weapons using metal cartridges did not enjoy an immediate success; this was due to the poor quality of the cases used. Here too techniques — among them that of stamping — had to be improved before sufficiently strong cases were produced.

The first attempts to produce cartridges on an industrial scale involved the names Smith, Wesson and Winchester. The latter, who was a total stranger to the gunsmiths' world, secured the services of one B. T. Henry who developed the first .44 calibre rim-fire metal cartridge. This cartridge then enabled him to perfect the system of the Smith and Wesson Volcanic repeating pistol and come up with the Henry carbine which, not long after, was to become the famous 1866-model Winchester. The slightly earlier Spencer rifle was also endowed with excellent features. Both these guns were equipped with tubular magazines and their repeater-action was controlled by an under-lever.

In Europe there was a preference for a breech-locking repeater-action. A large number of models appeared in the wake of the Chassepot and Dreyse guns; in fact every country boasted its own model. France replaced the Gras rifle in one fell swoop by the Lebel which, when it was adopted in 1886, was undoubtedly the best gun available. But it was fitted with a tubular magazine in those days, and the drawbacks of this system compared to the loading-clip developed by Mauser in 1888 were soon shown up. This clip was to be fitted to all military weapons produced at the end of the century.

As far as the revolver was concerned, Lefaucheux used the pinfire metal cartridge as from 1851. On the other side of the Atlantic, Colt and Smith developed the first double-action systems using centre-fire metal cartridges. In 1876 Wood devised, for Winchester, the first revolver with a laterally swinging cylinder.

The nineteenth-century sporting gun

Sporting guns also benefited from the technical advances that we have just discussed. In 1822 Pauly developed a breech-loading system which was subsequently improved by Lefaucheux. In 1831 the Robert rifle appeared as a new improved version of this mechanism. In the same year Lefaucheux patented his rifle in which the barrels were opened by dropping them down on a hinge in the breech. The great merit of this gun lay in the fact that for the first time the breech-barrel locking mechanism was really efficient. From 1836 onwards this gun fired the pinfire metal cartridge.

In 1845 Lefaucheux improved his gun by using Pottet's invention of the centre-fire cartridge. Various systems were tried out to improve and strengthen the barrel drop-down assembly. The lock became smoother and more effective, particularly through the addition of a stirrup

connecting the large percussion spring and the tumbler bearing the hammer. For centre-fire cartridges, the hammers were made to rebound at the end of their travel, thus freeing the pins, which reassumed their 'rear' position and made it possible for the barrels to be dropped down without first cocking the hammers. After Purdey's invention of a so-called 'top-lever' locking system on top of the lock, in 1875, Anson and Deeley came up with a so-called 'Hammerless' model where cocking was automatically carried out by dropping down the barrels. Even today nearly all the drop-down guns being manufactured throughout the world are of this type. Deeley further improved his Hammerless model in 1876 by equipping it with an ejector. At the same time Holland and Holland produced an ejection mechanism and a lock, still not improved upon.

In 1870, or thereabouts, and apparently quite by chance, the discovery was made in England of the choke-bored muzzle which created a more effective cone of fire for shot. Numerous other types of guns were studied, in France especially, and some of these are still being used today: for example there was the fixed-barrel system by Darne, and the Idéal shot gun of the Manufacture Française d'Armes et Cycles de Saint-Etienne. In Switzerland and Belgium the major improvements were made above all to competition guns, in particular by Francotte and Martini.

Towards repeaters using smokeless powder

In about 1880 the appearance of pyroxiline or 'smokeless' powder made it possible not only to improve ballistic performances but also to reduce and then almost totally eliminate the hard residue caused by combustion. This residue had proved to be the major obstacle both to the various loading systems and to automatic or manual repeating systems. These, sometimes known as controlled rapid-fire systems, immediately benefited from this discovery. Self-loading came on the scene in 1880, or so it would appear, the year when the Clair brothers of Saint-Etienne developed a gas-based system. Automatic and semi-automatic weapons consequently multiplied across the board. Among those responsible for their increased production, which focused chiefly on machine-guns and pistols, one must mention Borchardt, Mauser, Mannlicher and, in particular, Browning. In the course of his fifty-year career, the latter developed machine-guns, pistols, competition carbines and sporting guns which are still widely used today. World War I, for its part, promoted the study and production of the first individual automatic weapons. These were improved in the inter-wars period.

Reading this brief history it is noticeable that after a period of slow progress the firearm has advanced in leaps and bounds since the nineteenth century. Like most craftsmen and artisans since the industrial revolution, the gunsmith has been able to realize ideas (often of long standing) which only modern industrial techniques have enabled to come to fruition. This differential between the principle and the means of application is incidentally still to be found in research work carried out in connection, for example, with automatic weapons which use selfcombusting ammunition; the idea would seem to be ahead of the available means of realization. Modern weapons offer us a wide variety of types and systems, most of which are less than a century old. The use of top-quality steels, light alloys and modern techniques such as cold-boring or sheet-stamping, gives them qualities of reliability, handling and resistance which their predecessors did not have.

As they stand today they give rise to certain observations: in the old days a gun could be used for both hunting and war; today guns are specialized. Their conditions of use have been limited, either in actual practice, or by the authorities. Sporting guns, which are now practically perfect, are subject to rules and regulations in many countries which lay down specifications to restrict their destructive capacity and thus protect wild life. Their development is thus also restricted. Competitive shooting, considered as a sport, is also carried on within limits fixed by various federations and the International Shooting Union. The only guns where the search for greater effectiveness is the criterion are military weapons; it is in this field that we see the greatest volume of research being carried out and the greatest number of problems being solved.

In conclusion we can in this day and age confirm a phenomenon that is often noted in other respects: the survival of ancient solutions alongside present-day solutions: hence the demand for and continual production of sporting guns with centre-fire systems and external hammers. And one paradoxical feature of our times is the fact that the rules for the purchase of hand-guns have revived pre-1870 percussion models in several countries.

The Henry carbine used during the
American Civil War.

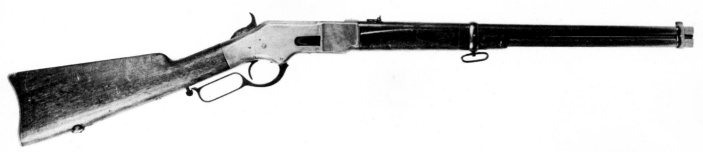

The 1866-model Winchester
carbine was to be the first of a
whole line of famous carbines.

A Swiss competition carbine,
signed Rudolph Hämmerli.

Left: The model No 1, *first issue*,
Smith and Wesson, made in 1867,
was the first American revolver to
use the metal cartridge.

A 'Schützenfest' (shooting match)
German carbine.

2
handguns

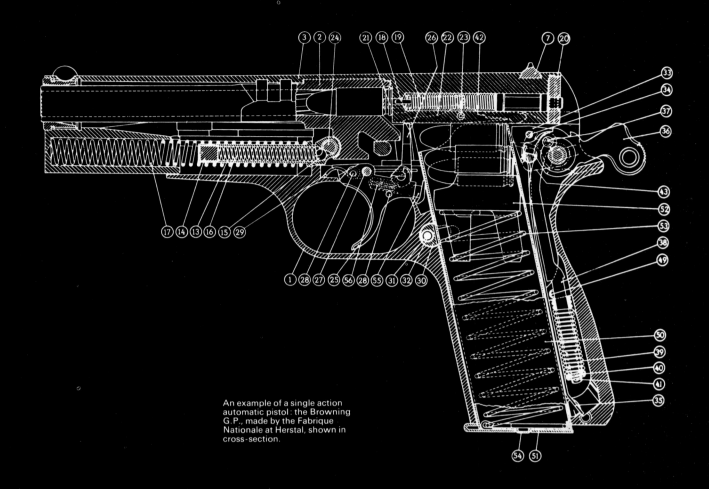

An example of a single action automatic pistol: the Browning G.P., made by the Fabrique Nationale at Herstal, shown in cross-section.

Section of the German double action Mauser HSc automatic pistol.

Since the coming of the firearm, gunsmiths have used their skills to produce guns which are as light and easy to handle as possible, and sufficently powerful at the same time — the ideal being to devise a personal weapon, easy to carry, and capable of being fired quickly. In addition to these qualities, a gun must be safe and dependable.

The modern handgun, in its various forms, is the outcome of these criteria, and it meets all the above requirements.

If we disregard the various specialized guns which are manufactured in limited editions mainly for competition use, the bulk of current production consists of two categories of repeating handguns: automatic pistols and revolvers.

Automatic pistols

This term, so commonly used, is peculiar in as much as it describes not an automatic handgun but a gun in which the cocking and feeding take place automatically after the first shot has been fired. The term 'semi-automatic', which is incidentally used to denote rifles with a similar mechanism, would thus be more accurate. For the sake of simplicity we shall however stick to the term 'automatic pistol'.

These are guns with cocking and loading mechanisms operated after each shot is fired by the residual energy of the ammunition. Varying numbers of rounds are loaded either in a magazine (which is generally integral with the gun) or in a clip in the grip. When a bullet is fired, the reaction causes the bolt to recoil; the empty case is extracted and ejected; the recoil spring is compressed; and the hammer is cocked. There is then a second movement: the compressed recoil spring pushes the bolt back to the initial position and simultaneously feeds another round in to the chamber.

We should mention at this early stage that if a gun is to function smoothly, the ammunition used must be of good quality and a standard type. Widespread use of automatic pistols is due solely to the industrial production of improved quality ammunition.

Although the basic principle outlined above applies to all hand-guns known collectively as automatic pistols, the mechanisms vary. This is not the place to discuss each one of them, so we shall single out just two systems: single-action models; double-action models.

Single-action models

These are undoubtedly the most commonly used, because they are the most simple. The firing action of these guns is based on the recoil of the bolt which, as described above, cocks the hammer. But unlike the 'automatic' weapon (in the precise meaning of the term), the bullet is fired independently of the forward travel of the bolt. If the bolt does not close completely — and this is the most common cause of accidents with this type of gun — a part called the disconnector disconnects the trigger from the sear, which controls the hammer, thus preventing the gun from being fired.

Single-action mechanisms feature a lighter trigger pull than double-action mechanisms, and the trigger travel can be reduced to a minimum. This latter characteristic can greatly improve on-target accuracy by reducing the stress to be applied to the trigger; it also makes it possible to achieve a very rapid rate of fire. But because single-action guns can only be fired when the bolt has completed its full travel, even before the first shot, the overall action of these guns is slower. When 'cocked' these guns are sensitive, and thus pose a greater risk when being used by inexperienced hands. On the other hand this sensitivity is a welcome feature for the competitor in a shooting match. As we shall see later on, actions of this type equip all match automatic pistols.

In effect, depending on to what use they are put, the degree of sensitivity of these guns becomes either their principal quality — in shooting competitions —, or else their major defect — when used for self-defence or police-work. One is reminded of the case of Pierre Lourmel, known as 'Pierrot le Fou' who, as France's public enemy No 1, managed to slip through the police net which had been spread right across France, time and time again, until in the end he fatally wounded himself while sliding a cocked gun of this type into his belt.

Double-action models

In these models the hammer or the firing mechanism is cocked by the action of the finger on the trigger, quite separately from the stroke of the bolt. We should however point out that in most models the gun functions in practical terms on the single-action principle once the first shot has been fired: the backward stroke of the bolt cocks the hammer. The most common guns working on this system are the Walther PP, PPK and P 38. The best-known pistol in France is called 'Le Français', and was made by La Manufacture d'Armes et de Cycles de Saint-Etienne; this is a double-action pistol in which the cocking of the firing mechanism is *always* separate from the bolt movement. Automatic or manually operated safety devices on these different models make it possible to lock the firing mechanisms for as long as is necessary.

Models which incorporate only the double-action are the least common. They may not require manual cocking for the first shot, but among their disadvantages are a long trigger travel and a comparatively heavy trigger pull (3.5–7kg). Both these features can affect accuracy and the rate of fire. Among this type of gun are the CZ 45, made in Czechoslovakia, the Steyr-Daimler-Puch, made in Austria, and the new Heckler und Koch VP 70 and VP 71, made in Germany.

Some inventors have tried to combine the advantages of the two types of lock: single- and double-action. The best-known is Fritz Walther with the PP, PPK and P 38 models just mentioned and now world famous. In view of the success of these guns, several manufacturers have also marketed double-action guns with a selective lock: here the first round may be fired on either the single- or double-action principle, and the following rounds by single-action. Among the best known of these are the Mauser, Sauer and Sohn, Beretta, Ceska Lbropowka, Heckler und Koch, Bergmann, Smith and Wesson, Astra and Makarov — the last model being copied in East Germany with the Borsig trademark. This type of gun, being a combination of the single- and double-action systems, is comparatively more expensive than less sophisticated models, but it is likely to supersede all other models whose good points it has adopted and whose bad points it has sidestepped.

Classifying automatic pistols

Whatever system is involved, automatic pistols can be divided into three groups:

1. Small calibre (.22 LR, .22 long and short, 6.35mm [.25 ACP]) compact (pocket) pistols. In some cases the calibres have been reduced still further, particularly by German and Austrian manufacturers: the Kolibri, for example, chambers a 3mm round and the Lilliput, by Mentz, in production since 1927, takes 4.25mm calibre ammunition.

2. Police pistols: 7.65mm (.32 ACP, USA), 9mm short (.380 ACP), or 9mm Browning.

3. High-power combat pistols, using ammunition with high ballistic qualities. At the present time the calibres vary between the 7.62mm Soviet and the .455 (11.45mm) Webley (Navy). These are mainly automatic pistols issued to the armed forces. The calibres mentioned above should not be taken too literally for each of the categories used. In fact, in some countries, the army has for a time used small calibre weapons, in particular the 7.65mm; and, conversely, the standard issue for modern police forces in various countries tends towards large calibre weapons.

The above classification is thus functional and intended to help simplify what follows. We trust the reader will forgive us if we mention similar guns in the various chapters of this book, depending on the place, time and use. This will apply particularly to the Webley and Scott automatic pistol which remains more or less the same gun, whether it be called the 6.35mm Vest Pocket, the 7.65mm Metropolitan Police or the .455 Webley Mk 1 Self-Loading pistol—thus covering all the categories outlined above.

Compact pocket pistols

The undisputed master behind the introduction of automatic mechanisms in guns is John Moses Browning. His patents were used to advantage by many American firms — especially Colt and Winchester — but he himself moved shop to Belgium as a 'moral émigré' so to speak, because of certain differences which caused him to oppose the trends of the Winchester Repeating Arms Co. In Belgium he was keenly welcomed by the Fabrique Nationale d'Armes de Guerre at Herstal-lez-Liège. As his part of the marriage contract John M. Browning laid the plans of two sensational new guns on the table: an automatic repeating sporting rifle, still manufactured by the Fabrique Nationale, and an extra-slim automatic pistol, known as the Browning 1900, which was to become a permanent fixture on the international market.

Five years later, and at the prompting of the 'man from Ogden', the Belgian company marketed the 6.35mm Browning (.25 ACP), the first repeating pocket-gun which used an equally new type of ammunition. This new, compact automatic pistol was the first real rival to the wide range of small revolvers being manufactured in Europe and in the United States. Both the gun and the new type of ammunition enjoyed instant success. Every arms manufacturer went to great steps to get a footing in a market with apparently considerable outlets. It became the thing to do, to own a small calibre compact hand-gun. Arms purchasers were flooded with demands for the 6.35. Colt, in the United States, started to manufacture this bestseller under licence issued by Browning and put it on the market in 1908, calling it the Colt Auto Pocket and the Colt Vest Pocket. Spanish manufacturers, with their long tradition of borrowing ideas, modified their production tools in readiness to turn out copies of the most successful models without a moment's delay. In Germany, Carl Walther, with his well-established reputation for sporting guns dating back to 1886, also decided to manufacture a gun of this type; but he was keen to put up some effective opposition to the success of the Brownings, and so he turned his thoughts to an even smaller and lighter pistol. In 1908 the German firm put their Model 1 on the market, and a year later added Model 2, an improved version of the original. And these models were indeed smaller and lighter than their Belgian rival. Realizing the threat, Browning cut down both the size and the weight of his Browning 6.35mm and marketed the Baby Browning, which managed to outclass the German competition. This pistol is still manufactured by the Fabrique Nationale in Belgium. Its sales top two million, undoubtedly a sales record for this class of gun.

In France the Manufacture d'Armes et de Cycles at Saint-Etienne finally joined the bandwagon in 1910 and launched the automatic, double-action pistol with a dropdown barrel and a calibre of 6.35mm, known as Le Français. This gun was made up until about 1965 and became the standard-issue for certain officers in the Criminal Investigation Department in France. Even the 'long-barrelled' version was quite compact, and there was the added advantage of being able to carry it about with a round up the spout, ready for emergency action. Its low velocity was made up for by a high degree of accuracy, exceptional for a double-action gun. Once Models 1 and 2 had been launched, Carl Walther became involved for a time with 7.65mm police weapons: shortly before the outbreak of World War I he reverted to a 6.35mm calibre with his Model 5, an improved version of Model 2. When war was declared, arms manufacturers had to adapt their production programmes to high power military weapons. Carl Walther directed his energies to his Model 6, using the 9mm Parabellum cartridge. For the first time in the history of the Thuringian firm, the gun was a resounding 'flop'. Carl Walther followed this failure to the grave shortly afterwards in 1915; he was 57. But the firm carried on under the direction of his sons, Fritz, Erich and Georg. To meet demands from the Kaiser's officers during the war, the Model 6 was converted back to a 6.35mm calibre and marketed in 1917 as Model 7. The firm's frenzied production was interrupted by the 1918 armistice, and the lines had to be reconverted to defensive weapons. The 6.35mm Model 8 and then the Model 9 were both extremely successful in 1920 and 1921 respectively. By 1936 more than 200,000 Model 8 pistols had been sold. For eight years the German firm refrained from putting any new models on the market, and simply enjoyed the successes of Models 8 and 9. Then came the PP (Polizei

The VP 70 automatic pistol with its holster-stock. The selector is clearly visible at the top of the stock.

The Heckler and Koch VP 70 automatic pistol, 9mm Parabellum calibre (note 1).

The 9mm Parabellum calibre Borsig automatic pistol; this gun, currently manufactured in East Germany, is a copy of the Soviet Makarov PM double action pistol.

The Walther HP automatic pistol, 9mm Parabellum calibre. This was a pre-war commercial version of the standard Walther P.38 military pistol.

The Webley and Scott Mark I automatic pistol. This was the standard-issue equipment of the Royal Navy from 1912–1945.

The Webley and Scott automatic pocket pistol. Satisfied by the new line brought out for the standard Royal Navy pistol, Webley and Scott repeated it for the pocket pistol.

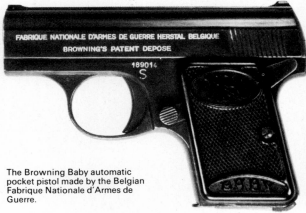

The Browning Baby automatic pocket pistol made by the Belgian Fabrique Nationale d'Armes de Guerre.

The Walther no. 9, no. 101 automatic pistol. There were two other versions: the 102 engraved; the 123 de luxe model, engraved, with ivory grip plates.

The Mentz Lilliput 1927 automatic pistol.

The compact single-shot Liberator Flare Projector of the American O.S.S.

Pistole), a 7.65mm calibre gun which produced a certain change of course.

For many years to come Walther was to concentrate almost exclusively on the production of increasingly powerful guns. The fact was that during these years the previously fashionable small calibre pistols were apparently failing to attract the same wide clientele, because the market had been virtually saturated by German and Spanish guns of uneven quality, but mass-produced.

Keen to put an end to the Walther record, the August Mentz company, in Suhl, marketed the Lilliput, smaller than the Walther No 9, using a 4.25mm cartridge. The Austrians went one better with their Kolibri Automatic, using a 3mm cartridge, which was nicknamed the 'armpit pistol'. These dangerous playthings likewise fell victim to the dictates of fashion; in addition their lack of power accelerated their disappearance, because of the way people's taste in guns developed. It was not long before catalogues no longer listed them. Mentz reconverted his Lilliput to a 6.35mm model and the Kolibri vanished for good.

Quite recently Kolibris and Lilliputs have become valuable firearms, mainly because of their original designs which are of interest to collectors.

Weapons produced by Browning and Walther bred a considerable amount of competition in the field. As a result arms manufacturers throughout the world made large numbers of fairly successful 6.35mm pistols in the inter-war period. It would be tiresome to list them all, and this is not the purpose here in any event. But it is worth mentioning the Mauser WTP 1 (Westen Taschen Pistole) and the 1910 model. The latter was heavier and larger than its counterparts, and without doubt one of the better finished pistols of the day. Elsewhere, the Lignose Einhand embodied some interesting technical research; it was conspicuous above all for the bolt which was activated by the cocking-lever (in fact the trigger guard), itself an integral part of the bolt. Lastly there were the Bayard pistols which remained for many years on the list of La Manufacture d'Armes et de Cycles de Saint-Etienne.

Well before World War II manufacturers in the United States were concentrating on .22 guns, which were very popular across the Atlantic. These were essentially sporting rather than pocket pistols and the .22 (5.5mm) cartridge was not widely seen on the European market before 1939.

In 1940 western Europe was suddenly confronted with the 'German threat'. During the Occupation the production of pocket pistols was interrupted; most of the existing pistols were handed over to the occupying forces, who also controlled all arms production and concentrated exclusively on military weapons. While traditional guns continued to be manufactured, a new type of gun emerged during this period. It was the Allies, in fact, with their agents parachuted into occupied Europe, who concentrated on the development of compact and inexpensive guns. Their research gave birth to a whole new generation of pistols, designed for the exclusive use of Allied intelligence services. From these we should single out the Liberator or Flare Projector, made on the orders of the OSS (predecessor to the CIA); this single-shot gun used the standard US .45 ACP (11.43mm) cartridge and

carried 10 rounds in the grip. More than one million such pistols were manufactured in record time by the Guide Lamp Corporation, at a unit cost of $1.75.

American influences were strong after 1945, and European manufacturers resumed production of compact pocket guns, mainly .22 pistols, with a view to getting a foothold in the American market. The 6.35mm cartridge was not very popular in the United States, but it was nevertheless retained for the regular European clientele.

At the present time the trend for this type of gun favours the .22 calibre (Short or Long Rifle). This tendency is not hard to understand if one considers the following points: (a) .22 rounds are as or more powerful than 6.35mm ammunition; (b) the cost price of .22 ammunition is low; (c) legislation in force in some European countries allows across-the-counter sale of .22 ammunition, but exercises strict control over 6.35mm cartridges.

Pistols for self-defence and police use

Hugo Borchardt's automatic pistol which went on the market in 1893 had one major drawback: its bulkiness. The breech block located behind the grip threw it out of balance and considerably increased its size. Aware of the need to produce a smaller gun, the German Theodor Bergmann consequently produced his 1894 model, the mechanism of which was directly influenced by that of the revolver, with the cylinder replaced in this instance by a vertical magazine situated in front of the trigger guard. This gun was made to fire a variety of medium-power cartridges. Unfortunately it is quite impossible to find them these days.

Its feed system, deriving from the Laumann patent of 1890, seems to have inspired the Feederle brothers in their creation of the 1896 Mauser high power automatic pistol. Although the 1894 Bergmann was reasonably successful as soon as it appeared, it still only represents a fleeting phase in the development of the automatic pistol.

The arrival in Liège of John M. Browning, whose decisive role in the development of the hand-gun we have already discussed, was to bring about an important step forward in pistols designed for self-defence, with the help of the Fabrique Nationale d'Armes de Guerre de Herstal. In spite of its undeniably martial title, F.N. attached far more importance to civilian markets than to possible military contracts. As a result this company swiftly started production of the small Browning pistol known as the Browning 1900 which the man from Ogden had brought with him in his luggage. This weapon also used a new type of ammunition for the time: the 7.65mm Browning (.32 ACP in the United States). It was a dazzlingly successful gun. Its compactness made it a perfect weapon for the purposes of self-defence, and as such it was both effective and unobtrusive. In Central Europe it dominated the entire market thanks to its mechanical qualities and low price. The Belgian army adopted it as a standard issue. It also cropped up in a less commendable market, when gangsters abandoned the revolver in favour of the Browning and used it for their violent purposes and to settle their differences. When the first motorized hold-up in history occurred, Jules Bonnot, leader of the Bonnot gang, was armed with one of these guns. Undoubtedly jealous, the French police of the day also equipped themselves with this gun and some years later Bonnot was himself killed by

The Browning 1900 model
automatic pistol made by the
Belgian Fabrique Nationale
d'Armes de Guerre This gun was
sold by the Manufacture d'Armes
et Cycles de Saint-Etienne.

An adaptation of the .32 Colt
Pocket Model automatic pistol for
use by British secret agents who
carried it in their belt. Firing was
carried out by a release device
fixed to the finger by a ring; the
control cable ran down the sleeve
of the user.

The German Dreyse 1907
automatic pistol. The clip for this
gun contained eight 7.65mm
calibre rounds.

The Beretta 1915–19 automatic
pistol.

The Spanish Izarra automatic
pistol supplied to the French
government during World War I.
Despite its official use, this gun
was never a standard issue in the
French army.

The Manurhin PP automatic pistol,
under Walther licence.

The Browning 1922 automatic
pistol, supplied to the Yugoslav
government.

The Turkish Kirikkale automatic
pistol. This gun is a copy of the
Walther PP 7.65mm calibre pistol.
There is a 9mm Short calibre
version too.

a Browning 1900.

But for the military authorities this weapon had one major drawback: it could not be stripped by hand, and as a result the business of servicing and cleaning it presented certain difficulties in wartime use. In 1902 this problem was solved by another Browning patent and the development of a new model. In addition the 7.65mm round, which was not considered powerful enough for military purposes, was replaced by the 9mm Browning. The F.N. manufactured this new model with the trade name Browning 1903. It is worth noting in passing that the features of the 7.65mm and 9mm Short round were more or less the same, with an approximately 30kg muzzle energy; and the performance of the military Browning over the civilian models was only marginally higher. In the United States Colt brought out the 1903 model, with the trade name of the .32 Colt Automatic Pistol, Pocket Model, with a 7.65mm calibre.

The Browning 1903 became the standard issue arm of the Belgian army, and in 1907 was also adopted by the Swedish army and made under licence from this year by the Husqvarna company with the reference m/07. It was also used by the Danish, Dutch and Turkish police forces. In a very different context, the Browning 1903 hit the sad headlines on 28 June 1914 at Sarajevo, being the gun with which Gavrilo Princip fired the assassin's shots which killed Archduke Francis Ferdinand of Austria, heir to the Austrian throne, and his wife, the Princess von Hohenberg. World War I was the result . . .

In the face of the acclaim given to the Browning and the new 7.65mm ammunition, European arms manufacturers attuned themselves to the taste of the day and to a greater or lesser extent 'enlarged' most existing guns with a 6.35mm calibre to fit the 7.65mm round. The Spanish turned out to be pastmasters in this respect and during World War I supplied the French army with large quantities of Star and Ruby pistols as well as other makes, chambered to fire the 7.65mm; the French army at the time, as far as hand-guns were concerned, was equipped with 1873 and 1874 revolvers which were out of date and used an 11mm black-powder round, and with 1892 revolvers in 8mm calibre, whose lack of power was notorious.

The United States, for their part, continued to concentrate their arms production in revolvers, which had shown their paces for three-quarters of a century, and had earned considerable glory during the conquest of the West. The 'six-shooter' is still as much a part of American folklore as it ever was and has still not been deposed by automatic pistols, despite the praiseworthy efforts of a good number of American arms firms, such as Colt, Smith and Wesson, Savage, etc.

The Browning 1910, an improved version of the 1903 model, appeared in Europe in 1912. This gun is virtually foolproof and still figures in the F.N. catalogue as the Model 10. This Belgian novelty arrived just at the right time to compete with the German 1910 Mauser which was beginning to earn a well-deserved reputation for itself. World War I, which most historians consider to have been the first conflict of modern warfare, somewhat upset traditional military notions and exposed the need for high-power personal military hand-guns. This was made conspicuously clear in the Kaiser's armies, who from the

outbreak of war clamoured for powerful weapons which could be used at normal combat distances. In Germany the manufacture of 9mm Parabellum calibre guns took precedence over small calibre manufacture.

Even before the invasion of Belgium by German troops, John M. Browning had returned to his native America where he developed the renowned automatic Colt Government Model of 1911 in .45 ACP (11.43mm) calibre which equipped the soldiers in the US expeditionary corps in 1917 and 1918. After the Armistice, the terms of the Treaty of Versailles forced Germany to make considerable cutbacks in its arms production. For several years no new models appeared east of the Rhine. During this period Browning returned to Belgium and shortly afterwards the F.N. put a variant of the model 1910 on the market: it had a longer barrel and an increased clip capacity, and was referred to as the Browning 1922. This gun was adopted by many countries, among them the new state of Yugoslavia. It is still in production today in Belgium, with the trade name 10/22, and is still used by police forces in several European countries. France, for example, in the Paris police headquarters, still uses some 2000 of these guns.

During this period in Italy, at Gardone, Pietro Beretta was re-adapting his 1915 automatic pistol which was standard issue for the Italian army, and offering the civilian authorities his new 1915/19 model, chambering a 7.65mm Browning round. In France, the Manufacture d'Armes et Cycles de Saint-Etienne, not to be confused with the Manufacture d'Armes de Saint-Etienne (the State arsenal), had for some time been offering its Le Français 7.65mm calibre automatic pistol, known as the Policeman model.

In 1923 the Manufacture d'Armes des Pyrénées Françaises (Unique) came into being and started producing automatic pistols influenced by the 1903 Browning. By 1929 the Walther company had overcome the various post-war difficulties and brought out the famous Walther PP (Polizei Pistole) on the German market. With this gun the Carl Walther Waffenfabrik introduced a double-action device which had only featured on revolvers and the small Le Français automatic pistol until then. Two years later the PP was joined by the PPK, a smaller version of the former. Both these pistols are still being manufactured, and are available in .22LR, 7.65mm and 9mm Short calibre. The Walther PP and the Walther PPK (Polizei Pistole Kriminal) are both remarkable guns and enjoy such a high reputation that they have long been being made under licence by numerous arms manufacturers, among which are Manurhin for France, Hämmerli in Switzerland and Kirik-Kale in Turkey. In 1933 the Manufacture d'Armes de Bayonne (MAB), spurred on by its director Barthe, brought out its model C, derived from the 1910 Browning, and model D, derived from the 1922 Browning, in 7.65mm calibre. Since 1921 this company had been marketing its 6.35mm calibre A and B models. Like Walther, the Waffenfabrik Mauser at Oberndorf had to cut back its production of weapons after 1918; once the tricky post-war situation was over, it once again started manufacturing hand-guns and police weapons. The 1910 model became the 1934 model, and was more refined and better made than its predecessor. But in other respects the Mauser had to contend with the challenge posed by its

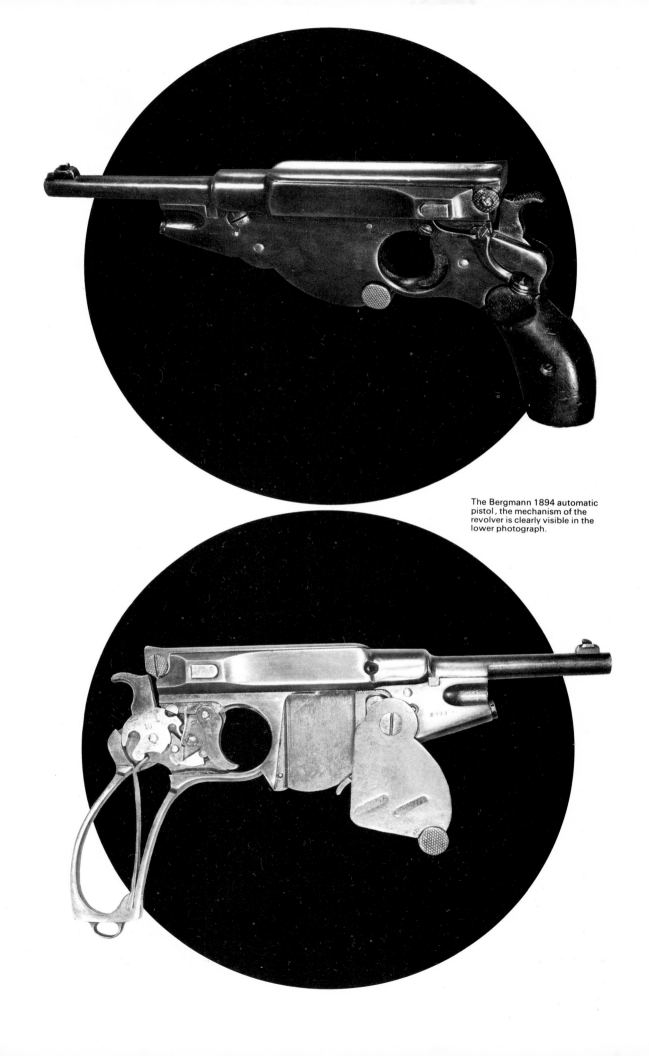

The Bergmann 1894 automatic pistol, the mechanism of the revolver is clearly visible in the lower photograph.

nearest rival, Walther, which seemed to have gained a head start by bringing out its PP and PPK models.

Created in 1937, the HS (Hahn Selbstspan) automatic pistol was the first double-action Mauser. After one or two modifications it became the HSa, then the HSb, and subsequently, as the HSc, has enjoyed many years of success and is still being manufactured in 7.65mm calibre (8 rounds) and a 9mm Short calibre (7 rounds). During the French occupation of Württemberg at the end of the last war, 2000 of these guns were delivered to France as war damages. A rather ugly version of this gun, called the 'Triangle Pistol' because of its shape, was all the same distributed to the most esteemed SS officers in the 'Burgen' (politico-military training schools) where the SS elite was formed. This model is extremely hard to find nowadays, and consequently highly prized by collectors.

World War II caused the development of the police gun to mark time, and production was directed mainly towards high-power combat pistols. The factories in occupied Europe nevertheless continued to operate 'at full steam' for the German troops. Although the hand-gun for the German army was specified as being of 9mm Parabellum calibre, many officers preferred to carry lighter weapons; they forsook the heavy P-38 and of their own accord used 7.65mm guns such as the German PP, PPK or HSc, the Czech CZ, and the HP 7.65mm, either made or influenced by Browning. So it was that all the hand-guns being produced in France, Belgium, Czechoslovakia, Hungary, Poland etc. found themselves stamped with the eagle and swastika. In 1945 German factories were ordered to hand over virtually all their production as war damages. Little by little the conditions of the Armistice became less harsh and commercial deliveries started up once more. Convinced of the effectiveness of large calibres, the national police force abandoned the 7.65mm calibre as time went by in favour of the 9mm Parabellum. In other respects, the 6.35mm gun, considered too ineffectual for the purposes of self-defence, was more or less replaced by the 7.65mm. Faced with a worldwide craze for the Parabellum automatic pistol (also known as the Luger or P.08), the Erma Werke company of Munich came up in 1964 with a replica of this highly thought-of weapon in a .22 calibre calling it the EP 22. The ET 22 Marine with a 30cm barrel, adjustable sights and wooden fore-end appeared slightly later. In 1968 the Erma KGP 68, a lighter version of the EP 22, made its appearance in 7.65mm and 9mm Short calibres.

Since 1865 the Italian company Vincenzo Bernardelli, at Gardone, had been renowned for its sporting guns. On the initiative of its director, this major firm decided shortly after World War I to enter the hand-gun market. In 1928 the firm won a contract for the development and manufacture of a standard gun for the Italian army. As well as revolvers influenced by trans-Atlantic models, which we shall discuss at a later stage, Bernardelli put an automatic pistol, known as the Baby, on the market in 1949. It is still in production. In 1950 a series of Standard 7.65mm and 9mm Short calibre models failed to gain a foothold in the market. Since 1959, and in order to remedy the failure of the Standard, Bernardelli produced the model 60, in .22 LR, 7.65mm and 9mm Short calibres. Slightly modified to comply with American legislation concerning the importing of foreign arms into the United States, this gun, with an external hammer, was known as the USA model.

High-power combat pistols

Most high-power combat pistols work on similar general principles to those discussed for hand-guns and guns used for self-defence. But because the ammunition develops considerable power, it is always necessary to reduce the blowback action on the breech bolt; to achieve this, and mechanisms differ from type to type, the breech-opening mechanism is delayed until the pressure exercised on this part is compatible with the safety of the gun. Whatever delaying mechanism is used, all such guns have what is known as the 'closed bolt' action. The most common method of closing the breech is to make the bolt and the mobile barrel interlock during the first recoil phase; the two parts separate after a short movement backwards and as from this moment the breech bolt travels alone. This device is known as the 'short recoil mechanism'.

These automatic pistols are characterized by a more or less foolproof action, usually simplified sighting mechanisms, and a so-called 'safe' trigger mechanism. They are generally chambered to fire high-power ammunition such as the 7.62mm Tokarev (or 7.63mm Mauser), 7.65mm Parabellum (.30 Luger), 9mm Parabellum (9mm NATO), .38 Colt Super Auto, 9mm Largo (Spanish service calibre) and .45 Colt Automatic (11.43mm), and have been devised to meet military requirements. The primary purpose of these guns was thus to be the standard hand-gun of one or more national armies.

We have just rapidly looked at the most common calibres for this category of guns; but we should add a few words about the 9mm Parabellum calibre. In the following pages we shall, as is usual, use this general term, but it should be stressed that guns manufactured before 1945 in this calibre were chambered to take the 9mm German Parabellum; the dimensions of this round are slightly different to what we currently call the 9mm Parabellum, which is in fact the 9mm NATO, the standard calibre used by the Atlantic Treaty Organization. For this reason the old P-08 or P-38 are ill-suited to modern manufactured ammunition.

The famous Germans

The first mass-produced high-power automatic pistol was the model which Hugo Borchardt made for the D.W.M. (Deutsche Waffen- und Munitionsfabriken), and which was marketed by them from 1893 onwards. The inventor, who had worked for several years at New Haven in the United States at the Winchester Repeating Arms Co., seems to have been influenced by the first Winchester carbines in developing the 'toggle' mechanism in his pistol. Fitted with a vertical clip holding seven 7.65mm Borchardt rounds (a special round very like the present-day 7.65mm Parabellum), a long barrel and a bulky recoil spring housing situated behind the grip, the gun was not very easy to handle and lacked balance for precision firing. The addition of a carbine butt made it more suitable for this kind of shooting by turning it into a short-barrelled carbine. But as a result the gun lost its position as a hand-gun. But one should still consider the Borchardt as the first valuable automatic pistol, even if it was virtually unusable as such.

The Mauser 1896 automatic pistol was the brainchild of the brothers Fidel, Friedrich and Joseph Feederle. The project for this gun got off the ground in 1893 at

A Parabellum copy made by Erma Werke and known as the Model KGP .68, chambering the 7.65mm Browning round.

The Mauser HSc double action automatic pistol, 7.65mm calibre, as made before the war.

The Mauser 1943 automatic pistol. This pistol, which is striker-fired, is a variant of the 1910 model. The marking 'M' surmounted by the eagle and swastika indicates that the gun was destined for officers of the German navy.

A sectional view of the Bernardelli automatic pistol.

Created as a result of SIG-Sauer cooperation, the new P.230 double action automatic pistol comes in 9mm Police, 9mm Short, 7.65mm and .22 Long Rifle calibres.

Oberndorf in the offices of Paul Mauser, though he knew nothing about it, for he would never have allowed his employees to waste a minute of their working-day for anything other than the making of repeating rifles. Once the project had reached a satisfactory stage, Fidel Feederle embarked on the task of producing a prototype. This prototype was well advanced when the 'boss', Paul Mauser, got wind of these 'secret' goings-on. His initial reaction was brutal, and it was only the friendship between him and the three Feederle brothers which saved the project from being dumped. Quick to grasp the interest implicit in their study, Mauser gave their work the go-ahead, for he had seen a chance to secure a footing in the hand-gun market. On 15 March 1895 the finished prototype released its first bullet. The gun fully, or as good as, satisfied its authors and was patented that same year (No 90430). It retained its basic look until the end of its career in about 1945, undergoing only minor modifications in fifty years. The magazine, placed in front of the trigger-guard and holding ten rounds (sometimes six or twenty) with the help of a loading-clip influenced by those on Mauser repeating rifles, improved the balance of the gun and reduced the disturbance when discharged. The addition of a wooden holster-stock and the use of the powerful 7.63mm Mauser round enabled it to fire at distances of up to 1000m, with of course relative accuracy. In fact the only feature that left anything to be desired was the way the pistol sat in the hand. The shape of the grip partly explains this shortcoming.

The 1896 Mauser and its numerous derivatives are mechanically excellent. The one-piece barrel and slide frame and internal mechanism are machined in a block and assembled without the aid of screws; the only screw used for the assembly of the gun is the one which holds the grip plates. Considered to be too heavy and unnecessarily bulky by the German military authorities, who preferred the D.W.M. Parabellum pistol, the 1896 model did not enjoy the military career on which its makers were reckoning. Mauser aimed his production at civilian markets. The 1896 model became the ideal weapon for the colonies; the budding young officer Winston Churchill owed his life to one during an engagement against the Dervishes in September 1898 in the Omdurman plain, during the war in the Sudan. In an attempt to curry favour with the various military authorities, the Waffenfabrik Mauser proposed a lighter version of the 1896 model: a shorter barrel, six-round magazine and flat sides. But, like its predecessor, this model did not interest the military. For a while the 1896 model was also offered in the form of a carbine with a detachable stock to compete with the Parabellum carbine which the D.W.M. had just put on the market. The two carbines were never as successful as their respective manufacturers hoped. Rejected by the military, the 1896 model was proposed by Mauser on the commercial market in several countries. Von Lengerke and Detmold in New York ensured a certain sale of the gun in the United States. In France, the Manufacture d'Armes et Cycles de Saint-Etienne offered it to its clientele as 'the most powerful gun currently existing in the category of automatic pistols . . . This is an ideal weapon for settlers, explorers, and anyone who requires a weapon for self-defence which is at once very powerful and relatively light.' In England, Westley Richards was Mauser's agent

and made a very respectable job of selling the 1896 Mauser.

Shortly after the appearance of the 1896 Mauser automatic pistol, a serious rival came on the scene in the Kaiser's Germany: the Parabellum automatic pistol. If it is true that certain guns have won their letters patent of nobility throughout the world, it is as well to make special mention of Georg Luger's Parabellum automatic pistol. Who, nowadays, expert or layman, has not heard of the Luger or Parabellum? We come across them in virtually every spy thriller, and certain journalists use the term Parabellum as a generic designation for automatic pistols in general; just as some use the word Colt as a synonym for revolver.

The Parabellum or Luger, which is sometimes also called the P-08, although all three terms define one and the same gun, has had the effect, since the day it appeared, of an almost magical spell for those who have a liking for handsome guns. Is it the original shape, the curious 'toggle' breech, its exceptional handling ability, or the fact that so many imaginary heroes use it, that have surrounded this gun with a sort of mythical aura? We do not know which, but few people remain unimpressed by this little mechanical jewel whose performance is nevertheless, and sadly, often erratic. It was in about 1898 that Georg Luger, sales representative-cum-inventor working at Ludwig Loewe of Berlin, presented the Swiss authorities with an improved model of the Borchardt pistol, whose sales he had promoted both in the United States and in Europe. The Borchardt-Luger outclassed the Mauser, Bergmann, Mannlicher and other pistols during tests and trials carried out by the Swiss general staff. A further series of tests carried out by the Swiss army confirmed its superiority in 1899 and resulted in an order for 3000 pistols placed with Ludwig Loewe, which had in the meantime become the D.W.M. (Deutsche Waffen und Munitionsfabriken). Switzerland was the first country to adopt the Parabellum, chambered to fire the 7.65mm Parabellum, as a standard-issue hand-gun.

Keen to find a standard-issue automatic pistol the United States army tried out the Parabellum in 1907, together with the Colt pistol which was to become the renowned Government Model of 1911, and obviously came out in favour of the latter. On the civilian market Stoeger of New York became D.W.M.'s American agent and importer of the Parabellum, which was christened the Luger after the name of its inventor, to the United States. Models sold on the other side of the Atlantic then bore the American emblem on top of the chamber. At about the same time D.W.M. proposed a carbine variant of its Parabellum pistol. The only success scored by this gun has been among present-day collectors.

In 1904 the German navy (*Kriegsmarine*) was the first branch of the German armed forces to adopt the Parabellum as a standard-issue weapon. The first pistols delivered under the terms of the contract were the 1900 model fitted with a 15cm barrel. From 1906 the Parabellum Marine was supplied in the 1906 version (where a helical recoil spring replaced the old leaf spring, and the sides of the cocking knobs were entirely knurled.) Most of the old models already in service underwent this special modification. All the Parabellum Marine pistols were chambered for the 9mm Parabellum round, fitted with a

Mauser 1896 automatic pistol, 7.63mm Mauser calibre. This is one of the very first types, identifiable by the shape of the hammer, the long extractor and the sight graduated from 50—500 metres.

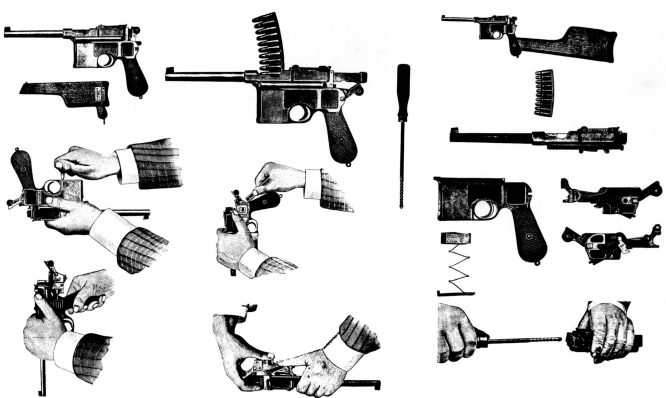

Instructions for use and stripping supplied with the 1896 Mauser when it was first marketed.

The Parabellum P.08/14 automatic pistol.

The Borchardt automatic pistol by Ludwig Loewe of Berlin.

Derived from the 1896 model, the Mauser 1912 automatic pistol is shown here with the breech open for loading the ten 7.63mm Mauser rounds.

The Mauser 1896 automatic pistol with 6-round magazine. This model has no sights, and was not cut for stock.

Mauser 1912 automatic pistol with stock fitted and sight adjusted for 1000 metres.

A Mauser carbine derived from the 1896 automatic pistol chambered for the 7.63mm Mauser. It had a 37cm barrel, detachable stock and sight graduated from 50–500 metres.

sight which was adjustable on the toggle joint, and delivered with a removable stock for long-distance use.

European trends in the pre-war period

It was at Steyr in Austria that the Mannlicher Waffenfabrik had brought out its 1905 model a year earlier. The grip of this gun incorporated an 8- or 10-round magazine loaded by means of a loading clip similar to that of the 1896 Mauser pistol. Although it used a special kind of ammunition, the 7.65mm Mannlicher, this gun won numerous orders, particularly in South America. For a while it was the standard weapon for the army in Argentina. The Roth-Steyr, successor to the 1905 model, went on to steal the show, conspicuously outclassing its elder brother. It was adopted from 1907 onwards by the Austro-Hungarian cavalry as a standard issue. Likewise, using a special 8mm round, it was fitted, like the 1905 model, with a magazine in the grip fed by a clip loader. It was very popular in the Balkan countries, and was carried by many a partisan during World War II, although its production had long since been halted.

Arms manufacturers in Italy could not remain aloof from this upsurge of high-power automatic hand-guns. The Italian navy had already ordered 5000 1896 model Mausers for its own requirements. In 1906, at Brescia, the Brixia automatic pistol was developed which seemed to be derived partly from the 1896 Mauser, as far as its mechanism was concerned, and partly from the Parabellum, as far as its looks were concerned. The Brixia chambered a special round, known as the 9mm Glisenti, which was interchangeable with the 9mm Parabellum but much less powerful. Although it was not yet adopted by the German army, the Parabellum caught the attention of a number of potential users: Vickers Limited started manufacturing it in the Netherlands from 1906 onwards. The Parabellum was to become a standard weapon in many countries: the Netherlands, Portugal, Bulgaria, Japan and so on, as well as Switzerland, where the army had been already using it for more than six years.

The French army, for its part, was 'coddling' its own darling – the 1892 service revolver – and was little concerned with adopting an automatic pistol for which it had little time, and which was equally disparaged by the British military authorities. The German army finally adopted the Parabellum in 1908 and called it the P-08. (Since its reorganization by Bismarck the German army denoted its standard-issue weapons by the initial or initials of the generic name of the weapon and the year of its adoption as a standard issue – P-08 for the Pistole 1908, K 98 for the Karabine 1898, MP-40 for Machine Pistole 1940. These references will recur throughout this book.) Returning to the P-08, it differed from its predecessor, the 1906 model, by doing away with the grip safety and reversing the operation of the thumb safety-catch. In 1914 the P-08 was equipped with a warning device at the end of the clip which blocked the bolt in the open position after the ejection of the case of the last round. The P-08/14 was certainly the most widely used of all the types of Parabellum pistol: in fact more than 2,000,000 of these pistols were manufactured from 1914–18. All the military pistols produced in Germany bear the year of manufacture engraved on the upper part of the chamber.

In Belgium, in about 1908, the Anciens Etablissements Pieper, at Herstal, started production under licence of the whole range of Bergmann pistols, none of which was a standard-issue west of the Rhine. In 1910 a new model was brought out influenced by both the Bergmann, whose revolver lock it retained, and the 1896 Mauser, from which it adopted the breech system and the magazine located in front of the trigger-guard. Chambered for the 9mm Bergmann-Bayard round (9mm Largo, the standard Spanish calibre), this pistol was equipped with a detachable clip holding six, eight or ten rounds, which could also be loaded by the system used on the 1896 Mauser, from the top of the gun, by means of a clip loader. This pistol was simultaneously manufactured in Germany and Belgium and became the standard equipment for the Danish and Spanish armies.

Having, for its part, tried out the numerous pistols offered by the major arms manufacturers throughout the world, the United States army finally adopted the Colt .45 ACP pistol. Like its rare forebears, such as the 1902 Colt Sporting model, this pistol derived from John Browning patents. It saw service in France in 1917 and 1918 with the Americans, and has been used on almost every battlefield up to the present day. During the 1930s gangsters in Chicago and other cities carried it together with the Thompson sub-machine-gun. The Colt .45 ACP remained standard equipment for the American GIs when certain minor modifications had been made to it in 1926, namely: (a) the back of the grip was rounded; (b) the frame, behind the trigger, was milled to give the forefinger a better position; (c) the hammer was shorter and less curved; (d) the upper part of the grip safety was lengthened.

All parts remained interchangeable between the two versions. This heavy, efficient and accurate gun saw service on the 1939–45 battlefields, in Korea, Indo-China and Vietnam, and so on. Less spectacularly, the Colt 1911 A1 'surplus' was the basic weapon in France in the years following the Liberation. It is still used by many a crook because this gun is of impressive size, is remarkably accurate, and is uncommonly effective because of the huge power of the impact of the 11.43mm round, as evidenced by Antoine Guerini, former gang-leader in the Marseilles area, who was gunned down in a service station by two gangsters who riddled him with fourteen .45 ACP bullets.

Shortly before World War I, Don Venancio Lopez de Ceballos y Aguirre, Count of Campo Giro, and a lieutenant-colonel in the Spanish army, equipped the army with its first standard-issue automatic pistol in the shape of the 1913 Campo-Giro, which chambered the 9mm Largo round.

World War I

The 1914–18 war was to highlight the superiority of the high-power pistol over the obsolete revolvers used by the Allies: the Enfield, and Webley made in Great Britain, the standard-issue French 1892 model, and the 1874 Italian Glisenti. The Allies south of the Alps had the standard 1910 Glisenti automatic pistol, derived from the Brixia. This was a highly complicated gun which, after the war, was superseded by the 1915 Beretta automatic pistol, chambering the 9mm Glisenti round. This 1915 Beretta was also marketed as a non-military model in 7.65mm

The Parabellum 1900 automatic pistol used by the Swiss army, in 7.65mm calibre (note 2).

Top-view of the Parabellum 1900 (so-called American Eagle) automatic pistol (note 3).

The Parabellum 1900 automatic carbine in 7.65mm Parabellum calibre shown without its detachable stock.

The Parabellum 1906 automatic pistol as made by Vickers Ltd.

The Parabellum Marine automatic pistol, 9mm Parabellum calibre.

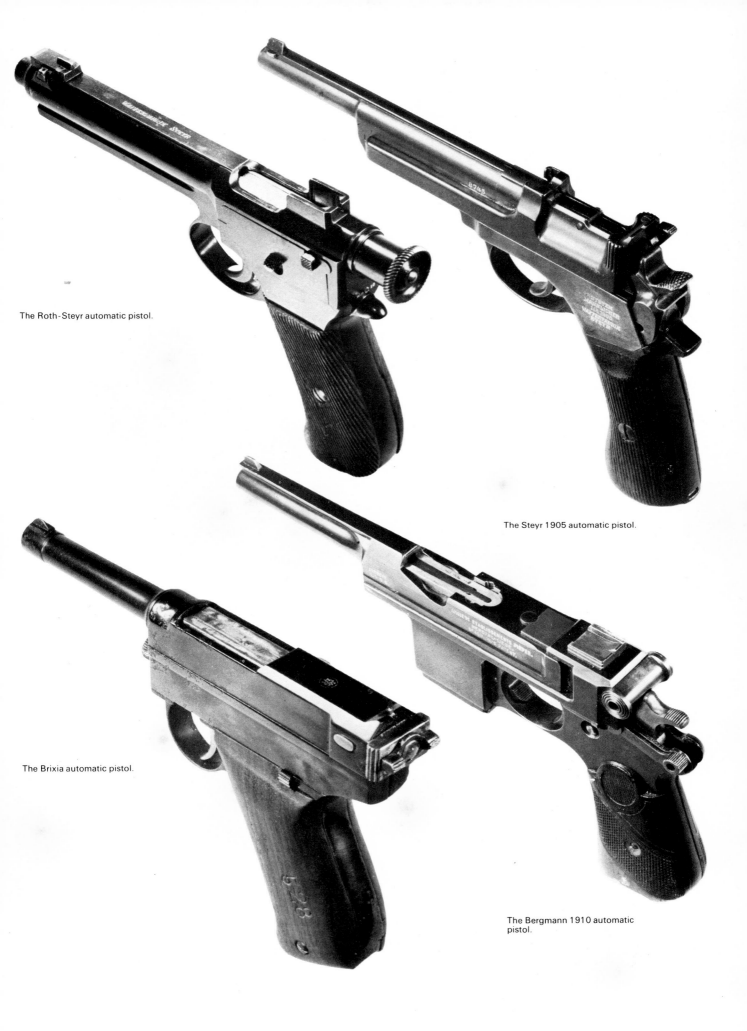

The Roth-Steyr automatic pistol.

The Steyr 1905 automatic pistol.

The Brixia automatic pistol.

The Bergmann 1910 automatic pistol.

The Colt 1902 Sporting model automatic pistol, manufactured in the United States in accordance with the Browning patents.

One of the 5000 Mauser 1896 automatic pistols supplied to the Italian navy.

The Italian Glisenti 1910 automatic pistol.

The transformation of a Mauser 1916 pistol by changing the original barrel for a Parabellum pistol barrel.

The Italian Beretta 1915 automatic pistol which replaced the Glisenti in the Italian army.

The Parabellum 1914 automatic pistol, known as the artillery Parabellum, with a snail-drum magazine holding thirty-two 9mm Parabellum rounds.

Browning calibre. In 1914 the Kaiser's artillery in its turn adopted the Parabellum, which was already in service with the navy and the infantry. But it was an ideal weapon for the artillery, although derived directly from the P-08/14; it had a 20cm barrel and an adjustable sight (up to 800 metres) fixed on the barrel in front of the chamber. The gun was supplied with a special clip, known as a snail-drum magazine, with a 32-round capacity. This drum, designed specially with artillerymen in mind, did not appear to satisfy its users, who generally preferred to use the normal 8-round clip, which could also be used on this model. The artillery model, when equipped with a holster-stock, could be swiftly transformed into a mini carbine.

During the war Germany swallowed up a huge number of Parabellum pistols and, unable to meet the demand, the D.W.M. was bolstered by Mauser, Krieghoff, Simson and Co., and the Erfurt Arsenal. Was it because of the urgent need for hand-guns of all sorts, or was it because the Parabellum revealed certain flaws, when in use, which it had hitherto managed to conceal? It is hard to say, but the fact remains that in 1916 the Waffenfabrik Mauser saw its 1896 pistol finally adopted by the imperial general staff. An order for 150,000 guns was placed with it, but these guns, which looked identical to the 1896 model, were chambered for the 9mm Parabellum. To differentiate them from the other variants, a figure 9 was engraved and painted in red on each grip plate. These guns saw much active service in 1917–18 in the field. The 1918 Armistice and the Treaty of Versailles put a halt to German production of military weapons. A large number of Mauser and Parabellum pistols ended up in the scrapyard. But some were saved to equip the 100,000 troops of the Weimar Republic. One of the clauses in the Treaty of Versailles concerning armaments stipulated that hand-guns should be fitted with barrels no longer than 10cm, which amounted to an indirect confirmation of the effectiveness of the weapons used by the Kaiser's army, as witnessed with much loss of life by the Allied troops. Mauser barrels were therefore reduced from 14cm to 10cm. Some were even equipped with Parabellum barrels; this transformation was so meticulously carried out that the screw-assembly of the new barrel can only be detected by X-ray examination.

The Parabellum 08/14, in the infantry version with a 10cm barrel, was not affected by the restrictive clauses of the Treaty, and some officers were equipped with it.

The post-war period

During their engagements against the German troops, Russian troops had, at their own expense, had a chance to see the effectiveness of the Mauser automatic pistol. After the war the new regime purchased fairly large quantities of these guns. Some have seen this as the origin of the reference Bolo (Bolshevik) for these short-barrelled Mausers with no sights and a modified grip. We can give them the benefit of the doubt, but shall not speculate further. Without any military supplies from Germany, for the reasons outlined above, the various countries in the Far East, and China in particular, produced their 1896 Mausers on a hand-made basis. Apart from some .45 ACP models made by the Shansei arms factory and the Taku Docks, these guns were in the main of very mediocre

quality. Faithful to their tradition, and keen to exploit the Asian market which the Germans could no longer supply, the Spanish went to work. In 1928 the firm Unceta y Cia (Astra) took out a patent for an automatic pistol which, in its looks, was strangely similar to the 1896 Mauser. But the lock and assembly of the gun were conspicuously different; simpler than its German forebear, this pistol was easier to dismantle and strip. The Chinese markings on the sides of these guns leave one in no doubt as to their destination. Under the trade name of the Model F Astra, this gun was also available as a machine-pistol (cf. the chapter 'Sub-machine-guns'). It was without any doubt one of the best guns produced by the Spanish arms industry. It was, in particular, used during the Spanish Civil War (1936–9), by both sides. When the Republic fell a large number of these weapons 'crossed' the Pyrenees and some of them ended up in the hands of the resistance groups in the south of France. It is also worth mentioning the vain attempt, made in about 1929 by the Manufacture d'Armes et Cycles de Saint-Etienne, to get the French army to adopt its Le Français automatic pistol, Army type, chambered for the 9mm round. The authorities who, shortly thereafter, were to adopt 7.65mm calibre weapons, rejected this gun as 'lacking power'! But for their own personal use a good many officers had guns of this type when war was declared in 1939.

The Swiss, who had previously been supplied with standard-issue pistols by the D.W.M. in Germany, decided in 1929 to make their own Parabellum which was christened the 1929 model. This gun chambered the 7.65mm Parabellum round. Made by the Waffenfabrik-Bern, it quite closely resembled the German Parabellum, whose general features it had borrowed; but it differed in as much as the grip, with plastic plates, was straight in shape, the grip safety was longer than on the 1900 and 1906 Parabellums, and the thumb safety had a non-scored button. In addition the parts were not interchangeable with those of previous models. The 1929 Swiss Parabellum was produced to the tune of 27,941 models for the needs of the Swiss army; in addition to this, 1916 pistols were put on the civilian market. These latter are identifiable by the letter *P* which precedes the series number. During the tests, prototypes of this model were made with a 9mm Parabellum calibre, but were not satisfactory.

German re-armament and its consequences

Keen not to have Spanish competition in markets which it considered to be its own, the Waffenfabrik Mauser retaliated strongly with its 1896 model, duly brought up to date. The new model appeared in 1930. It was in the first instance fitted with its usual fixed magazine (first 1930 type), but was very quickly modified to take detachable 10- and 20-round clips (second 1930 type). This model is identifiable by its barrel which is screwed on to the slide, its new so-called 'universal' safety device which makes it possible to uncock the hammer without any risk of striking the round, and the presence of the Mauser emblem on the left side of the receiver above the grip. This model was made in 7.63mm Mauser and 9mm Parabellum calibres; the two types can only be told apart by close examination of the boring of the barrel.

Concerned about its independence, the young Soviet State neither could nor was to remain dependent on foreign nations for the supply of automatic pistols to the Red Army. Fedor V. Tokarev, ex-Cossack officer in the Imperial Russian army and subsequently arms engineer at the Toula arsenal, set to work and in 1930 produced the TT-30 pistol (Toula-Tokarev). The gun chambered a 7.62mm (so-called F) round, very like the 7.63mm Mauser, with which it was interchangeable, though slightly more powerful. The barrel assembly, which was somewhat modified in 1933, gave rise to the TT 1933 model. The Petter patent for the removable lock, and the Browning patent for the barrel and bolt assembly seem to have influenced the Soviet engineer. In spite of the high rates of production in World War II, the gun remained remarkably well finished during this period, which says a lot for the Soviet arms industry. After the war several countries which fell within the orbit of the USSR adopted the 1933 Tokarev as a standard weapon. Some of them manufactured it in their own factories, which was the case with Red China and Yugoslavia. In the latter, the firm Zastava is currently producing its model 60 in Soviet 7.62mm or 9mm Parabellum calibre. The TT 1933 has been technically superseded and replaced by Makarov and Stechkine automatic pistols, the latter capable of firing bursts of 9mm Parabellum rounds.

Since 1922 John M. Browning had made three applications in Belgium for patents covering a 'high power automatic pistol'. This brilliant inventor died in Liège in 1929, at the age of 71, and never actually saw his posthumous child, the G.P., which represents the high point of Belgian arms manufacture. Because circumstances in the post-war period were unfavourable to arms plans, the project remained on the F.N. shelves while that company played for time. The rise of Adolf Hitler to power and the threats posed by Germany to world peace led, in 1935, to the production lines grinding into action to produce the Browning Grande Puissance or Browning G.P. After the occupation of Belgium by the German forces the Canadian government sub-contracted G.P. production for the armament of Canadian, British and Chinese troops. The Herstal factory was forced, by Germany, to continue to turn out the G.P. to equip the Wehrmacht and, later, the SS. 200,000 pistols with adjustable sights and hallmarked with the eagle and swastika were delivered to Germany. Simple in conception, tough, and mechanically sound, the Browning G.P. has considerable fire-power with its 13-round clip holding the 9mm Parabellum in a staggered arrangement. It attracted favourable attention from numerous armies and police forces. Adopted by more than fifty countries, among which numbered nearly all Commonwealth members, it is still manufactured by the F.N. The G.P. comes currently in five versions: Vigilant, Capitan, Sport, De Luxe Model and engraved De Luxe Model. All are available in 9mm or 7.65mm Parabellum calibres. A new clip with a 20-round capacity has been recently put on the market and increases the fire-power of this remarkable gun still further.

It was also in 1935 that the French army decided to equip itself with a standard automatic pistol. Some years before it had rejected a 9mm model for lack of power, and the general staff naturally selected a 7.65mm calibre. But it

should be pointed out in this respect that this calibre, known as the 7.65mm Long, is conspicuously more powerful than the 7.65mm Browning. The weapon chosen by the French army was referred to as the Model 1935 A standard issue automatic pistol. It was made by the Société Alsacienne de Constructions Mécaniques, using a patent filed by an employee in this company, C. Petter, which covered the detachable lock.

The Société Industrielle Suisse (SIG) at Neuhausen undertook to manufacture this gun under licence, and brought out the Petter model, the first in a long line of SIG automatic pistols, the last of which – the Model P-210 – represents the culmination.

In France the Model 35 A underwent certain restyling of the frame and bolt, and mechanical alterations – the suppression of one small link for tilting the barrel – as well as changes in outward looks with a new surface treatment obtained by means of phosphating. It subsequently became the 1935 S which, like its predecessor, chambered the 7.65mm Long round, later used for the MAS 1938 sub-machine-gun.

It would seem that the year 1935 was a lucky year for the production of new automatic pistols. In fact it was in this year that Poland, as a result of the F. N. Herstal technicians' cooperation, made its F. B. Radom pistol (Radom being the name of the arsenal where it was developed). The Radom made the most of the latest improvements introduced by the most recent Browning patents and was immediately adopted by the Polish army as the Model 35. Chambered for the 9mm Parabellum, this excellently finished pistol was one of the best pre-war models. When the Germans marched into Poland they showed great interest in it and production carried on under their aegis; the guns were used to equip German troops on the Eastern front and all bore the Nazi eagle. Production of this gun did not cease until the arrival in Poland of the Russians, at the end of the war.

World War II
In 1937 an automatic double-action pistol appeared in Germany, chambering 9mm Parabellum ammunition, which was devised and made for the army of the Third Reich: it was the Walther HP (HeeresPistole) and was instantly adopted by the Wehrmacht, the Kriegsmarine and the Luftwaffe. What is more it was also selected as the hand-gun equipping the various para-military organizations of the Nazi party. And lastly, as soon as it came out at the beginning of the war, the SS adopted it too. The old Parabellum had to step down in the face of this substitute. In battles fought by the German army from 1939 to 1945 in every type of climate there was ample occasion for those using the Walther HP to appreciate the gun's high degree of reliability, endurance and effectiveness. The German general staff called it the P-38, for reasons explained earlier. Like the P-08 during World War I, the Walther P-38 was in great demand for Germany's operational troops, and was manufactured by all the major German arms factories and also by certain factories in occupied Europe. The products of the various factories can be told apart by their respective initials: Walther: 'ac'; Spree Werke: 'cyq'; Brno: 'dov'; the Belgian F.N.: 'ch'; and Mauser: 'byf' and 'svw'. The French police force was supplied with a large

The Campo-Giro, first standard
automatic pistol of the Spanish
army.

The so-called 'Bolo' Mauser
automatic pistol.

The transformation of a Mauser
1912 model automatic pistol into a
7.63mm Mauser calibre in
accordance with the stipulation
drawn up at the Treaty of
Versailles.

The Mauser 1916 model
automatic pistol and its holster-
stock. This gun chambered the
9mm Parabellum and was less well
finished than commercial pistols.

The Parabellum P.08/14
automatic pistol made by the
D.W.M. in 1920, shown with the
bolt open and the toggle folded.

The Mauser 1930 automatic pistol
(first type) chambered for the
7.63mm Mauser.

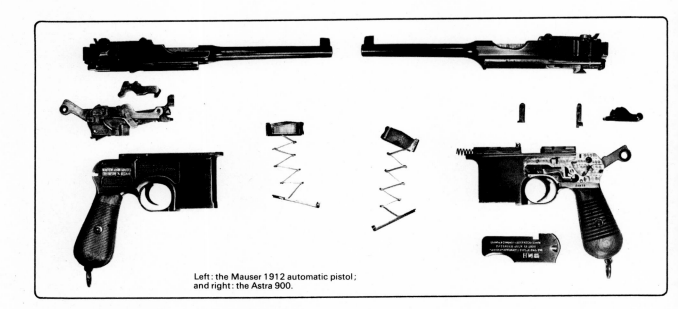

Left: the Mauser 1912 automatic pistol;
and right: the Astra 900.

The Astra 900 automatic pistol in
7.63mm Mauser calibre.

The Parabellum 1929 Swiss-made
automatic pistol.

number of guns bearing the initials 'svw' as war damages. The total production of P-38 pistols during the last war is estimated at more than one million.

When the American troops reached Thuringia they found the Walther factory at Zella-Mehlis completely devastated by bombing raids with the exception of the water-tower, which had miraculously escaped the bombs. When Germany was divided up, and the town of Zella-Mehlis was found to be in the Soviet zone (now East Germany), Fritz Walther emigrated to Ulm where he set up shop once again. At the present time production of the P-38 automatic pistol has been resumed and the gun is a standard issue in the Bundeswehr. The P-38 also comes in a civilian version, either engraved or not, with a steel or light alloy frame.

The lessons of the war

The war had conclusively demonstrated the superiority of the 9mm Parabellum round. It is very compact and represents a compromise between small calibres and the American .45 ACP, which is considered to be unnecessarily powerful and heavy in Europe. In about 1953 there was a rumour abroad in the United States that the army was thinking of adopting a standard-issue automatic pistol in a smaller calibre than the .45 ACP. Smith and Wesson of Springfield (in the United States) worked on a double-action automatic pistol chambering the 9mm Parabellum round and marketed it as the Model 39. It would seem that the rumours about a possible change of standard calibre were unfounded, because the old Colt .45 Government Model was replaced by neither the Model 39, nor any other model. As far as the Colt is concerned, it is still made by Colt, but it should be pointed out that during World War II, and for reasons identical to those which, in Europe, led to the manufacture of the P-38 by numerous factories, the Colt has been manufactured under licence by several arms factories in America (Remington Co., Ithaca, Springfield Armoury, etc.). Most of the high-powered automatic pistols made after 1950 are still being made today, as are a certain number of their predecessors. We have thus decided to include them, or some of them, in the technical data sheets, representing a selection of the most typical guns in this category. There are also target models derived from some of these guns: in this case they are fitted with a swifter lock and adjustable sights. The best-known in France are the Swiss SIG P-210 and the French M.A.B. P-15 Competition, as well as the Smith and Wesson M.52 chambered for the .38 Special Wad Cutter (target round for revolvers). In America and South-East Asia, the Colt National Match Gold Cup, available in .45 ACP and .38 Auto, is also very popular.

Revolvers

The revolver, which has been industrially manufactured ever since Samuel Colt's famous invention in 1836, has been threatened for eighty years by its young rival, the automatic pistol; but the revolver has held its ground, and according to some specialists still has a long career ahead of it. This, at any rate, would seem to be the view of the numerous manufacturers who, particularly in Europe, have been trying since the war to get a foothold in the market alongside the American giants. But although one cannot call the revolver an old arm, it did achieve its present degree of development well before the invention of smokeless powder. The improvements made to it in the course of the twentieth century have been of a primarily technological nature: the use of improved steels adapted to very powerful cartridges, and machining methods which make it possible to mass produce top quality arms.

The advances made where the revolver is concerned have been much less spectacular than in the case of the automatic pistol; for this reason we have preferred to deal more fully with the fundamentally modern weapon embodied by the latter. The revolver, by name, derives from the English verb *to revolve*, and has a distinctive feed system consisting of a cylinder which turns and has several chambers containing the cartridges. The rotation of this cylinder is controlled either by manually cocking the hammer (single action), or by the action of the finger on the trigger (double action).

If the first American revolvers had only a single action mechanism, most current models offer both single and double actions. Some contemporary guns, on the basis of the theoretical use to which they are put, use only one of these principles: modern replicas of old revolvers only have the single action; the Smith and Wesson Centennial, whose hammer is concealed, only has the double action, as do the Webley revolvers manufactured during the last war for the British commandos – these were without a full cock notch, at the request of the British general staff, thus making the double action (which was quicker) obligatory. In broad terms, the single action is used at the range, for accuracy, and the double action in more active military operations. As far as the single action is concerned, and compared with automatic pistols, revolvers offer a certain number of advantages which cause most sporting competitors using large calibres to prefer them: clean, easy trigger-pull, manufacturing quality, low wear and tear and reliability. The double action of a revolver is used for rapid return fire and for continuous rapid fire. The features of a good double action lock have been defined by, among others, Raymond Caranta and Pierre Cantegrit in their book *Aristocratie du pistolet*. Of these features the most essential one is the supple nature of the mechanism. The American company Smith and Wesson of Springfield (Massachusetts) has for more than seventy years been a pastmaster in the manufacture of top quality double action revolver mechanisms. Few other revolvers can compare with its production; though one should note the Colt Python, where the lock parts are manually adjusted.

American revolvers

The North Americans tend to dominate this type of firearm, in particular Colt, and Smith and Wesson. We would ask the reader to excuse us if we take a brief step backward so as to set the scene for the two most famous American revolver manufacturers somewhat better.

The Colt's Patent Fire Arms Manufacturing Co.

The ill-informed nowadays tend to call all revolvers 'Colts', even if the gun in question is the thoroughbred product of some 'Spanish hardware store'. This 'error' may be taken as a posthumous homage to Samuel Colt who

Colt Government Model automatic pistols. Top: the 1911 World War I
model. Below: the 1911 A1 model manufactured during the last war.

The Colt 1911 automatic pistol.

The Smith and Wesson 39
automatic pistol.

The German standard-issue
Walther P.38 automatic pistol in
9mm Parabellum calibre.

The Tokarev TT.1933 7.62mm
calibre automatic pistol.

The SIG-Sauer automatic pistol.

The Radom Vis 35 automatic pistol, standard equipment of the pre-war Polish army.

The first standard automatic pistol of the French army: the model 1935A.

The 1935 S standard French automatic pistol.

The so-called Petter model automatic pistol manufactured by the Swiss firm SIG under licence and derived from the 1935A standard French model.

The Walther P.38 automatic pistol. Manufactured by Mauser, by way of war damages, this gun was supplied to the French police force.

The Tokarev TT.1933 automatic pistol.

The Browning G.P. automatic pistol made by the Fabrique Nationale d'Armes de Guerre at Herstal in Belgium. This is the variant known as the 'Capitan' which is being made at the present time.

was the first man fully to develop a truly functional revolver. It is true that some time before him, and particularly in the golden age of the old firearms, gunsmiths had made repeating guns fitted with a cylinder which was rotated manually after each shot. The results achieved by Samuel Colt quickly attracted the attention of the American military authorities, and all the more so because his inventions emerged at a particularly troubled moment in history. The Colt Walker, Colt Navy 1851, Colt Army 1860 and Colt Navy 1861, as well as certain civilian models, dominated the hand-gun market in the mid-nineteenth century. When the Hartford master died in 1862 his successors continued the task and in particular brought out various less military-orientated models. The patent filed by Rollin White and transferred to Smith and Wesson did not expire until 3 April 1869; before this The Colt's Patent Fire Arms Manufacturing Co. could not market a revolver firing metal cartridges. So the debut of this gun was prepared down to the very last detail, the aim being to put on sale, on this date, a revolver which would outclass its rivals.

In 1872, after comparative tests with other revolvers, the Ordnance Department of the US Army adopted the new Colt revolver in .45 Long Colt calibre and placed an initial order for 8000 guns to equip the US Cavalry. Some of these guns were carried by General Custer's men at the battle of Little Big Horn, but this was not enough to deter the Indians, who outnumbered them ten to one, and 260 soldiers lost their lives, among them Custer himself. The famous Colt Single Action Army revolver, known as the Peacemaker, thus embarked on a long and noteworthy career which it still enjoys today in the hands of shooting enthusiasts. The Colt Frontier, very like the Army model, was not chambered for the .45 LC, contrary to the belief of a good number of misinformed people, but for the .44-40 WCF, which meant that it could use the same ammunition as the 1873 Winchester carbine, whose inseparable mate it was throughout the West. Like the Army model, this revolver was a single action model only, and cocking was manual. It is characterized by the individual ejection of the empty cases, controlled by means of a movable rod fixed along the barrel, as on French Lefaucheux and Service 1873 revolvers. Sturdily made, and immortalized by the cinema, it is the cowboy's standard equipment in American folklore. The Colt Bisley, a competition version of the Single Action Army revolver, had been specially designed to rival Smith and Wesson's New Model Target, but failed to get the better of it. It would be almost impossible and in any event tedious to list here all the models produced by Colt, so we shall mention only the best-known: the Colt New Navy, the Colt Army Special, the Colt New Service, the Colt Officer's Model Target, the Colt Police Positive and the famous Cobra. It was a Cobra with which Ruby killed Lee Harvey Oswald, the presumed assassin of J. F. Kennedy, president of the United States.

At the present time North American police forces use the Colt Trooper and, more particularly, the Colt Python, whereas the Colt Officer's Model Match is frequently pitted against the Smith and Wesson K.22 on European shooting ranges.

Smith and Wesson

In 1864 this firm brought out the first repeating pistol, later to become the Volcanic. Smith and Wesson later sold the patent to a business consortium, which included Oliver F. Winchester who was at the time a shirtmaker. Smith and Wesson subsequently turned their efforts to the development of a metal cartridge which they felt was urgently needed, and a gun capable of using such ammunition. First they brought out the .22 Short ammunition which can still be purchased today at any gunshop. The acquisition of the Rollin White patent for a cylinder with chambers bored right through it secured them — in the United States — a comfortable lead over their rivals who were forced to mark time until 1869, when the patent expired. First came the Model no. 1, then the model no. 2, firing a .32 calibre rim-fire cartridge, and the model 1 1/2, a smaller version of the no. 2. With their no. 3 model Smith and Wesson moved away from small calibres and produced a very powerful gun using a .44 calibre centre-fire cartridge; numerous versions of this model were then manufactured, with the Russian, .45 Schoefield, the New Model, and the famous New Model Target on which the first world shooting records were based.

Then came the series of .32-20 Hand Ejector models. At this time the major development was the creation of the .38 cartridge, designed for a new gun. Then came the Military and Police model, a remarkably effective weapon, which is still enjoying a brilliant career which started in 1899. It has undergone numerous improvements in its details, but still retains its original appearance.

During World War II Smith and Wesson supplied several thousand Military and Police .38 Special calibre revolvers for American troops. This model is known as the Victory Model. In April 1940, with a contract for several thousand guns (the exact number is not known), Great Britain purchased from Smith and Wesson a variant of the revolver known as the K-200. This weapon was a standard issue in the British army during the war, and chambered the ordinary .38 round. At the present time the range of Smith and Wesson production includes more than forty different models, most of which are designed for target shooting.

Other American revolvers

Lorded over by the two super-firms described above, other American arms manufacturers have, since the appearance of the revolver, been forced to accept a small market: neither Harrington and Richardson nor Iver Johnson have been able to rally against their powerful rivals. With his .38 model firing triangular-section plastic bullets feeding, via a clip, a rotating cylinder, Dardick introduced a new idea which never really got off the ground in a commercial sense. For some years a new firm in the United States, Sturm Ruger and Co. — well known in other respects for its rifles — made an effort to market top quality guns which, in certain fields of their respective range of production, provided competition for Colt, and Smith and Wesson. With, in particular, its Blackhawk and Security Six models, the former with single action and the latter with double action, Sturm Ruger and Co. offered extremely well-made revolvers at reasonable prices which incorporated certain original features.

European revolvers

In Europe the first standard-issue revolver designed to fire

The French 1892 model service revolver

The American Remington New Model revolver, single action, which was the forebear of our present-day revolvers.

The Smith and Wesson 40 Centennial revolver, currently being produced (note 4).

The Spanish Llama Martial double-action revolver, of modern manufacture.

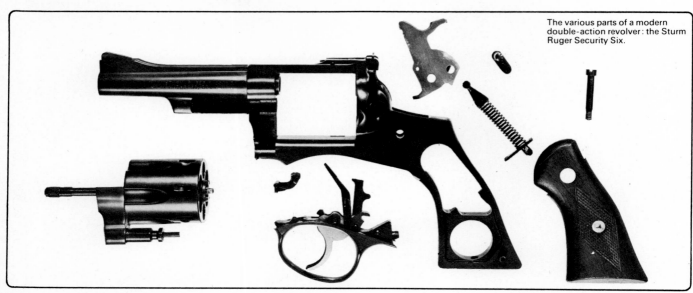

The various parts of a modern double-action revolver: the Sturm Ruger Security Six.

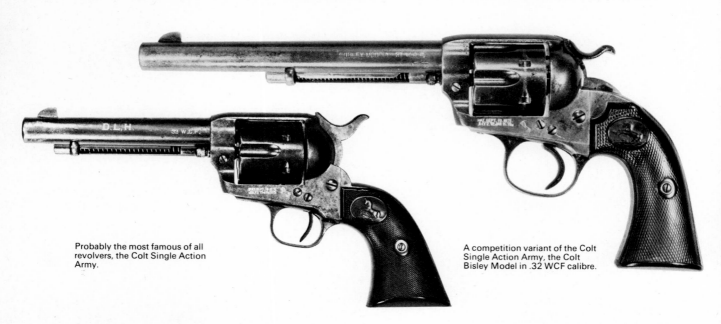

Probably the most famous of all revolvers, the Colt Single Action Army.

A competition variant of the Colt Single Action Army, the Colt Bisley Model in .32 WCF calibre.

a cartridge loaded with smokeless powder and jacketed bullet was without any doubt the French 1892 model manufactured by the Manufacture d'Armes de Saint-Etienne (the State Arsenal). This revolver, adopted by the army in 1892, was standard equipment until 1935 when it was decided to replace it on a gradual basis by the 1935 model automatic pistol. This replacement was so gradual that many officers were still carrying the 1892 model at the outbreak of World War II. It was, for all that, a well-made gun, which differed from its rivals abroad in that the cylinder swings to the right. If one is to go by the French Army instruction manuals, this distinctive feature is explained by the fact that an officer holds his sabre in his right hand, and must therefore use his revolver with his left hand. This conception of the use of hand-guns explains why the cylinder swings to the right. This was the gun carried by French officers during the period of colonial expansion and some countries continued to produce it, using recovered parts, when they had achieved independence from French colonial rule.

Among what might be called modern European revolvers, only the English Webley models have their distinct personality, although aesthetically speaking their appearance may perhaps be a little too Victorian in the eyes of the continental enthusiast. In his remarkable book, *The Handgun*, Geoffrey Boothroyd, an English handgun expert, draws a parallel which deserves mention. 'Undoubtedly the strongest of the hinged frame revolvers, the service life of the six Government Webleys was entirely honourable and there is no doubt that, if the same attention had been devoted to the stories and legends of the British Empire as has been devoted to the opening of the American West by the Movie Moguls, the Webley Government Models could truly be said to have been the "Peacemakers" of the British Empire.'

As custom has it in the British Isles, modifications made to a gun are recorded either by a change of type name (Mark I, Mark II, III, etc., when the modifications are major ones), or by the addition at the end of the name of one or more asterisks when the modifications made are considered minor ones. In view of this, and unless one is an expert in English guns, the amateur tends to get lost in a veritable jungle of designations. Neither Webley nor Enfield escaped the net, and so we have preferred to simplify our presentation of the most distinctive revolvers by regrouping them. When World War II looked like being a long, drawn-out affair, the Enfield Arsenal took up the idea of the old Delhaxhe pistol of the last century (the 'Apache' type) and produced a prototype of a hand-gun designed for the British commandos. This gun in addition acted as dagger and knuckle-duster, and had a cylinder holding four 9mm Parabellum rounds.

Although Europe was and still is the favourite territory of the automatic pistol, there has in recent years been a revival of interest in revolvers. Pressured by a demand which does not correspond to the self-defensive arms market but corresponds rather to the competition and collectors' market, European manufacturers are toying with the revolver market to satisfy increasing demands. Thus it is that after the appearance of the first Italian and Spanish copies, numerous European manufacturers, unabashed more often than not, reproduce — usually by making certain modifications — the mechanisms of Smith and Wesson revolvers. In Germany this trend is marked by the appearance of firearms such as the latest .357 Magnum Korth, an undeniably original gun, and the well-made Sauer and Sohn. The manufacturing techniques of German arms manufacturers have earned them their letters patent of nobility in the international field at the highest level and have introduced certain new solutions notable for the finished quality of the product, which is part and parcel of German tradition. The Italians base their sales policy on good quality at a modest price. The same goes for Llama products in Spain, and the Astra Cadix revolver has an ingeniously simple lock.

With the exception of certain German models, all these revolvers have simultaneous ejection. They are generally chambered for the .22 Long Rifle (5.5mm), .32 SW Long, .38 SW, .38 Special and .357 Magnum. The .44 Magnum (11mm) calibre is more of a ballistic curiosity than a weapon which is actually used, and the Colt .45 is little known outside the United States. The single action revolver survived for more than a century in the form of the Colt Single Action Army and its derivatives. It is of course reproduced in Europe by Hämmerli, Jager, Uberti, Sauer and Sohn and others. All these single action guns are 'six-shooters' and usually chamber .22 Long Rifle, .22 Magnum, .38 Special, .357 Magnum, .44 Special, .44-40 WCF, .44 Magnum and .45 Long Colt ammunition. Certain models are equipped with an adjustable sight, both for height and direction, which gives them extremely accurate performance. As well as these models, the European arms industry has for some years, and especially in Italy and Belgium, been manufacturing large quantities of reproductions of Colt and Remington percussion revolvers. These models date from the mid-nineteenth century. Here the bullet, powder and percussion cap are separate. Designed originally for export to the American market, these models are widely known in countries where legislation permits their sale. Shooting clubs where 'black powder' is still used have sprung up in many countries, with the result that though technically obsolete they are more popular than ever today.

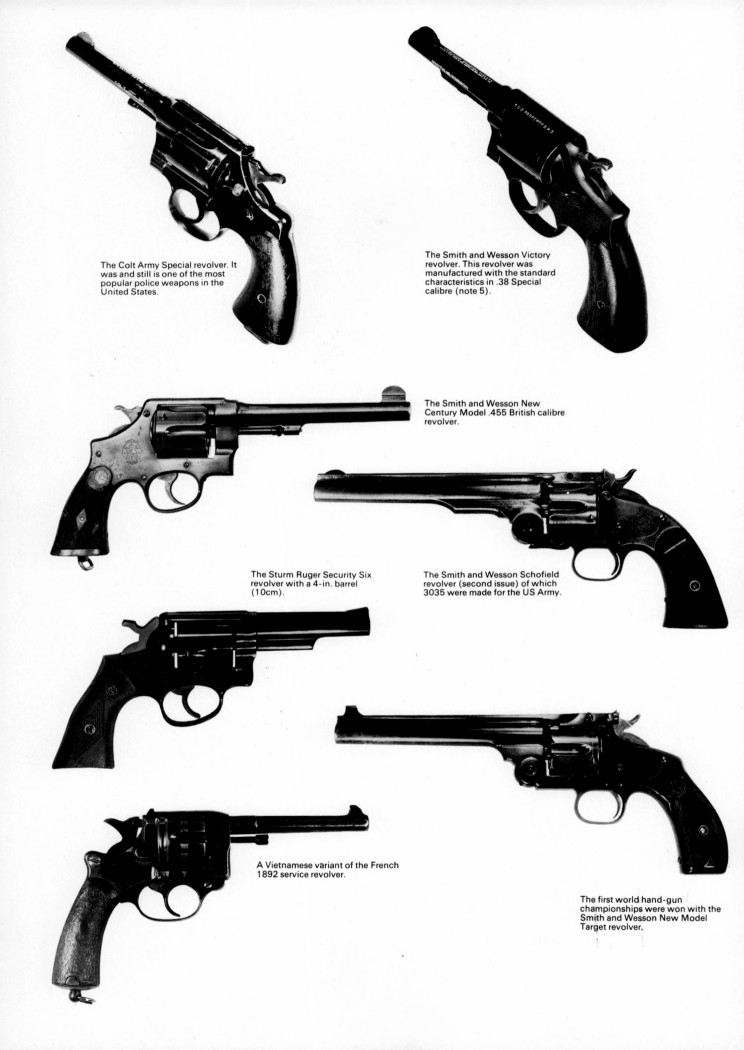

The Colt Army Special revolver. It was and still is one of the most popular police weapons in the United States.

The Smith and Wesson Victory revolver. This revolver was manufactured with the standard characteristics in .38 Special calibre (note 5).

The Smith and Wesson New Century Model .455 British calibre revolver.

The Sturm Ruger Security Six revolver with a 4-in. barrel (10cm).

The Smith and Wesson Schofield revolver (second issue) of which 3035 were made for the US Army.

A Vietnamese variant of the French 1892 service revolver.

The first world hand-gun championships were won with the Smith and Wesson New Model Target revolver.

The Webley WG Target Model
revolver. This gun was a variant of
the Webley WG.1/4 (note 6).

The Sturm Ruger Blackhawk
revolver with a barrel of 4 5/8in.
(11.7cm) and a .357 Magnum
calibre.

The Webley and Scott WS Army
Model revolver. This was the
standard issue for the British army
1915–27, when it was replaced by
the Enfield no. 2 Mark I revolver
(note 9).

The Webley-Fosbery 1902
automatic revolver, made by
Webley and Scott with patents
belonging to Col. G. Vincent
Fosbery of the British army (note
7).

The Webley and Scott Mark VI
revolver, sectional view showing
the mechanism. Somewhat
anachronistically this commercial
model has military markings; in
fact it was used for training
recruits.

The Enfield no. 2 Mark I revolver.
The gun shown here has the series
1 number. It appeared in 1927 and
was followed by thousands of
others until 1957, having
undergone one or two
modifications (note 8).

The future of the handgun

And now, what is the future of the handgun? In order to give a rough answer to this question we must single out three uses of the handgun: sport, defence and the army. Where competition shooting is concerned, legal restrictions do not seem to be slowing up the boom. The aspirations of marksmen to possess well-adapted guns and firearms, enabling them to practise their chosen pastime or sport, seem justifiable and the powers-that-be in most countries appear to admit it. At most these administrations take due measures to stop the weapons falling into the wrong hands. As far as self-defence is concerned, legal restrictions concerning purchase, possession and carrying of such guns in advanced countries cause them to lose their interest for the individual. In the military field, the handgun is at present considered more often than not as an individual means of self-defence, and is greatly appreciated as such since the sub-machine-gun replaced it as a hand-to-hand combat weapon.

It would seem that one can expect to see the development of the specialized competition gun and the military handgun being carried on, but as a weapon of self-defence the handgun will tend to become slowly obsolete, except for administrative or police use.

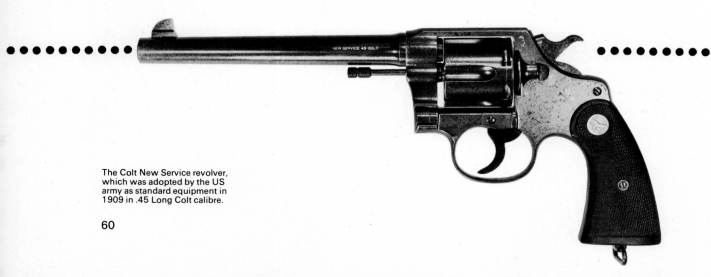

The Colt New Service revolver, which was adopted by the US army as standard equipment in 1909 in .45 Long Colt calibre.

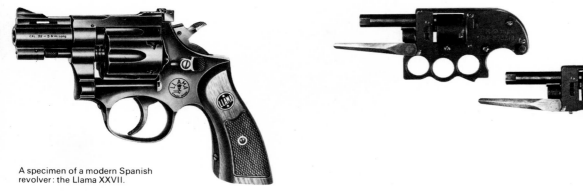

A specimen of a modern Spanish revolver: the Llama XXVII.

A prototype of the Enfield D.D.(E) 3313 revolver designed for the commandos during World War II.

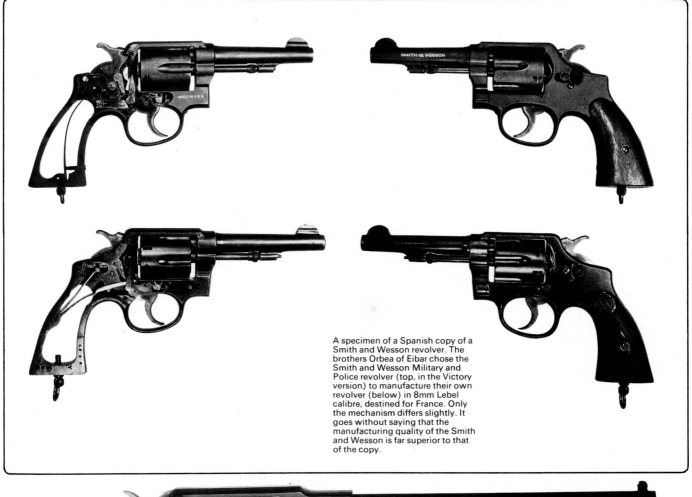

A specimen of a Spanish copy of a Smith and Wesson revolver. The brothers Orbea of Eibar chose the Smith and Wesson Military and Police revolver (top, in the Victory version) to manufacture their own revolver (below) in 8mm Lebel calibre, destined for France. Only the mechanism differs slightly. It goes without saying that the manufacturing quality of the Smith and Wesson is far superior to that of the copy.

The Italian Euroarms revolver. A present-day replica of the Remington New Model Army revolver. This gun is made in .44 and .36 calibres. It is designed only for black powder, and fires lead bullets.

The MBA Associates Gyrojet Mark II automatic pistol.

The SIG P-210 automatic pistol in the de luxe version, engraved and gold damascened.

Automatic pistols and revolvers: technical data

Walther Model TP

Country	West Germany
Type	single-action automatic pistol
Designation	Walther model TP
Calibre	6.35mm or .22 LR
Weight	340g
Length	overall 13cm, barrel 6.5cm
Capacity	6 rounds
Remarks	joining the 6.35mm tradition Walther brought out this gun which is still being manufactured today

Walther Model TPH

Country	West Germany
Type	double-action automatic pistol
Designation	Walther TPH
Calibre	6.35mm or .22 LR
Weight	325g
Length	overall 13.5cm, barrel 7.1cm
Capacity	6 rounds
Remarks	this pistol is the last pocket version of the PPK

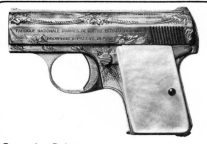

Browning Baby

Country	Belgium
Type	single-action automatic pistol
Designation	Fabrique Nationale d'Armes de Guerre—Herstal—Browning 'Baby'
Calibre	6.35mm
Weight	370g (with full clip)
Length	total 10cm, barrel 5cm
Capacity	6 rounds
Remarks	this gun has been made since 1910 with virtually no modifications

Deringer Hi. Standard

Country	United States
Type	double-action, double-barrelled pistol
Designation	High Standard, Deringer
Calibre	.22 LR, .22 Long, .22 Short or .22 Magnum
Weight	310g
Length	overall 12.5cm, barrels 8.8cm
Capacity	two rounds
Remarks	this small pistol represents a Deringer revival; these guns saw their heyday in the hands of professional gamblers in the West

Smith and Wesson 61 Escort

Country	United States
Type	single-action automatic pistol
Designation	Smith and Wesson 61 Escort
Calibre	.22 LR
Weight	400g
Length	overall 12.2cm, barrel 5.4cm
Capacity	5 rounds
Remarks	latest of the automatic pistols made by the great Springfield firm, the small Escort is a pocket gun of excellent quality

Beretta 950

Country	Italy
Type	single action automatic pistol
Designation	P. Beretta 950
Calibre	6.35mm or .22 Short and .22 LR
Weight	280g in 6.35mm, 250g in .22
Length	overall 11.5cm, barrel 6cm
Capacity	8 6.35mm rounds, 6 .22 rounds
Remarks	this drop-barrel model has no extractor, the backward movement of the bolt making up for this omission

Bernardelli 68

Country	Italy
Type	single-action automatic pistol
Designation	V. Bernardelli, 68
Calibre	6.35mm, .22 Short or .22 LR
Weight	270g
Length	overall 10.7cm, barrel 6cm
Capacity	5 .22 Short or Long rounds
Remarks	the shape of this pistol, influenced by the Browning, makes it a 'classic', extremely well-finished gun

Unique, Mikros

Country	France
Type	single-action automatic pistol
Designation	Unique 'Mikros'
Calibre	6.35mm, .22 Short or .22 LR
Weight	265g light alloy frame, 350g steel frame
Length	overall 11.2cm, barrel 5.7cm
Capacity	6 rounds
Remarks	although the name sounds German, the Mikros has the features common to all the French Unique models

Mauser HSc

Country	West Germany
Type	double action automatic pistol
Designation	Mauser HSc
Calibre	7.65mm or 9mm short
Weight	660g
Length	overall 16cm, barrel 8.5cm
Capacity	8 rounds in 7.65mm, 7 in 9mm
Remarks	produced in 1938, this gun is still being made today

Walther PP

Country	West Germany
Type	double-action automatic pistol
Designation	Walther PP
Calibre	7.65mm, 9mm Short or .22 LR
Weight	660g
Length	17cm, barrel 9.8cm
Capacity	8 rounds in 7.65mm and .22 LR, 7 in 9mm
Remarks	still made by Walther, this gun is also made under licence in France by Manurhin

Walther PPK

Country	West Germany
Type	double-action automatic pistol
Designation	Walther PPK
Calibre	7.65, 9mm Short or .22 LR
Weight	590g
Length	overall 15.5cm, barrel 8.3cm
Capacity	7 rounds in 7.65mm and .22 LR, 6 in 9mm Short
Remarks	still made in Germany, like the PP this pistol is manufactured under licence in France by Manurhin

Browning 1910

Country	Belgium
Type	single-action automatic pistol
Designation	F. N. Herstal 1910 model or Model 10
Calibre	7.65mm or 9mm Short
Weight	580g
Length	overall 15cm, barrel 9cm
Capacity	7 rounds in 7.65mm, 6 in 9mm Short
Remarks	still manufactured by the F.N., this pistol is still used by some police forces, and is one of the grand old men in its category

Browning 1922

Country	Belgium
Type	single-action automatic pistol
Designation	F. N. Herstal, model 1922 or 10/22
Calibre	7.65mm or 9mm Short
Weight	700g
Length	overall 18cm, barrel 11.5cm
Capacity	9 rounds in 7.65mm, 8 in 9mm Short
Remarks	still made by the F.N., this pistol still equips certain police forces

Beretta 70

Country	Italy
Type	single-action automatic pistol
Designation	Beretta 70
Calibre	7.65mm
Weight	575g
Length	overall 16.5cm, barrel 9cm
Capacity	8 rounds
Remarks	thanks to its light metal frame and compactness the 70, in current production, is an excellent gun for the purposes of self-defence

Bernardelli USA

Country	Italy
Type	single-action automatic pistol
Designation	Bernardelli USA
Calibre	.22 LR, 7.65mm or 9mm Short
Weight	760g in 7.65mm calibre
Length	overall 16.4cm, barrel 9.4cm
Capacity	10 rounds in .22 LR, 8 in 7.65mm, 7 in 9mm Short
Remarks	this model owes its name to the fact that it conforms with American legislation concerning firearms imports

Unique L

Country	France
Type	single-action automatic pistol
Designation	Unique L
Calibre	.22 LR (Ld), 7.65mm (Lc), 9mm Short (Lf)
Weight	560–800g depending on calibre and frame
Length	overall 16cm, barrel 9cm
Capacity	10 rounds in .22 LR, 7 in 7.65mm, 6 in 9mm Short
Remarks	manufactured with light metal or steel frames, this simply designed gun has a very strong mechanism

Unique Police

Country	France
Type	single-action automatic pistol
Designation	Unique R 51 Police
Calibre	7.65 and 9mm Short
Weight	750g
Length	overall 14.5cm, barrel 8cm
Capacity	9 rounds in 7.65mm, 8 in 9mm Short
Remarks	in the 7.65mm version this pistol was designed for use by the French police; it is carried by most members of the urban divisions and public security units

Unique Bcf 66

Country	France
Type	single-action pistol
Designation	Unique Bcf 66
Calibre	7.65mm or 9mm Short
Weight	750g
Length	overall 16.5cm, barrel 10cm
Capacity	9 rounds in 7.65mm, 8 in 9mm Short
Remarks	in principle designed to replace the R 51 for local police forces, and made more accurate when compared with the R 51 by the use of a longer barrel, this gun has the singular feature of being able to change the calibre (7.65mm and 9mm) by simply switching barrels and clips

HK P9S

Country	West Germany
Type	double-action automatic pistol
Designation	Heckler and Koch, P9S
Calibre	9mm Parabellum
Weight	875g
Length	overall 13.7cm, barrel 10.2cm
Capacity	9 rounds
Remarks	there is also a single action version. The special feature of the P9 and P9S consists in the fact that their barrels are not rifled but have a polygonal section. This modern pistol, which calls on the latest techniques for plastics and stamped metal, is perfectly suited to military use

Korriphila HSP 70

Country	West Germany
Type	double-action automatic pistol
Designation	Korriphila HSP 70
Calibre	9mm Parabellum
Weight	900g
Length	overall 20cm, barrel 12cm
Capacity	8 or 9 rounds, depending on model
Remarks	this gun is produced on a small scale and despite its excellent quality has not managed to offer serious competition to its elder rivals

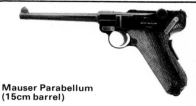

Mauser Parabellum (15cm barrel)

Country	West Germany
Type	toggle-bolt, single-action automatic pistol
Designation	Mauser Parabellum (Luger)
Calibre	7.65mm Parabellum, 9mm Parabellum
Weight	870g
Length	from 19–24cm depending on length of barrel (10, 12.7, 16 and 15cm)
Capacity	8 rounds in 9mm, 9 in 7.65mm Parabellum
Remarks	although out of date in military terms this gun has been manufactured since 1969 by the Mauser Jagdwaffen factory in Oberndorf, basically to meet the demands of the American market where the Luger, with its legendary reputation, is very sought after

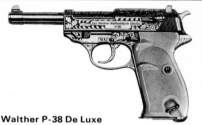

Walther P-38 De Luxe

Country	West Germany
Type	double-action automatic pistol
Designation	Walther P-38
Calibre	.22 LR, 7.65mm Parabellum, 9mm Parabellum
Weight	800g
Length	overall 21.6cm, barrel 12.9cm
Capacity	8 rounds
Remarks	currently made in three calibres (without loading indicator in .22 LR) this excellent pistol is still standard equipment in Germany and in certain other countries. It can be supplied with a light alloy frame

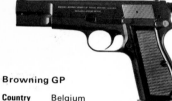

Browning GP

Country	Belgium
Type	single-action automatic pistol
Designation	Fabrique Nationale de Herstal, model GP 35; shown here is the Vigilant
Calibre	7.65mm Parabellum and 9mm Parabellum
Weight	1080g
Length	overall 18.6cm, barrel 11.8cm
Capacity	13 or 20 rounds depending on clip
Remarks	this excellent automatic gun, whose clip capacity has recently been increased to 20 rounds, is currently manufactured under licence in several countries (Canada in particular). There are several versions, depending on the use the purchaser has in mind. At the present time it is the most widely used standard pistol

Llama VIII

Country	Spain
Type	single-action automatic pistol
Designation	Llama VIII (9mm and .38 Super) or IX A(.45 ACP)
Calibre	9mm Largo, .38 Super Auto and .45 ACP
Weight	1000g in 9mm and .38 Super, 1100g in .45 ACP
Length	overall 21.6cm, barrel 12.8cm
Capacity	9 rounds in 9mm and .38 Super, 7 in .45 ACP
Remarks	a very faithful copy of the Colt Government Model 1911, this automatic pistol owes its elegance to the addition of a ventilated rib

Star M

Country	Spain
Type	single-action automatic pistol
Designation	Etcheveria, Star
Calibre	7.53mm Mauser or 9mm Largo
Weight	1100g
Length	overall 22cm, barrel 12cm
Capacity	8 rounds in 7.63mm Mauser, 8 in 9mm Largo
Remarks	the Star is greatly influenced by the Colt 1911, but has a simpler mechanism. In the M version, with an adaptable holster-stock, it is extremely accurate. This gun currently equips the Spanish army and some police forces. It is quite popular in Africa and the Far East

Colt 1911 A1

Country	United States
Type	single-action automatic pistol
Designation	Colt, Government Model of 1911 A1
Calibre	.45 ACP
Weight	1100g
Length	overall 22cm, barrel 12.7cm
Capacity	7 rounds
Remarks	grand old man of high-power pistols in current production, the Colt 1911 comes in competition models as well: National Gold Cup and Mk IV/Series 70. Its power and reliability often make it more popular than more modern pistols

Colt Commander

Country	United States
Type	single-action automatic pistol
Designation	Colt Commander
Calibre	9mm Parabellum, .38 Super Auto or .45 ACP
Weight	750–800g
Length	overall 18cm, barrel 11cm
Capacity	7 rounds in .45 ACP, 9 in .38 Auto, and in 9mm Parabellum
Remarks	a shortened and lighter version of the Government Model, this pistol is made of steel or light alloy

Gyrojet Mark I

Country	United States
Type	single-action automatic pistol
Designation	MBA Associates, Gyrojet Mark I
Calibre	13mm
Weight	450–370g depending on barrel length
Length	overall 14.3cm to 21cm, depending on barrel: 5 and 12.7cm
Capacity	6 rockets introduced directly in the butt
Remarks	a revolutionary gun using rockets, this pistol, which would seem to need further development, is not very accurate by comparison, does not stand up well to damp, and is not altogether reliable. The firing pin is fixed and when the hammer is lowered it pushes the 'rocket' on to the firing pin, thus causing firing

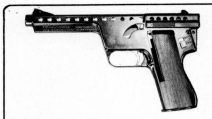

Gyrojet Mark II

Country	United States
Type	single-action automatic pistol
Designation	MBA Associates, Gyrojet Mark II
Calibre	12mm
Weight	420g
Length	overall 21cm, barrel 13cm
Capacity	7 rockets, introduced directly in the grip
Remarks	an improvement on Mark I, this pistol suffers from the same problems as its predecessor; with the latter it undoubtedly represents the first step towards a whole new generation of handguns

MAB P 15

Country	France
Type	single-action automatic pistol
Designation	Manufacture d'Armes de Bayonne, model MAB P 15
Calibre	9mm Parabellum
Weight	1110g
Length	overall 22cm, barrel 11.5cm
Capacity	15 rounds
Remarks	also made in a competition version, this excellent pistol was brought out to rival the Belgian GP 35. At the present time it is quite popular in the USA. In France it is sometimes carried by officers and some policemen

MAC 50

Country	France
Type	single-action automatic pistol
Designation	Manufacture d'Armes de Châtellerault, MAC 50
Calibre	9mm Parabellum
Weight	960g
Length	overall 19.5cm, barrel 11.2cm
Capacity	9 rounds
Remarks	standard equipment since 1950 in the French army, this tough pistol also equips other national armies in former French colonies. It is also carried by certain police forces

Tokagypt

Country	Hungary
Type	single-action automatic pistol
Designation	The Hungarian State Arsenal, Tokagypt 5
Calibre	9mm Parabellum
Weight	900g
Length	overall 21cm, barrel 12cm
Capacity	8 rounds
Remarks	a copy of the Russian TT 33 (Tokarev) pistol, this gun has been made at the request of Egypt, its name being a merger of Tokarev and Egypt. It uses the 9mm Parabellum and not the 7.62 S like its predecessor

Beretta Brigadier

Country	Italy
Type	single-action automatic pistol
Designation	Beretta 1951 Para, known as the 'Brigadier'
Calibre	9mm Parabellum
Weight	820g
Length	overall 20.4cm, barrel 11.4cm
Capacity	8 or 10 rounds
Remarks	adopted in 1951 by the Italian army and navy, this gun was also adopted in the same year by the armies of Israel and Egypt. The use of light alloy has considerably reduced its weight

SIG 210-2

Country	Switzerland
Type	single-action automatic pistol
Designation	SIG (Schweizerische Industrie-Gesellschaft), model P210–2
Calibre	9mm Parabellum, 7.76mm Parabellum and .22 LR
Weight	850g
Length	overall 21.5cm, barrel 12cm
Capacity	8 rounds
Remarks	one of the best-finished guns in the world, the SIG P 210-2 is the standard weapon of the Swiss army. The change of calibre is obtained by replacing the barrels and clips. A conversion arrangement enables it to fire the .22 LR on the 9mm and 7.65mm Parabellum models

Brigant

Country	Czechoslovakia
Type	single-action automatic pistol
Designation	The Czechoslovak State Arsenal, model 52, so-called Brigant
Calibre	Czech 7.62mm
Weight	900g
Length	overall 21cm, barrel 11.5cm
Capacity	8 rounds
Remarks	derived from the Tokarev TT 33, this pistol uses 7.62mm Czech ammunition with 20 per cent more power than the Soviet 7.62mm round. It was adopted in 1952 by the Czech army

Arminius HW 5

Country	West Germany
Type	single- and double-action revolver
Designation	Arminius HW 5
Calibre	.22 LR, .22 Magnum or .32 S and W Long
Weight	780g in .22 LR and .22 Magnum, 725g in .32 S and W Long
Length	overall 22cm, barrel 10cm
Capacity	8 rounds in .22 LR and .22 Magnum, 7 in .32 S and W Long
Remarks	sold at a relatively low price, this gun is made in many versions by Weihrauch

Colt Single Action Army
(here the .357 Magnum)

Country	United States
Type	single-action revolver
Designation	Colt, Single Action Army (.357 Mag. and .45 Colt), Single Action Army New Frontier with de luxe finish and competition sighting device
Calibre	.357 Magnum and .45 Colt
Weight	from 1000–1500g, depending on barrel length and calibre
Length	variable: barrels of 7.6 to 33cm (Buntline model)
Capacity	6 rounds in all versions
Remarks	also made as the Colt Single Action Frontier Scout in .22 Short, .22 Long and .22 LR calibre. The most famous revolver manufactured since 1873

Hi. Standard Sentinel Snub Nose

Country	United States
Type	single- and double-action revolver
Designation	Hi-Standard, Sentinel Snub Nose
Calibre	.22 LR
Weight	500g
Length	overall 15.5cm, barrel 6cm (2 3/8in.)
Capacity	7 rounds
Remarks	available in bronze or nickel finish in .22 LR calibre only

Ruger Blackhawk
(here in .357 Magnum with 7.5in. [19cm] barrel)

Country	United States
Type	single-action revolver
Designation	Sturm Ruger and Co, Blackhawk .357 Magnum (+9mm Parabellum) and .45 Long Colt (+.45 ACP)
Weight	1050 to 1300g depending on calibre and barrel length
Length	from 23–30cm depending on barrel (11.7–19cm)
Capacity	6 rounds in all versions
Remarks	calibre changeover is carried out by simple replacement of cylinder

Ruger Security Six
(here with 4in. [10cm] barrel)

Country	United States
Type	single- and double-action revolver
Designation	Sturm Ruger and Co., Security Six
Calibre	.357 Magnum
Weight	920–1000g depending on barrel length
Length	overall: 20–28cm, depending on barrel; barrel, 7, 10 and 15cm
Remarks	6 rounds
Remarks	available with or without adjustable sights, this sound gun is only sold in the .357 Magnum calibre (and can use the .38 S and W and the .38 Special)

**Smith and Wesson
Military and Police (Airweight)**

Country	United States
Type	single- and double-action revolver
Designation	Smith and Wesson, Military and Police Model and Military and Police Airweight Model
Calibre	.38 Special and .41 Magnum
Weight	Military and Police: 825–925g; Airweight Model: 520–565g
Length	18.5–34cm for steel model (barrel of 5, 10, 12.7 and 15cm) and 18.5–23.5cm for Airweight model (6 or 10cm barrel)
Capacity	6 rounds
Remarks	in the .41 Magnum calibre there is a 10cm barrel, and the gun weighs 1160g with a steel frame

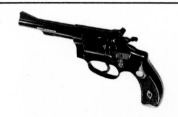

**Smith and Wesson 1953
.22/32 Kit Gun**

Country	United States
Type	single- and double-action revolver
Designation	Smith and Wesson 1953 .22/32 Kit Gun
Calibre	.22 Short, .22 Long, .22 LR and .22 Magnum
Weight	650g with 10cm barrel
Length	20–25cm with barrels of 5, 9, 10, or 15cm
Capacity	6 rounds
Remarks	there is an Airweight version of this model with a 9cm barrel only in the different calibres

**Smith and Wesson 27
.357 Magnum**

Country	United States
Type	single- and double-action revolver
Designation	Smith and Wesson 27 .357 Magnum
Calibre	.357 Magnum
Weight	1160–1330g depending on barrel length
Length	22, 26, 28 or 35cm (barrels of 9, 13, 15 or 21cm)
Capacity	6 rounds
Remarks	this currently made revolver was the first one designed to fire the .357 Magnum round

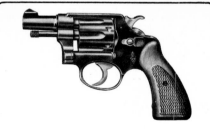

Bernardelli pocket revolver

Country	Italy
Type	single- and double-action revolver
Designation	Bernadelli, VB pocket model
Calibre	.22 LR or .32 S and W Long
Weight	545g in .22 LR and 490g in .32 calibre
Length	overall 16cm, barrel 5cm
Capacity	6 rounds
Remarks	pocket model derived from VB, available in same calibre with barrels of 80, 110 and 150mm

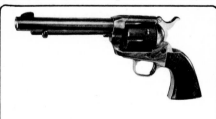

Hämmerli Dakota

Country	Swiss
Type	single-action revolver
Designation	Hämmerli, Dakota
Calibre	.357 Magnum and .45 Long Colt
Weight	1000–1200g depending on barrel length and calibre
Length	26, 28 or 33cm (barrels of 8, 11, 14 or 19cm)
Capacity	6 rounds
Remarks	a modern Swiss replica of the Colt Single Action Army, this gun is finished with all the care for which the Hämmerli company is noted

3
sub-
machine-guns

Machine pistols, otherwise known as sub-machine-guns, came into being when it was deemed necessary to increase the fire power of the infantryman in close combat or hand-to-hand fighting. As any such improvement of fire power could not entail any excessive increase in the bulk and weight of the weapon, the sub-machine-gun was, from the outset, physically restricted in both volume and weight. Since World War II it has replaced the handgun in its tactical use, but in fact represents a compromise between the traditional automatic weapon – the machine-gun – and the individual weapon – the rifle.

To all appearances it is relatively easy to make distinctions between handguns, with their differing initial purposes; but the same does not apply to sub-machine-guns which have all been originally conceived with military functions in mind. In other respects the mechanical principles are the same. Given these basic facts, any attempt to call distinctions between them would involve plunging into subtle technical details with which we would be reluctant to bore the lay reader. We have thus preferred to write an outline of the history of the machine pistol on a chronological basis, with the aim of broadly tracing the development which, in slightly more than half a century, has culminated in the modern sub-machine-gun.

World War I and the birth of the sub-machine-gun

The ill-informed public generally thinks that the sub-machine-gun came originally from the United States, because most laymen's acquaintance with it has been through American films made between the two wars. In reality the first 'modern' sub-machine-gun came into being in Europe and, more specifically, in Italy in about 1915, when it was christened the Villar Perosa after the name of the factory which manufactured it on a small scale at Pinerola, not far from Turin.

With its two twin barrels, it was the brainchild of an Italian colonel, Bethel Abiel Revelli, who had devised it to equip Bersaglieri cyclist units with extremely light automatic weapons. When the Villar Perosa was adopted as a standard weapon by the mobilized Italian army, a new era was ushered in for a truly individual weapon which was relatively light and capable of firing in bursts. Its weight was way below that of the machine-gun, which had gone into service at an earlier date. The use of automatic pistol ammunition instead of the ammunition fired by military rifles made it possible considerably to reduce the bulk and weight of this new gun. With mobile warfare grinding to a swift halt in the first months of the war, cyclist troops dug themselves into trenches, where the sub-machine-gun showed its paces in terms of handling ability and its remarkable fire power in hand-to-hand combat. It was also used in the air in the first biplanes belonging to the *Regia Aeronautica*. Despite its rate of fire of 3000 rounds per minute, the fire power of the Villar Perosa was still considerably inferior to that of the machine-guns with which some were keen to equate it. The 9mm Glisenti round for which the gun was chambered was undoubtedly partly to blame in this shortcoming, because although this ammunition was mechanically interchange-

able with the 9mm Parabellum, it was twenty per cent less powerful than its German counterpart. Beyond the narrow confines of the Austro-Italian front the appearance of this new weapon does not seem to have found much of a following among the staffs of the warring nations. The ballistic power of the ammunition fired by it was laughable when compared with that used by military rifles and subsequently used by machine-guns, and every army was obsessed with the task of increasing the numbers of machine-guns. Nevertheless, the lack of mobility and clumsiness of the Hotchkiss, Maxim, Vickers, Schwartzlose and other types of machine-gun were a source of constant worry for the ordnance corps of the nations at war. The importance of these problems increased dramatically when it was time to mount an offensive action. In the end, and in conditions of the utmost secrecy, every country set about finding a solution to the problem of the light automatic weapon.

In their efforts to solve these difficulties the English reduced the weight of their machine-guns as much as possible and issued them to their troops in the form of the Lewis Mark I .303 machine-gun; the French, on the other hand, adopted the light machine-gun.

The Germans, for their part, seem to have suffered numerous disappointments with their lightened Maxim and made wide use of Parabellum and Mauser pistols, equipped with holster-stocks and large capacity clips. But these weapons were not capable of firing in bursts and were in addition costly and complex to manufacture.

These factors combined spurred an engineering technician, Hugo Schmeisser, to produce his first machine pistol, which looked like a kind of massive carbine. The new weapon, which was called the MP.18-1, appeared in the German lines in the closing months of World War I in very small numbers; chambered to take a 9mm Parabellum, it used the 'snail-drum magazine' of the artillery Parabellum. These clips were far from being satisfactory on the weapon for which they were originally intended, and it is not hard to imagine how functionally reliable they were once mounted on a different weapon by means of an adaptor sleeve.

The MP.18-1 was destined to spawn a whole generation of German and foreign sub-machine-guns, the lines of which were based on this model; the last of the line was the Lanchester, the patent for which was applied for at the London Patent Office in April 1941.

The English and French do not appear to have been particularly impressed by the appearance of these German sub-machine-guns. What is more, snowed under at the time by victorious images of riflemen depicted as soldiers in extended order and spraying the enemy lines with short bursts of fire as they followed the tanks into battle, high ranking officers could dream only of individual machine-guns using the Lebel round. Hugo Schmeisser's sub-machine-gun must have struck them as some desperate attempt by the central European powers to equip their assault troops with a cheap gun with a ridiculous ballistic capability.

Towards the end of the war the Esercito Italiano approached various national firms with a view to producing a gun which was lighter and easier to handle than the Villar Perosa. As a result the Officine di Villar Perosa manufactured the O.V.P. sub-machine-gun (the initials of

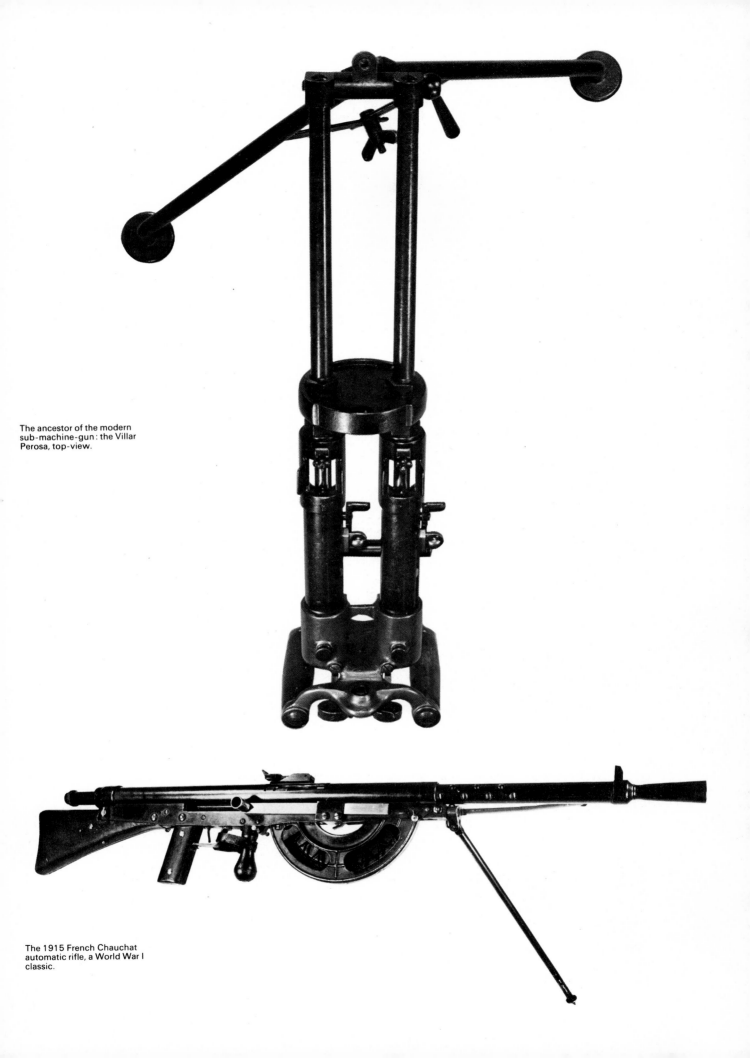

The ancestor of the modern sub-machine-gun: the Villar Perosa, top-view.

The 1915 French Chauchat automatic rifle, a World War I classic.

Schmeisser MP-18.1
sub-machine-gun.

The O.V.P. sub-machine-gun.

The Revelli/Fiat sub-machine-gun.

The 1918 Monogrillo Beretta
sub-machine-gun.

The 1918 Bigrillo Beretta
sub-machine-gun.

72

The prototype of the Thompson sub-machine-gun.

The 1921 Thompson sub-machine-gun with the 100-round drum magazine.

The 1928 Thompson sub-machine-gun with a 20-round clip and Cutts deflector.

The 1928 Thompson sub-machine-gun with a 30-round clip.

The 1928 Thompson A1 sub-machine-gun adopted by the US Army.

The 1911 Colt 45 A1 automatic pistol transformed on a somewhat makeshift basis for full automatic fire.

The Spanish Astra F machine pistol.

The Astra F machine pistol with the stock plates removed to show the fire regulator mechanism.

the factory), a single-barrelled version of the Villar Perosa. The mechanism remained virtually the same as that of its predecessor; a lengthened barrel, the addition of a stock and a cooling sleeve somewhat refined the general line of the gun. Produced in about 1918, this weapon enjoyed a modest career in North Africa in the hands of the Italian troops there during World War II.

The Fiat Company in Turin, together with the Pinerila company, seems to have become interested in changing the Villar Perosa into a single-barrelled version. But the research undertaken did not get beyond the prototype stage and pre-production series. The feeding system used was that of the Villar Perosa, with the same clip-locking system and downward ejection of empty cases, but a sheet-metal deflector had been added to protect the hand of the user. If one can judge from an examination of the gun, which it has been impossible to undertake, a selector placed above the trigger would have made it possible to select semi-automatic fire or full automatic fire, with the third position being the safety position.

The Pietro Beretta company of Gardone also took part in the improvement of the Villar Perosa. Its experience in portable arms, covering more than two and a half centuries, could only make a positive contribution.

It was a young engineer called Tulio Marengoni who was responsible for the 1918 model Beretta sub-machine-gun which was produced in two versions:

1. the 1918 model Monogrillo (with one trigger) which fired only full automatic. In order to give it a more martial appearance, the standard bayonet for the 1891 Italian rifle had been added to it. This gun became a standard issue weapon in the Italian army, and equipped the *Arditi* assault troops, who hung on to it until the onset of the 1939–45 war;

2. the 1918 Bigrillo (with two triggers). One of the triggers was used to control semi-automatic fire, the second for full automatic fire. The folding bayonet was replaced by a lug for attaching a removable bayonet. The ejection chute for the empty cases was a more complex shape than its Monogrillo equivalent.

With these models Beretta took its place in the business of manufacturing sub-machine-guns and consequently proceeded to climb to the top of the list as far as the Italian production of this type of weapon was concerned, as well as playing a dominant role on the international market.

In 1917 the United States reinforced the Allied armies against Germany. The Franco-British military authorities showed little interest in the new weapon, but the Americans – practical and pragmatic people if ever there were – reacted to it quite differently. Colonel John Taliafero Thompson, a West Point graduate, was too old for active duty, and was instead nominated director of the U.S. armaments division with the rank of general. For several months he had been nurturing the idea of equipping the US infantryman with a light portable gun capable of full automatic firing which would rout the enemy with a hail of fire and lead. The B.A.R. (Browning Automatic Rifle) had just appeared and a handful of U.S. soldiers had a chance to use it on the French front. But the B.A.R. was not easy to handle and very cumbersome. With the assistance of T. H.

Eickoff and Oscar V. Paine, and the financial backing of Thomas Fortune Ryan, Thompson worked incessantly on his Persuader. The breech-locking mechanism was prompted by a discovery made by John B. Blish and the feed mechanism followed the technique of contemporary machine-guns, using a belt. Studies ended in near-failure until a satisfactory solution emerged in the form of a straight clip, hastily produced, containing the .45 ACP round which Thompson had helped to have adopted by the army. Like Dr Gatling fifty years earlier, Thompson believed he had found the absolute weapon and shared the preference of the military authorities of the day for hip firing which, theoretically, made it possible to get the better of the enemy by brisk and well-sustained fire. The end of the war came just when he was in the thick of the experimental stage with his gun, which was thus unable to take part in the final victory.

These first three sub-machine-gun models – the Italian Villar Perosa, the German Schmeisser and the American Thompson – already had the features generally to be found in all later models to have appeared in the following fifty years: they all fire from an open bolt position, which simplifies the mechanism and reduces overheating (at the same time slightly increasing the trigger-pull); they cover the three principal options for clip and magazine mounting known to date: (a) the Villar Perosa clip is situated above the gun, with the sights accordingly at the side, but this enables the firer to keep a low profile when firing on the ground; (b) the Schmeisser clip has a lateral attachment, with normal sights as a result, but this arrangement increases the width of the gun out of all proportion and makes it laterally unbalanced; (c) the Thompson clip is situated beneath the receiver, which makes it naturally balanced and allows for the classic sighting system, but it is not best suited to prone position firing.

Inter-war development of the sub-machine-gun

Relatively speaking, the 1918 Armistice dampened the warring spirits of the countries which had been at war and European armament factories marked time for some years. The same desire for peace also made itself felt in the United States, but the demobilized John Thompson persisted in the development of his fearsome weapon. Early in 1919, the Auto Ordnance Corporation at Bridgeport (Connecticut), a company newly formed by the association of the main figures behind the development of the Thompson sub-machine-gun, brought out some prototypes known as the 1919-model Thompson. The gun even at this stage offered the outward appearance with which we are familiar today, except for the removable wooden shoulder-piece which did not appear until the 1921 model.

The Auto Ordnance Corporation sub-contracted a section of its production to the Colt's Patent Fire Arms Mfg. Co., which explains why some of these sub-machine-guns bear the mark of that famous Hartford company. Then came the 1927 and 1928 models, the latter being sometimes fitted with cooling fins. The front grip in some cases disappeared and was replaced by a wooden fore-end, which made it look something like a rifle – a look

The Mauser 'Schnellfeuer' machine pistol with a 20-round clip in 9mm Parabellum calibre and the holster-stock fitted.

The Mauser 'Schnellfeuer' machine pistol with the 7.63mm Mauser calibre 20-round clip (note 10).

The Mauser 'Schnellfeuer' machine pistol with the 9mm Parabellum 10-round clip.

The Erma EMP sub-machine-gun.

The Bergmann MP.35/1 sub-machine-gun.

The 1933 Brøndby sub-machine-gun.

The SIG MKPO sub-machine-gun.

which became it, in the eyes of some contemporaries. The post-war circumstances were not favourable to armament development, and the American military authorities kept their distance from this new gun, which was neither rifle nor machine-gun. With a keen interest in the Thompson's fire-power, the Irish Republicans tried to smuggle it into Ireland where there was heavy guerilla fighting against the British troops. The discovery at New York of a hidden Thompson shipment on board a ship heading for Dublin almost led to a break in diplomatic relations between the United States and Great Britain. But tensions gradually eased, although the reputation of the Auto Ordnance Corporation emerged somewhat tarnished by the regrettable incident.

With no individual automatic weapons, I.R.A. partisans sometimes transformed 1911 A1 Colt automatic pistols to make up for this shortcoming.

It was at about this time that gang warfare hit the streets of Chicago. In the trigger-happy hands of henchmen of Al Capone and other American underworld bosses, the Thompson acquired a reputation which its authors could well have done without. The St Valentine's Day massacre of the Bugs Moran gang by Al Capone's men firing Thompson sub-machine-guns caused much adverse publicity for the Auto Ordnance Corporation, which took many years to restore its image. A certain stock of 1928 Thompsons was supplied to the U.S. mail service for the protection of its convoys and trains. Later these guns were transferred to the U.S. Marines who made conspicuous use of them in the defence of the U.S. Legation at Shanghai. As a result of this incident the U.S. Navy and then the U.S. Army both officially adopted the Thompson, which became the *US Model of 1928 A1*. The British and Belgian authorities put the Thompson sub-machine-gun through intensive testing with a view to adopting it too; there was even a plan to make it in 9mm Parabellum calibre to meet European demands. But no orders were forthcoming, although the results of these tests, attended by Winston Churchill in person, were convincing enough.

German re-armament and its consequences
In Europe the euphoria of peacetime was slowly giving way to fears about the 'next and last' confrontation; after its defeat Germany was shamelessly re-arming itself, despite the stipulations of the Treaty of Locarno; fearing reprisals by the 'German spirit of revenge', the rest of Europe followed suit.

Not content with having copied and in some respects improved the 1896 model Mauser automatic pistol, the Spanish, more particularly the Esperanza y Unceta company, put a version of their own gun, capable of full automatic fire, on the market in about 1930: it was known as the model F. Chambered for the 9mm Bergmann Bayard Spanish round, this gun had a rate of fire regulator in the grip which, by means of a leaf spring, controlled the return of the hammer. The selector located on the right hand side of the frame, above the grip, allowed for semi-automatic and full automatic fire. Equipped with a wooden holster-stock, the model F to some extent constituted the first real machine pistol. In response to this competition offered by its Spanish rivals, the Waffenfabrik Mauser in Oberndorf adapted its 1930 model, itself derived from the 1896 model automatic pistol, to automatic fire. On 25 Novem-

ber 1930, Josef Nick acquired a German patent for a gun capable of 20-round automatic fire. The prototype and a few pre-production models were made to satisfy the ever-growing demands of the Asian market where the Spanish were starting to gain a dangerous foothold. It was not until the application for the Westinger patent of 13 April 1932 that the Schnellfeuer assumed its final form with its half-moon selector giving semi-automatic fire in position *N* and full automatic fire in position *R*. From 1933 to 1934 a hundred such machine-pistols were supplied to Yugoslavia. Chambered to take the 7.63mm Mauser and the 9mm Parabellum, they were christened the Model S.

When the Nazis seized power, the party's elite detachments – the SS and the SA – were equipped with the Schnellfeuer. Nazi and Fascist sympathizers in Europe benefited from the goodwill of the new German overlords and large numbers of Schnellfeuer models were supplied to extreme right-wing terrorist organizations. It was incidentally with one of these guns that Vlada Geogejev, alias Cernozenski, alias Petrus Kalemen, shot King Alexander I of Yugoslavia and Louis Barthou, the French Minister of Foreign Affairs, who had gone to Marseilles to greet the king on 9 October 1934, on the orders of the Croat Oustava, led by Ante Pavelitch. Interest in the Schnellfeuer was revived towards the end of World War II when 12,000 of these guns were ordered for the SS Waffen units fighting on the Eastern front.

Fired by Ludendorff, Hindenberg and Adolf Hitler, the pan-Germanic dream was laid openly on the table and in 1935 German munitions factories were once more achieving their cherished rates of production. Erma of Erfurt plunged into the production of its Vollmer sub-machine-gun which had been being hatched since 1927. Improved by the addition of a cooling jacket made of perforated sheet metal, the Vollmer became the EMP-model Erma, production of which started in 1931 and continued until mid-1938, when it gave way to the MP .38. At the same time, Bergmann brought out in quick succession its MP .34/1 and, more importantly, its MP .35/1, fed by vertical 24- or 32-round clips introduced laterally on the right hand side of the receiver. Usually chambered for the 9mm Parabellum, these weapons were also manufactured for the 7.63mm Mauser, the 9mm Bergmann Bayard and the .45 ACP. These models enjoyed a brief career with the Negus of Ethiopia in about 1935, before being officially adopted by Denmark in 1939, with the Danish reference M 39, using the 9mm Bergmann Bayard round.

Sub-machine-guns were beginning to attract the attention of European general staffs, with the exception of Great Britain and France, where they were regarded with considerable scepticism. The hesitant attempts made in France with the E.T.V.S. came to nothing. The Scandinavian countries also took part in the development of this modern gun; Estonia equipped itself with the 1923 model Talinn, inspired directly by the MP .18/1 Schmeisser. As far as the Finns were concerned, they had already had the 1926 model Suomi, chambered to fire the 7.65mm Parabellum, for some time, as well as the M/1931 Suomi fed with 9mm Parabellum rounds by vertical clips or by a 71-round drum magazine which gave it a good capacity for well-sustained fire.

The Norwegians tried out the 1933 model gas-operated

Brøndby sub-machine-gun with a muzzle brake, but did not follow it up. The Czechs for their part started production of their ZK 383. Even the Swiss, sheltered as they were from war by their traditional stance of neutrality, eagerly embarked on studies for a sub-machine-gun. In 1933 the Schweizerische Industrie-Gesellschaft (SIG) at Rheinfall filed an application for a patent for a sub-machine-gun, the MKMO model, some of whose features, which were revolutionary for the day, still persist both with SIG and with other manufacturers. As an example there was the front-folding clip which this company was the first to use and which was later borrowed by the Czechs and the French. (This was the sub-machine-gun which was produced by the Manufacture d'Armes de Tulle, MAT 49.)

The MKPO model was a transposed version, intended for police use, of the MKMO model, designed for military use. The barrel had been shortened and the clip capacity reduced. The MKPO model was produced between 1935 and 1937 in 7.63mm Mauser, 7.65mm Parabellum, 9mm Parabellum, 9mm Mauser and 9mm Bergmann Bayard calibres. Anxious to achieve the highest possible quality, the golden rule of the firm, the SIG quickly halted production of the MKPO, the mechanism of which was not entirely satisfactory in the eyes of the 'weapons watchsmiths'. It was replaced by the new KMPS model, with an improved mechanism, and some minor external differences, such as the addition of a spherical button on the cocking lever and the increased clip capacity, now holding thirty-two rounds. It is nevertheless worth noting that this gun was produced only to fire the 7.65mm and 9mm Parabellum round. Like the MKPO sub-machine-gun for police use, the MKMO military sub-machine-gun underwent the same mechanical changes before it became the MKMS.

Apart from Beretta, several Italian armament factories started manufacturing sub-machine-guns, with varying success. For instance Armaguerra of Genoa produced a model 35, chambered for a 9mm Parabellum round, and designed exclusively for full automatic fire. All these new weapons had satisfied the various military authorities on the experimental range, but how would they perform in actual combat conditions? The Spanish Civil War, between 1936 and 1939, was to act as a laboratory and test-bed for weaponry, and here the sub-machine-gun established its reputation. The Vollmers, Bergmanns and Ermas carried by the Condor legion of German volunteers partly equipped pro-Franco troops and made it possible to develop the remarkable MP .38. On the other side, sub-machine-guns from every country proved their effectiveness. Manufactured in Spain, the Star 35, Labora 1938 and copies of the German MP .28/11 were, for instance, also used.

Under Mussolini, Italy also supported the nationalist troops of General Franco and profited from the war to perfect the 1938 Beretta sub-machine-gun, derived from the prototype produced in 1935 by Tulio Marengoni. Chambered to fit the 9mm Parabellum round, this gun was produced in three versions: the 1938 A, A1 and A11 models. It could fire a high-power round, the M 38, which had been specially designed for it. When it was officially adopted by the Italian army, the 1938 model was mass-produced until 1944.

World War II and the sub-machine-gun

From 1939 onwards the Germans made wide use of the new MP .38 which took the French and the English completely by surprise: both the latter were still issued with the 1916 carbine which was so much more powerful and accurate! As a last resort the commando patrols during the 'phoney war' were equipped with a 1924/29 light machine-gun. The technical branch of the French army had nevertheless by that time produced the MAS 1938 sub-machine-gun, manufactured by the Manufacture d'Armes de Saint-Etienne, chambered for the 7.65mm Long, but this had only just come into production. In fact it was only supplied in any appreciable quantity to the Armistice army. No sooner had Hitler marched into Paris victorious, than Germany, now at the height of its lightning military conquests, once more improved its MP .38 sub-machine-gun. The MP .40 called for modern construction techniques (maximum use of stamped, riveted and welded metal), which in turn made it possible to increase still further the production rates necessary to meet the requirements of the troops in the field. Between 1940 and 1945 more than a million MP .40s were manufactured.

It is interesting to note that a variant of this weapon, the MP .40/11 sub-machine-gun, was later produced and equipped with two twin 32-round clips, thus making it possible to fire sixty-four rounds continuously without changing clips. It is likely that this gun was intended to counter the 71-round PPsh-41 used by the Soviet army on the Eastern front.

During the war, under the pressures of experience and needs, the sub-machine-gun was subject to two clearly defined requirements: on the one hand, to produce a gun which was as compact as possible, intended to arm parachute troops, combat vehicle crews, officers and law enforcement agencies; on the other hand, to produce a gun with a wooden stock and a large clip holding powerful ammunition for assault troops.

The guns emerging as a result of this were, to start with, chambered for more powerful pistol ammunition, such as the 9mm Mauser or the 9mm Steyr. This solution was swiftly dropped for reasons of standardization. Later these sub-machine-guns were once again reinforced and equipped with breech-locking systems, and chambered for shorter rifle ammunition. This development was rendered possible by the new steel technology and new powders. The assault rifle, the direct forerunner of the modern combat rifle, was born. Under a new guise the individual weapon capable of full automatic fire that had been sought after as early as World War I by French tacticians had been produced.

When France was defeated in 1940, the German troops fanned out across the country, most of the British troops had been shipped back across the Channel in utter disarray, and the insular isolationism of the English was direly threatened by an imminent armada of German troops. If France had been defeated, it was quite conceivable that Great Britain would before long undergo the same fate. Having finally grasped the 'void' represented by the absence of individual automatic weapons among the

The Beretta 12 sub-machine-gun
with wooden stock and 40-round
clip.

The 57 sub-machine-gun with a
200mm barrel and foldable stock.

The SIG MKPS sub-machine-gun.

The SIG MKMS sub-machine-gun.

The Armaguerra 35 sub-machine-gun.

The Beretta 1938 A1 sub-machine-gun.

The Beretta 1938 A2 sub-machine-gun.

The Lanchester sub-machine-gun.

The MAS 1938 sub-machine-gun.

Sten Mark I sub-machine-gun.
Note that the front grip has been
removed from this weapon.

Sten Mark II sub-machine-gun.

Sten Mark III sub-machine-gun.

Sten Mark V sub-machine-gun.

MP-41 sub-machine-gun.

Suomi m/37–39
sub-machine-gun.

The Russian PPsh-41
sub-machine-gun.

1943 F.N.A.-B sub-machine-gun
with 40-round clip.

81

Beretta model 1 sub-machine-gun.

American M3 sub-machine-gun,
known as the 'Grease Gun'.

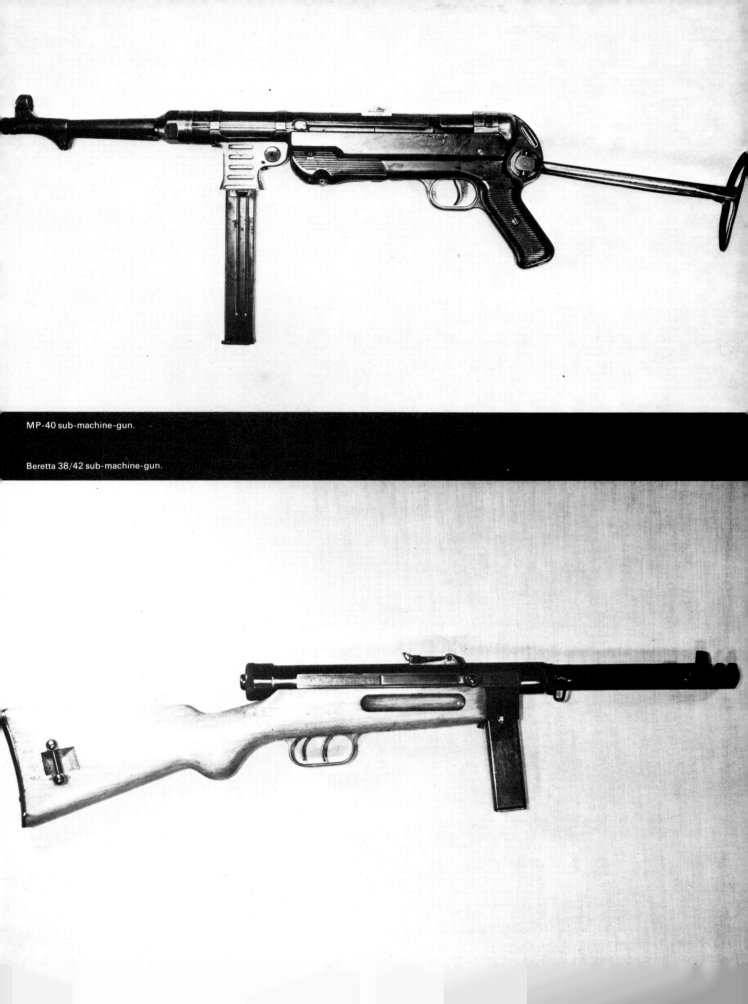

MP-40 sub-machine-gun.

Beretta 38/42 sub-machine-gun.

1943 F.N.A.-B sub-machine-gun with clip and stock both folded.

TZ-45 sub-machine-gun (shown without clip).

Variara sub-machine-gun with 40-round clip.

Variara sub-machine-gun with stock folded and clip in firing position.

Thompson M1 sub-machine-gun with 30-round clip.

Thompson M1A1 sub-machine-gun with 20-round clip.

ranks of its armed forces, His Majesty's Government took a keen interest in this gun which for so long it had viewed with disdain. Since the beginning of the war numerous sub-machine-guns had arrived from America to equip certain units in the British army. But these were just sporadic and expensive invoices for supplies which, at any given moment during the Atlantic crossing, could be sent plummeting to the sea-bed by a German U-boat. It was thus imperative that the majority of the sub-machine-guns urgently required by the army were supplied post haste by the munitions factories.

Although revised and modified by the Englishman George Herbert Lanchester and manufactured by the Sterling Engineering Company Ltd of Dagenham, Essex, the Lanchester sub-machine-gun was simply a copy of the MP .28/11, Hugo Schmeisser's German sub-machine-gun, itself a direct descendant of the 1918 model! Its inventor patented this gun in April 1941 at the London Patent Office. It was made in 9mm Parabellum calibre for the exclusive use of the Royal Navy. Faced with the latent danger of invasion, it was time to arm every citizen old enough to carry a gun just as quickly as possible. This weapon would have to have automatic fire and be very low-priced. If the Lanchester complied with the first condition, it certainly did not comply with the second: being complicated, it was costly to produce.

At the Enfield arms factory to the north of London two men, Reginald Vernon Sheppherd and Harold John Turpin, sat down at their drawing-boards and six months later came up with a sub-machine-gun in which all expensive machining had been eliminated and which could be produced in double-quick time, given its simplicity and low cost-price. All that remained was to christen this newcomer, which was soon to be on everyone's lips; the two inventors prefixed the first two letters of the arms factory where the new gun had been created with the initials of their own names and called it the Sten gun. Between mid-1941 and 1945 some 3,750,000 Sten guns of all models were manufactured, with the record production figures occurring in 1943 with a weekly production rate of 47,000 guns. To start with the Sten gun was issued only to British troops, but as production rates increased Sten gun stocks started to build up and tens of thousands of these weapons were dropped by parachute throughout occupied Europe, where the underground resistance groups, whose symbol they became, used them against the German troops. During this period the Sten gun fitted with silencer and canvas hand guard appeared. Although not entirely efficient, these extras considerably reduced the noise level; some allied commandos received these weapons as standard equipment.

Late in 1944 the Oberndorf Waffenfabrik Mauser in Germany received from the government of the Third Reich the order to make 25,000 Sten sub-machine-guns destined to be parachuted behind the allied lines to the last German resistance groups who were, albeit to no avail, trying to stem the victorious advance of the French, American and British troops. These sub-machine-guns, whose code name was Gerät Potsdam, were faithful copies of the Mark II Sten and even the original marks had been reproduced to make them more lifelike and deceive the enemy. This entire order was completed in less than three months. In the last months of the war, several German arms factories on their own account took up production of a variant of the Sten gun which was referred to as the MP .3008. This gun could use the MP .38 clip.

At the present time the Sten is outclassed by many other similar weapons. Nevertheless, even if most of the major powers in Europe have scrapped their Sten gun stocks, it still remains a favourite weapon in certain Third World countries; the Chinese have even reproduced it, seduced by its astonishing simplicity. During its fairly lengthy military career, the Sten underwent numerous modifications which, in accordance with the British method, were conveyed by different references. Thus, one after the other, came the Sten Mk I, Mk II, Mk II S, Mk III, Mk IV models A and B, Mk V and Mk VI.

The Berlin—Rome axis sets the technical pace
With the advent of the MP .40 the German sub-machine-gun had achieved the final standard which it was to retain until the end of the war. The MP .41 by C. G. Haenel of Suhl was never adopted by any of the German armies. This hybrid weapon boasted the salient qualities and advantages of the MP .40 and MP .28/11 sub-machine-guns; it kept the receiver and the feed mechanism and system of the former, as well as the selection mechanism and wooden stock of the latter.

Allied to Germany by the Berlin—Rome axis, Italy had no option but to submit to the influence of its powerful associate. Armaments were also affected by this alliance and thanks once again to Tulio Marengoni, Beretta brought out a sub-machine-gun in 1941 which was heavily inspired by the German MP .38 and MP .40. This gun, which was extremely well made but doubtless too expensive for a country at war, was called the Model 1. The Gardone company which, in spite of everything, seems to have staked all on this model, was in no time forced to interrupt its costly production and concentrate on production of the 38/42 model, which was just as effective and far less expensive. Many of the parts in it were identical to those of the 1938 A Beretta: the receiver, cocking lever, and double-trigger system. Grooves in the barrel made it lighter, although they made it more rigid, and made it possible to eliminate the cooling jacket.

On 22 June 1941 German columns crossed into Soviet territory, in spite of the non-aggression pact signed some months earlier. During their struggle against the Finns in 1939 the Russians had had a chance to appreciate the effectiveness of the Suomi sub-machine-guns. The Swedish firm Husqvarna Vapenfabriks A.B. was incidentally manufacturing the 1931 Suomi under licence; this was adopted by Sweden under the reference m/37-39 and later used by Norway, Denmark, Indonesia and Egypt. The 1931 Suomi undoubtedly considerably influenced the Soviet Shpagine and Sudarov models.

Destined to replace the PPD sub-machine-gun, previously studied by V. A. Degtyarev, the PPsh-41, devised by Georg Shpagine and produced from 1941 onwards, made wide use of stamped metal and was cheaper to produce than previous models. A massive production programme ensued, calculated at some 5,000,000 pieces. Although outclassed by more modern equipment, the PPsh-41 is still the traditional weapon in certain Warsaw Pact countries and even in Red China, where it is produced in a slightly different form. Like the PPsh-41, the PPS-42 and PPS-43 Sudarev sub-machine-guns are tough and simple models. Together with the Finnish and Italian sub-machine-guns they were among the best available during World War II.

The 38/42 Beretta sub-machine-gun was unanimously considered by troops on the Western front as the best designed and most accurate weapon in the war. The 38/42 model was like a very short carbine, with two triggers, one for full automatic fire and the other for semi-automatic fire. A small deflector restricted the disturbance while a wooden stock made it possible to fire the weapon from the shoulder without discomfort. It was fed by a 20- or 40-round clip. But although better placed, Beretta did not have exclusive rights for the production of sub-machine-guns in Italy. Among the rivals, some less reliable than others, to the 'lord' of Gardone, mention should be made of the F.N.A.B. sub-machine-gun, 1943 model, in 9mm Parabellum calibre. Devised and made by the Fabrica Nazionale d'Armi at Brescia, this gun, which was entirely machined, was extremely costly, and this restricted mass-production. It was nevertheless used by Italian and German troops in 1943 and 1944. In addition the TZ 45 sub-machine-gun by the brothers Toni and Zorzoli Giandoso, named after the initials of its authors, was produced in 1944 and used by the Italian army in the latter stages of the war. Italian partisans, who had come by large numbers of these guns, used them against the German and Fascist Italian troops. Shortly after the war, and in a somewhat modified form, this gun was adopted by Burma, where it is made as the BA 52. The TZ 45 had a safety catch mounted behind the clip holder. The Variara sub-machine-gun, in 9mm Parabellum calibre, was produced on a virtually hand-made basis during World War I. It was mainly used by Italian resistance groups.

The American wartime sub-machine-gun
The Americans were irrevocably drawn into the war on 7 December 1941 when Japanese aircraft destroyed the Pacific Fleet at Pearl Harbor. At that time the only sub-machine-gun available to the US Army was the Thompson M1, a very slightly simplified version of the 1928 A1 Thompson; a further internal alteration of the mechanism produced the M1A1 model. But as far as its production was concerned it was just as complex and expensive. As there was no time to be wasted, which excluded the development of a new type of sub-machine-gun, the Thompson M1A1 was mass-produced, and on an American scale to boot. It featured in virtually every theatre of war both in Europe and in the Pacific. The large stocks of Thompson guns were distributed to the Allies after the war, and the French Foreign Legion used it later in Indochina and at the beginning of the Algerian war.

In order to lower the cost of the US standard-issue sub-machine-gun, several American companies started manufacturing lighter and simpler arms to replace the Thompson, which was unnecessarily heavy and complicated. Such attempts in no way prevented the Tommy-gun from taking part in the various victories in the Pacific and in Europe. Among its rivals was the US Reising 55 sub-machine-gun, devised by Eugene G. Reising in about 1941. It was a direct descendant of the Reising 50 and was produced until 1945 by the Harrington and Richardson Arms Co. About 100,000 of these guns, both model

50 and model 55, and all in .45 ACP calibre, were produced by the end of the war.

The UD M-42 sub-machine-gun, chambering the 9mm Parabellum round (a few rare models were in .45 ACP calibre), was designed shortly before World War II by Carl G. Swebelius, founder of the well-known American company, Hi-Standard. About 15,000 of these guns were manufactured by Martin Firearms for the United Defense Supply Corporation, controlled by the US government. According to some authors, these guns were used by the Office of Strategic Services, the famous O.S.S., and parachute-dropped into Europe and the Far East. A certain number of these guns was supplied to the Dutch government which used them in its Far Eastern colonies.

All these attempts were to no avail once the M3 sub-machine-gun appeared on the military scene. This was the common brainchild of George J. Hyde and Frederick W. Samson, director of research at the General Motors Corporation. It came about as a result of a specification drawn up by the US Army Ordnance Service. Faced with the success earned by the British Sten gun and the MP .38 and MP .40 produced in Germany, the specification, which indicated a .45 ACP calibre weapon, was somewhat altered, so that the gun could use both the .45 ACP round and the 9mm Parabellum. The change-over is carried out on the spot by switching barrels — a speedy operation that requires no tools — and the breech, and by the use of an adaptor sleeve permitting use of the Sten clip. Some of these M3 sub-machine-guns were made directly in 9mm Parabellum calibre. In such cases the gun does not bear the standard Ordnance mark, nor the series number replaced by 'US 9mm' on the righthand side of the feed chute. Adopted by the US Army in 1942, the M3 underwent certain modifications and became the M3A1 model, which has no cocking-lever on the right, an ejection port and an overall cover somewhat larger. About 1000 of these weapons were made during the war for the O.S.S. The total wartime production of the M3 and M3A1 rose to some 650,000. Some of them were equipped with silencers and flash-hiders. A short barrel, influenced by the design of the MP .44 German assault rifle, was tried at the experimental stage. A compact and effective gun, the M3 was dropped by parachute to the underground resistance during the German occupation of Europe. During the Korean war the Ithaca Gun Co. supplied some 33,000 of these guns to the expeditionary units.

The three calibres most used by the nations at war during World War II for their sub-machine-guns were the 7.62mm Tokarev (USSR), the 9mm Parabellum (Germany, Great Britain, Italy, Finland, Hungary etc.) and the .45 ACP (USA). The Japanese made some hesitant attempts with 8mm Nambu calibre sub-machine-guns, but according to Americans who came up against them in the field, these guns were quite infrequent in the war in the Pacific.

Towards the modern sub-machine-gun

In the USSR where research had been directed since 1940 towards an assault rifle with a high fire-power, the sub-

(1) American parachute troops on the Normandy front, armed with the 1928 A1 Thompson (left) and the M1 (right).
(2) In Sicily, British troops storm a village with Thompson sub-machine-guns.
(3) Near Rome, during the Italian campaign, General de Gaulle congratulates a Moroccan tabor equipped with a Thompson M1.
(4) In the Pacific, during the battle for Okinawa Island, an American Marine with a Thompson covers his comrade who carries a Browning Automatic Rifle.

The M3 sub-machine-gun in 9mm Parabellum calibre. The detail shows the markings on this same weapon in .45 ACP calibre.

The Reising 55 sub-machine-gun.

The US M3 sub-machine-gun seen from the right. The cocking-lever and the open flap of the ejection window are clearly visible.

The UD M.42 sub-machine-gun.

The SIG MP-44 sub-machine-gun.

machine-guns of the years 1940–5 gave way to automatic rifles. They have virtually disappeared from the military inventories of the Eastern Bloc.

In Western countries, as a result of the excessive power required by NATO for infantry ammunition, which should be the same for the rifle and the machine-gun, the sub-machine-gun had something of a comeback in the post-war period. Because every European country had to restock with military equipment and arms, the NATO standardization policy was applied to the 9mm Para-bellum calibre, the most widespread at the end of the war. With automatic rifles, machine-rifles and machine-guns supplying fire-power at long and medium distances, the role of the sub-machine-gun was reduced to the weapon carried by the leaders of combat units and groups, by parachutists, vehicle crews and police departments; this in turn led to the development of weapons which were as compact as possible within the limits of reasonable efficiency.

It was in this new frame of mind that the Swiss firm SIG took up a modernized version of its MKPS model. The major apparent difference resided in the use of a stamped metal fore-end within which the clip was folded when the gun was not in the firing position. Nevertheless, a clear mechanical improvement had likewise been made by the introduction of a selective trigger with two bosses per-mitting semi-automatic fire on the first and full automatic fire on the second. Since this model, this type of selector seems to have been permanently adopted by the SIG. The lateral faces of the metal fore-end turned out to be insufficiently rigid when used, and the Rheinfall auth-orities decided to add some stiffening beads. The MP .44 thus became the MP .46 without any other modification being carried out to the gun. This solution was aimed at reducing the weight of the gun and its cost price. The aim was only partly successful and neither the MP .44 nor the MP .46 were particularly successful among potential buyers, who found them too heavy and too expensive, despite their remarkable finish and their impeccable work-manship.

Despite the restrictive measures imposed on Italy as far as arms manufacture was concerned, Beretta was auth-orized to continue its production of sub-machine-guns for supply to foreign countries. Towards the end of 1945, the Gardone company put forward its 38/44 model which was the same as the 38/42 model with certain internal modifications: the recoil spring used was similar to that of the Sten gun, the bolt was very slightly shorter, and at first glance the only distinguishing feature between the two models was the absence of the spring housing plug protruding behind the receiver. Syria, Pakistan, Iraq and Costa Rica purchased these weapons in 1948 and 1949.

With its model 48 sub-machine-gun, the SIG broke with the tradition of a gun made with intensive and costly machining. Calling on modern casting and moulding techniques, the renowned Swiss company managed to reduce its prices to a competitive level. For the first time the barrel of a SIG sub-machine-gun was entirely visible, the cooling jacket having disappeared; the clip still folded forwards but was no longer hidden in a metal or wooden fore-end, now considered superfluous and unnecessarily heavy. But unable to throw a hundred years of tradition entirely to the winds, the SIG engineers have retained their noble wood to enhance the look of the weapon.

At the same time, in Czechoslovakia, the ZK 466 sub-machine-gun was produced on a small scale by Zbrojovka Brno and offered no striking innovations. But it is worth noting that the the clip folded forwards for easier carrying. This feature, together with the relatively small overall length, reveals the purpose of this weapon: equipping airborne troops. Between 1948 and 1949, the Italian company Bernardelli of Brescia produced an improved copy of the 38/44 Beretta sub-machine-gun; only a few models were actually made. Bernardelli was unable to find a foothold in an arena where his neighbour and rival Beretta had reigned for several years. Although thoroughly well made, this gun offered no revolution-ary features.

Modern sub-machine-guns

Among the most successful attempts to reduce the bulk of the sub-machine-gun we should quote the achievements of the SIG and the Manufacture d'Armes de Tulle, in Switzerland and France respectively, using foldable clips.

The SIG sub-machine-gun, MP .310 model, is currently one of the best models on the international market, and the result of forty years continual improvement.

The French MAT 49 is also a remarkable design. Among other special features there is the automatic grip safety which prevents the weapon firing when it is not in the normal firing position. This 'P.M.', as it is familiarly called in the French Army, is the veteran of twenty years of military campaigning in the far-flung corners of the former French colonial empire.

In Czechoslovakia another attempt was made in about 1948 to reduce the bulkiness of sub-machine-guns and improve their stability when on automatic fire. Czech technicians built a whole generation of guns with a 'telescopic bolt' forming a sort of sleeve around the barrel when in the closed position. This ingenious arrangement made it possible to reduce the length of the receiver considerably, and hence the length of the whole gun. The centre of gravity, as a result, is pushed forward to a point which is very favourable to accuracy.

Thus the Czech models 23 and 25 sub-machine-guns came into being, chambered for the 9mm Parabellum. Improved during production and adapted to the 7.62mm Soviet round, which was 'standardized' in the Warsaw Pact countries, the 26 model with the extendable metal stock and the 24 model with the wooden stock made their appearance in 1952 and became the standard-issue weapons of the Czech army until 1960.

More tailored for the security forces, the modern Czech Scorpion 61 sub-machine-gun uses the same principle of a telescopic breech, but chambers the classic 7.65mm Browning round. The political circumstances of the post-war years made it impossible for western countries to purchase these improved weapons, and so arms tech-nicians in these countries hastened to follow the Czech example to take advantage of these new improvements. Thus emerged, at an early stage, the Uzi sub-machine-gun in Israel, production of which was taken on under licence by the Fabrique Nationale de Herstal in Belgium. Later the Italians brought out their new Beretta 12 sub-machine-

The SIG MP-46
sub-machine-gun.

The 38/44 Beretta
sub-machine-gun.

The SIG MP-48
sub-machine-gun.

The ZK 466 sub-machine-gun.

The Bernardelli V.B.
sub-machine-gun.

The IMI (Israeli-manufactured)
UZI sub-machine-gun, made for
export.

The French MAT 49 sub-machine-gun with folded clip and retracted stock.

The SHE 26 sub-machine-gun with 24-round clip and retracted stock.

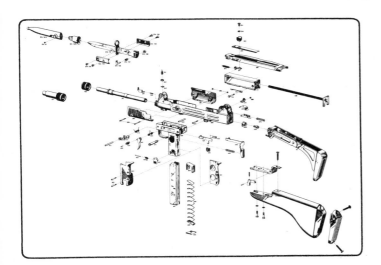

The Czech Scorpion 61 sub-machine-gun with the stock retracted.

The Walther MPK sub-machine-gun with the stock retracted.

An exploded view of the UZI sub-machine-gun with its bayonet and sheath.

The SIG MP-310 sub-machine-gun.

91

gun, heir to a whole line of prototypes sporting various systems. Lastly, there are two other similar weapons which are noteworthy: the Spanish Star 62 and the German Walther MPK or MPL, available in two lengths. These are both remarkably reliable weapons, made with great precision and highly accurate.

In England the long line of Sten guns virtually died out with the end of the war, and it was necessary to come up with a less primitive and more reliable sub-machine-gun to equip the British troops. It was the gun patented in August 1942 by George William Patchett, one hundred models of which had been produced at the end of the war, which was selected by the English authorities. It was of course steadily improved and went by the name of Sterling, the name of the company manufacturing it. The Sterling, which is well respected among European arms experts, offers no revolutionary features but is extremely well designed and made.

The Luxembourg Sola Super sub-machine-gun likewise offered no technical innovations. Made by the Société Luxembourgeoise d'Armes, and based on a design by one Jansen, it was never mass-produced. Some of these sub-machine-guns were smuggled into North Africa and used by the Algerian rebels. In about 1960 the Société Luxembourgeoise d'Armes (SO.L.A.) was converted for the production of plastic goods.

With no official source of arms supply, North Vietnam produced automatic weapons on an almost hand-made basis in the 1950s and 1960s. On the battlefield they recovered damaged weapons in which certain major parts were still serviceable, and the North Vietnamese then 'restored' these guns with any means at their disposal. As a result Vietnamese Thompsons and K 50s were found, as well as French MAT 49s rechambered for the 7.62mm Soviet and Chinese round, not to mention other makes whose reassembly was of the most rudimentary kind.

Among recent European guns, we should mention the Italian 57 model sub-machine-gun by Luigi Franchi, a well-known shotgun maker from Brescia. Chambering the 9mm Parabellum, this weapon is made with stamped and welded metal. Despite its compactness (42cm with the stock folded) this gun does not appear to have earned the success on which its authors reckoned. The Beretta 12 probably has more than a little to do with this commercial disappointment. There is a variant of the 57 model, equipped with a 40.5cm barrel for semi-automatic fire only. Any list must include the HK 54 (MP.5) and HK 53 German sub-machine-guns by Heckler and Koch. Newcomers to the arms industry, Heckler and Koch set up in business shortly after the war at Oberndorf/Neckar, in Mauser territory. Concentrating their efforts on the

CETME Spanish assault rifle devised by German engineers who had emigrated to Spain, Heckler and Koch adapted its production to ultra-modern techniques, based largely on stamped and welded metal and injected plastics. These techniques made it possible to achieve much higher production rates. The G 3 assault rifle thus came into being, leading to the HK 54 (or MP.5) sub-machine-gun, which is a reduced version of it; certain parts are common to both guns. Currently adopted by the German police, its price and quality seem to have guaranteed it a highly successful future. The HK 53 sub-machine-gun is a variant of it, chambered for the 5.56mm × 45 (.223) calibre round.

The future
of the sub-machine-gun

With the advent of the light automatic rifle, known as the 'assault rifle', in .223 calibre, the classic sub-machine-gun is in danger of being partly eclipsed in the military scene in the years to come. It will without doubt carry on for several years, in more compact versions, as the personal equipment of certain types of unit and of the forces of law and order, given its simplicity and its low cost.

The Heckler and Koch HK 54 (or MP-5) sub-machine-gun.

Above: Russian soldiers armed with the PPsh-41 during World War II.

The Luigi Franchi 57
sub-machine-gun.

Development of the Beretta
prototypes towards the Beretta 12.

Model 1953.

Model 10.

Model 12.

An Italian Special Branch
policeman armed with the Beretta
12 sub-machine-gun.

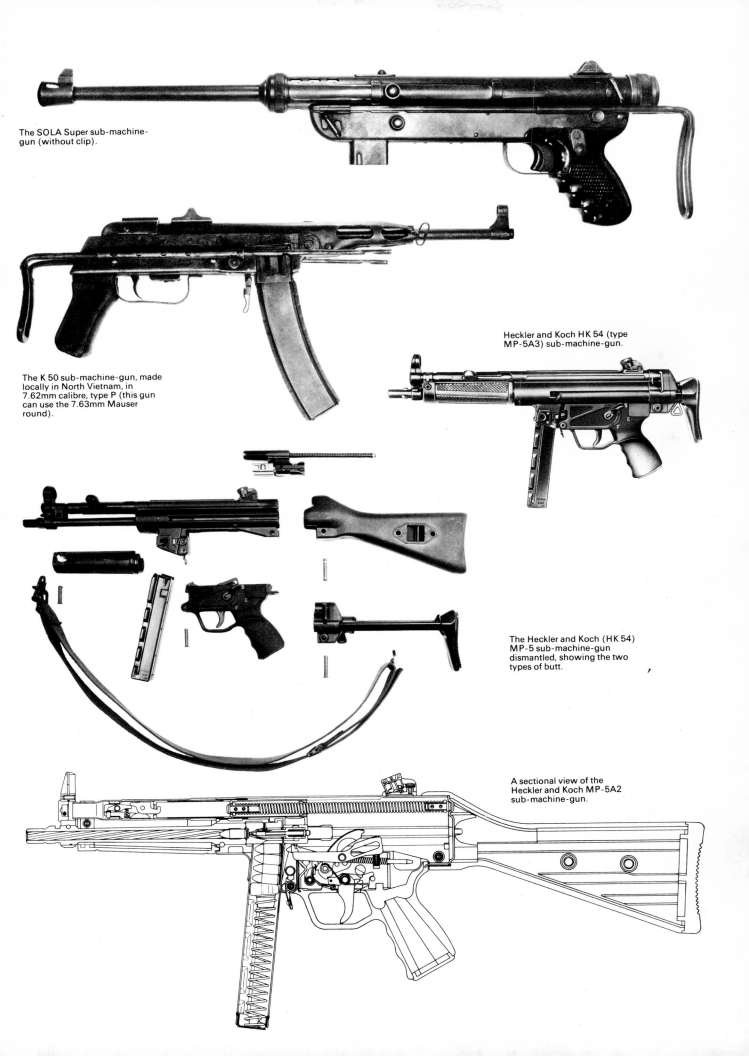

The SOLA Super sub-machine-gun (without clip).

The K 50 sub-machine-gun, made locally in North Vietnam, in 7.62mm calibre, type P (this gun can use the 7.63mm Mauser round).

Heckler and Koch HK 54 (type MP-5A3) sub-machine-gun.

The Heckler and Koch (HK 54) MP-5 sub-machine-gun dismantled, showing the two types of butt.

A sectional view of the Heckler and Koch MP-5A2 sub-machine-gun.

Sub-machine-guns: technical data

HK 54 (or MP.5)

Country	West Germany
Designation	Heckler and Koch HK 54 or MP.5 2 variants: MP.A2, plastic stock, MP.A3 telescopic stock
Calibre	9mm Parabellum
Weight	2.450kg for the MP.A2 and 2.550kg for the MP.A3
Length	overall 66cm (MP.A3) and 68cm (MP.A2), with a 22.5cm barrel
Capacity	30 rounds; cyclic rate of fire: 650rpm
Remarks	also made in .224 calibre, this sub-machine-gun has full automatic and semi-automatic fire controlled by a selector on the left-hand side. The stocks of the two variants are interchangeable

HK 53

Country	West Germany
Designation	Heckler and Koch, HK 53
Calibre	5.56mm × 45 (.223)
Weight	3.350kg
Length	overall 76.5cm, butt folded 56cm, barrel 28cm
Capacity	40 rounds, cyclic rate of fire: 600rpm
Remarks	derived from the HK54, differs only in respect of the technical arrangements required for use of the .223 round; this sub-machine-gun is one of Heckler and Koch's latest products; like the HK 54 it has semi-automatic and full automatic fire

Mauser MP.60

Country	West Germany
Designation	Mauser Werke, model 60
Calibre	9mm Parabellum
Weight	3.100kg
Length	stock folded 50cm, butt extended 77cm, barrel 25cm
Capacity	36 rounds; cyclic rate of fire: 750rpm
Remarks	this new gun from the Mauser Jagdwaffen seems at the time of writing to be in the pre-production stage. This sub-machine-gun on which a selector has been mounted to permit semi-automatic and full automatic fire, can fire anti-tank grenades when fitted with a special sleeve. The metal stock folds on top of the gun

Walther MPL (top) and MPK (bottom)

Country	West Germany
Designation	Walther MPL (long) and MPK (short)
Calibre	9mm Parabellum
Weight	MPK: 3.425kg; MPL: 3.625kg
Length	butt 28cm; MPL barrel 26cm; MPK barrel 17cm; overall, MPL 75cm, MPK 66cm
Capacity	32 rounds; cyclic rate of fire: 550rpm
Remarks	on the market since 1963 in both versions, this excellent sub-machine-gun has semi-automatic and full automatic fire. In the short version it is ideal for armoured vehicle personnel, and for police use

MAT 49

Country	France
Designation	Manufacture d'Armes de Tulle, MAT 49
Calibre	9mm Parabellum
Weight	3.500kg
Length	overall 72cm; stock folded 46cm; barrel 23cm
Capacity	32 rounds; cyclic rate of fire: 600rpm
Remarks	adopted in 1949 by the French army, this 'PM' also and in varying degrees equips most of the armed and police forces in the various former French colonies. It is likewise issued to certain divisions of the French police force. Under the name MAT 51 it has been manufactured with double triggers, wooden stock and lengthened barrel for use by uniformed French police. In the military version it only has automatic fire

Sterling Mk IV

Country	Great Britain
Designation	Sterling Engineering Company, Sterling Mk IV
Calibre	9mm Parabellum
Weight	3.500kg
Length	overall 71cm; butt folded 48cm; barrel 20cm
Capacity	34 rounds; cyclic rate of fire: 550rpm
Remarks	adopted in 1953 by the British Army, this sub-machine-gun, which has full automatic and semi-automatic fire, has undergone numerous modifications since its birthdate in 1942. As is the custom in Britain, such changes have entailed changes in the trade name

Uzi

Country	Israel
Designation	I.M.I. (Israeli Military Industry), Uzi, also manufactured under licence by the Fabrique Nationale Belge
Calibre	9mm Parabellum
Weight	4kg
Length	total 64 and 65cm; metal stock folded 45 cm; barrel 26cm
Capacity	25 or 32 rounds (the 40-round model is no longer in production); cyclic rate of fire: 600rpm
Remarks	manufactured since 1951 in Israel and then by the F.N. Belge, this sub-machine-gun, fitted either with a wooden stock or a foldable stamped metal stock, has been adopted by the West German army and by the Dutch army too. With a grip safety, the Uzi has full automatic and semi-automatic fire. In France it is issued to the Criminal Investigation Department of the police

Beretta model 4

Country	Italy
Designation	Beretta model 49, or model 4
Calibre	9mm Parabellum
Weight	3.250kg
Length	overall 80cm; barrel 21cm
Capacity	20 or 32 rounds; cyclic rate of fire: 550rpm
Remarks	improved version of the 38/44 to which a push-button safety has been added, this gun with two triggers giving semi-automatic and full automatic fire still currently equips certain units in the Italian army. It has been and still is in some countries the standard issue weapon for numerous national armies: West Germany, Thailand, Egypt, Indonesia etc

Beretta model 5

Country	Italy
Designation	Beretta model 5
Calibre	9mm Parabellum
Weight	3.250kg
Length	80cm; barrel 21cm
Capacity	20 or 32 rounds; cyclic rate of fire: 550rpm
Remarks	derived from the model 4, is practically identical except for the modification made to the shape of the push-button safety placed along the stock. Like the model 4, this gun is still in production

Beretta model 12, metal butt

Country	Italy
Designation	Beretta, model 12
Calibre	9mm Parabellum
Weight	3kg (metal butt) or 3.400kg (wooden butt)
Length	overall 65cm, metal stock folded 42cm; barrel 20cm
Capacity	20-, 30- or 40-round; cyclic rate of fire: 555rpm
Remarks	culmination of a series of prototypes (see previous photos), this sub-machine-gun which gives semi-automatic and full automatic fire is one of the most up-to-date in use. It relies widely on new casting and moulding techniques; it uses a variant developed by the Czechs in the 1950s: the telescopic breech

SIG MP.310

Country	Switzerland
Designation	SIG model MP.310
Calibre	9mm Parabellum
Weight	3.150kg
Length	51cm without stock; stock extended 74cm; barrel 20cm
Capacity	40 rounds; cyclic rate of fire: 900rpm
Remarks	latest of the SIG sub-machine-guns, the SIG MP.310 requires modern plastic-moulding techniques and metal-stamping methods. Its quality complies with the standards of the 'armament watchsmiths'. The MP.310 gives semi-automatic and full automatic fire, depending on the pressure applied to the trigger: first boss gives semi-automatic fire; final position, automatic fire

Scorpion

Country	Czechoslovakia
Designation	The State Arsenal of Czechoslovakia, model 61, known as the Scorpion
Calibre	7.65mm Browning (.32 ACP)
Weight	2.050kg
Length	stock folded 32cm; stock extended 62cm; barrel 12cm
Capacity	10 or 20 rounds; cyclic rate of fire: 700rpm
Remarks	very compact, this gun uses curved clips and has semi-automatic or full automatic fire. The Scorpion is one of the most recent Czech arms productions

At the FBI headquarters in Washington special agents train with the Thompson sub-machine-gun using tracer bullets.

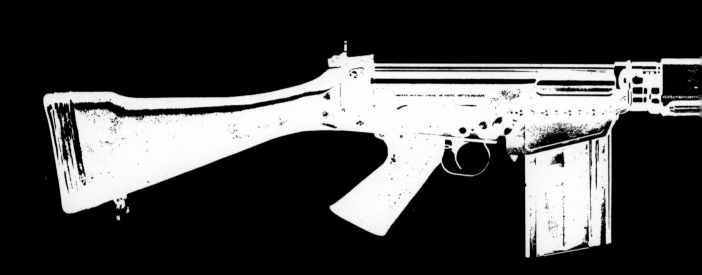

4
military rifles

The appearance of smokeless powder in Europe gave rise to a full-scale revolution as far as the military rifle was concerned. Revolvers and shotguns, on the other hand, did not undergo any radical changes as a result of this discovery. Although the actual shape of the rifle remained more or less the same, the major innovation consisted in the use of comparatively smaller calibres (as compared to those used hitherto) and considerably more powerful ammunition. But this increased power had a direct repercussion on the various bolt mechanisms, which now had to stand up to much higher pressures.

This development of the military rifle led in time to three different types of gun:

1. the repeating rifle;
2. the automatic (or semi-automatic) repeating rifle or carbine;
3. the automatic (or full automatic) or assault rifle.

The repeating rifle

In these guns the bolt, which is operated manually, carries out the following mechanical operations: (a) cocking the hammer; (b) chambering the cartridge fed from a magazine; the magazine may be either straight, and positioned beneath the breech-block, or tubular, in which case it is located in the stock or under the barrel.

When the gun is cocked the second time (i.e. when the first shot has been fired), the bolt, which usually contains an extractor, pulls the empty case on to an ejector, which is normally attached to the breech-block, and thus ensures that the empty shell is removed before the two operations mentioned above take place.

Rifles using smokeless cartridges

France, in 1886, was certainly the first country to adopt a military rifle which used smokeless ammunition. It was to replace the famous rifle known as the Gras, a large calibre gun designed for black powder. But the Ordnance kept a stock of these rifles in reserve, 'just in case . . .', which was why it re-emerged during World War I, where it was invaluable. During the 'phoney war' of 1939–40 a few Gras rifles were still being used in some sections of the French army . . .

It was succeeded by the Lebel rifle, which had a lengthy career, during which certain improvements were made to it. It was produced in large numbers during the 1914–18 war, and at that time was the symbol of the French trooper.

The German Paul Mauser devised a remarkably efficient bolt for his Gewehr 98, using Norris patents. This bolt was swiftly adopted by most simple repeating rifles, and still persists today, particularly in almost all big-game carbines chambered for extremely high power ammunition such as the .458 Winchester Magnum and the .375 Holland and Holland Magnum. It is also found in target rifles, as well as in numerous sporting rifles using .22 cartridges.

The Mauser 98 rifle was to become a worldwide classic, and it still remains so today. It was to be seen in every corner of the world in its various versions. It seems to have been recently manufactured once more in Eastern Bloc countries; it was the hallmark of the Third Reich; and in the late 1950s helped certain post-colonial guerrilla forces

to arm themselves, 'unobtrusively'.

During World War I the Mauser 98 meant as much to the 'Feldgrau' (German trooper) as the Lebel did to the 'Poilu' (French trooper). With a 7.92mm cartridge in the chamber, its excellent production quality and accuracy made it a formidable military weapon.

In 1891 Italy followed suit and also adopted a new standard-issue rifle. This was a 6.5mm calibre gun, commonly known as the 91, and it carved a well-deserved reputation for itself. It underwent one or two minor modifications, but its basic specifications remained the same. During World War I it was pitted against the Mannlicher rifles of the Austro-Hungarian armies.

In Switzerland Rubins and Schmidt in turn equipped their army with a rifle and a carbine — based on the old 1889 model — which came to be called the Rubins-Schmidt 1911 Model rifle and carbine. Both used the Swiss 7.5mm cartridge.

The bolt action repeating rifle during World War I

World War I was something of a testing-ground for the various weapons developed by the warring nations. Some divisions in the French Army were equipped with the standard 1892-M16 Model carbine. The capacity of the magazine, situated beneath the breech-block, was reduced to three 8mm Lebel cartridges, to avoid 'wasted ammunition'.

The English adopted the Lee Enfield No 1 Mark III rifle. This was without doubt the most widely manufactured standard British rifle: before the Armistice was signed in 1918, more than 4,000,000 had been produced. BSA halted production in 1943, but production continued until 1955 — when the FAL rifle made by the Fabrique Nationale in Belgium was adopted — in the Lithgow arms factory in Australia and at Ishapore in India.

The American expeditionary force landed in France in 1917, equipped with several thousand Springfield 1903 Model .30–06 calibre rifles. These could only be manufactured at Springfield Arsenal. Faced with growing demands, the Ordnance was keener to adopt a modified version of the Enfield 1914 Model rifle, then being made by Winchester for Great Britain. It was officially adopted by the US Army in 1917 as the US Enfield 1917 Model .30 calibre rifle, and in less than twenty months production of it totalled 2,202,423. This weapon was used to some extent in World War II as well; and in the post-war period it was even equipping certain European armies, which were being supplied by US arms factories.

In cleaning-up operations on captured enemy trenches the Americans resorted to using the Winchester 1912 Model pump-action shotgun, which they christened the 'trench rifle'. The use of shotguns brought a flurry of protest from the Imperial German Government, who regarded spraying their military personnel with buckshot to be in contravention of the Hague Conventions. The use of war gas must have struck the Germans as more humanitarian.

Military rifles between the wars

Gleaning whatever information they could from victory or defeat — depending which side they were on — arms experts only made very slight modifications to tactical

The French 1874 M 80/14 rifle known as the Gras rifle, which was used during World War I.

The French 1886 M 93 rifle, the Lebel rifle.

The German GEW 98 Mauser service rifle.

The French 1892 M 16 service carbine with its bayonet sheathed.

The British Lee Enfield no 1 Mark III rifle.

The American Springfield 1903 rifle.

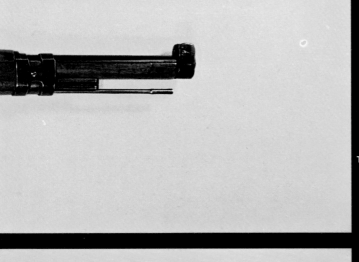

The German 1898 Mauser carbine.

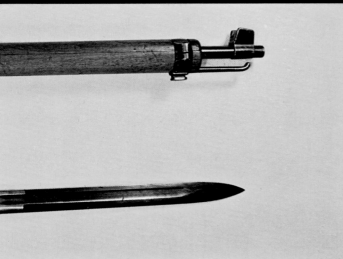

The Swiss Rubins-Schmidt 1911 carbine.

The US Springfield 1903 Mark I rifle.

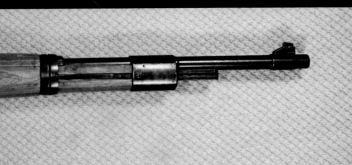

The standard German Mauser Kar.98 k carbine.

The American US Enfield 1917 rifle.

The American Winchester 1912 rifle, known as the 'trench rifle'.

The Italian 91-38 model rifle. A cross section showing the details of the mechanism.

The Italian Ballila training rifle used by Fascist youth groups.

weapons. Innovators were few and far between.

In Hitler's Germany the faithful old Gew.98 Mauser was readopted; one or two slight modifications were made, mainly with a view to reducing the cost price and increasing the production rate; and the result was the Kar. 98K. This weapon was manufactured in large numbers and used to equip the infantrymen of the Wehrmacht. But one branch of the German arms industry was undergoing rapid expansion: the sub-machine-gun, which, with its increased fire power, was to enable the shock-troops to win the *Blitzkrieg*.

After their conquest of Ethiopia the Italians gingerly brought their old 91 up to date, and called it the 91/38 Model. We might mention in passing that it was with a rifle of this type, fitted with a telescopic sight, all purchased at the government surplus store, that Lee Harvey Oswald allegedly assassinated US President, John F. Kennedy, in 1963.

When it came to training the para-military Young Fascists' 'Opéra Nazionale Balilla — children aged between six and twelve — a scaled-down version of the regulation rifle, 91/38 Model, was produced; this was a 6.5mm calibre gun, known as the Balilla Model, and it was manufactured in large numbers.

France, for her part, had finally given up making those numerous changes to her Lebel rifle. The Manufacture de Saint-Etienne had come up with a new rifle which was instantly adopted by the French General Staff: the M.A.S.36, which was to enjoy a long and successful career abroad.

World War II
When World War II broke out in 1939, the various warring factions set off for the battlefield with rifles which would have helped to win the Boer War.

Belgians, Poles, Germans, Czechs, Yugoslavs and Chinese went to war with simple Mauser repeating rifles; the French had a strange mixture of 7.5mm M.A.S. 36 rifles, 1886–93 and 07–15 Model Lebel rifles, 8mm 1892 and 1916 carbines, and it was not uncommon to see 1874 Model Gras rifles and 11mm Chassepot rifles in service, along with .433 calibre trusty old Remington Egyptians, which were used to train recruits and those on the home-front.

The English were equipped with a varied selection of .303 British (7.7mm) Lee Enfield rifles, while the Japanese and the Italians stood by their 6.5mm guns.

When the Japanese attacked Pearl Harbor the Americans were using their old 1903 Model 30–06 (7.62mm) Springfield rifle. This in effect was just a Mauser rifle which had been modified at great expense in American armouries, to give it its own special identity.

Paradoxically enough the Russians were the best equipped troops at the start of the war. Although they hung on to their 1891 Model Mossine rifle, which had been modified at various times down the years by the General Staff, they started to issue their front-line with new semi-automatic 1940 Model Tokarev rifles, which used 7.62mm rimmed cartridges.

Unable, for a variety of reasons, to come up with a reliable semi-automatic weapon, both the English and the Italians concentrated on the production of their regulation repeating rifles. In the early days of the war it was a battle between repeating rifles, and the winner was decided first and foremost on the basis of the quality of the rifle's performance. In tactical terms the various mechanisms left little to choose between them.

But the appearance of semi-automatic rifles and carbines on the battle-front tolled the knell for the traditional repeating rifle. As the war drew to a close, this latter enjoyed a final hour of glory in the hands of the various Resistance movements in Europe. After the war it was relegated to the armouries of those countries which, for one reason or another, were unable to bring their stock up to date as quickly as others.

France continued to use the repeating rifle in the various campaigns which heralded the independence of her ex-colonies; the MAS 36 underwent slight modifications and became the MAS 36–51, and was used in Indochina and Algeria together with more modern French and American rifles.

The classic repeating rifle was thus eventually outclassed by new technology, but it remains a much-respected museum-piece, and part of our glorious past.

Semi-automatic rifles and carbines

These weapons came into being because of the need to increase the rate of fire and the degree of accuracy. This could be achieved on the one hand by eliminating manual operation of the bolt and on the other by making it possible to keep the target in the line of sight. Thus the only non-automatic movement here is when the first round is chambered. When the first shot has been fired, the bolt mechanism, which is activated either by blowback or by a system which uses the gases in the barrel, ejects the empty case, cocks the hammer and feeds the next cartridge. But it is still necessary to press the trigger each time to release the hammer and thus discharge the round. The rapid rate of fire of these weapons gives them a definite advantage over the bolt action repeating rifle, but they are in turn inferior to the automatic rifle which can be fired in bursts.

The early days of the semi-automatic rifle
During World War I, three Frenchmen (Ribeyrolle, Sutter and Chauchat) developed the first French semi-automatic rifle, known as the 1917 Model. This was a heavy weapon, and frequent accidents were associated with it as a result of mechanical parts breaking. The 1918 Model, fitted with a clip which held five 8mm Lebel rounds, put these defects to rights. However, it played no actual part in the war, being manufactured in 1918, and never really had a chance to show its mettle.

Like their enemies, the Germans made cautious attempts to develop a semi-automatic rifle. These resulted in the Mondragon, a weapon of Mexican origin which was manufactured by the Swiss SIG company for the Kaiser's army.

Despite its excellent performance, the Mondragon was hurriedly taken out of service, whereas a short while later in France, the 1917 and 1918 Models were converted to repeating rifles.

These first experiments seem to have disappointed

The Italian 91/41 rifle.

The French semi-automatic 1918 rifle.

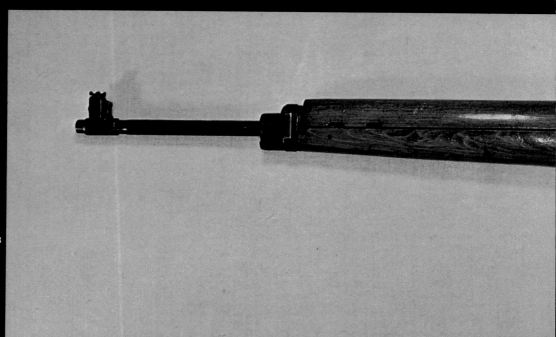

The Walther semi-automatic G 43 rifle.

A Swiss soldier on manoeuvres
with the SIG assault rifle.

The French MAS 36 rifle, model M 1936 CR 39, with folded stock. This model was particularly used by parachute units of the Foreign Legion in Indochina.

The French MAS 1936–51 rifle.

The Japanese Arizaka 38 carbine in 6.5mm Japanese calibre.

The 6.5mm calibre Italian semi-automatic Scotti (1931) rifle.

The 6.5mm Italian calibre Italian semi-automatic Genova Armaguerra 39 rifle.

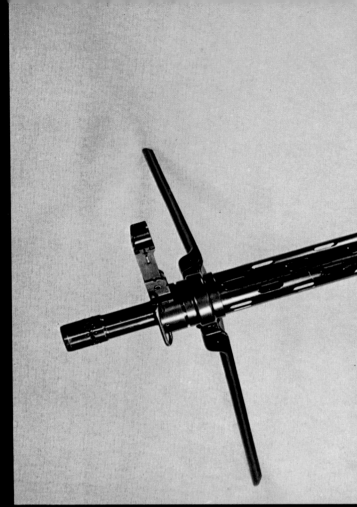

A member of the Welsh Guards outside St James's Palace, London, with the F.N. Herstal assault rifle manufactured under licence in Great Britain by the Enfield arms factory and BSA.

The Swiss SIG SG 510 assault rifle, chambered for the 7.62mm Russian round.

The Soviet Kalashnikov AK 47 assault rifle with accessories.

The MPIK assault rifle. This gun is the replica manufactured in East Germany of the Soviet Kalashnikov AK 47 assault rifle.

French and German designers alike, and for a time they abandoned their research in this field. The French turned their efforts to both medium and lightweight machine guns; the Germans concentrated on the machine-pistol. But in other countries arms manufacturers were keen to use the experience they had gained during the war to the best advantage. In Italy firms like Scotti, Genova Armaguerra and Beretta set to work to supply Mussolini's budding young army with a dependable semi-automatic rifle.

The Russians for their part were in no way discouraged by the failure of the Fedorov Avtomat automatic rifle with the Imperial Army, played for safety and turned their sights to the semi-automatic rifle and the machine-pistol. In 1931 Sergei Gavrilovich Simonov developed a prototype for an automatic rifle; it underwent certain modifications and eventually became the AVS automatic rifle which was adopted by the Red Army in 1936.

The reputation of the semi-automatic rifle and carbine is established (World War II)

As we saw earlier, the fighting in the young days of the war was conducted with 'conventional weapons': repeating rifles, machine-guns and light machine-guns, and so on. The only superiority as far as individual weaponry was concerned lay in the widespread use of sub-machine-guns by the German troops.

By the time 1941 came round things started to happen thick and fast. In fact when the German armies marched into the Soviet Union they found themselves up against large numbers of recently manufactured semi-automatic rifles – the 1940 Model Tokarev. Its ten-round clip gave this gun a fire-power which quite simply outclassed that of the old GEW or KAR 98 Mausers. But the German troops marched on and carried their banners right to the city walls of Moscow, because the infantryman's rifle was by no means the only decisive factor, as far as weapons were concerned.

However, the complex nature and awkward dismounting procedures for regular maintenance of the 1940 Model Tokarev saw it gradually disappear from the battlefront, where it was favourably replaced by the PPsh sub-machine-gun. But those at the head of the German Ordnance Corps were far from happy at the thought that their Wehrmacht was no longer able to boast the best rifle in the world.

The Americans joined in the war with a virtually out-of-date weapon in the shape of the 1903 Model Springfield and the 1917 US Enfield. It was a considerable stroke of luck for them that the Ordnance Service had a secret weapon in reserve. Experiments had been being conducted for some twenty years with semi-automatic rifles. Among them the rifle developed by John Garand, which came to be known as the M1, was put into service in the very first months of the war.

The overall production statistic for the war amounted to 4,040,000 rifles made by Springfield Armory, and the Winchester Repeating Arms Company. After the war 600,000 of these rifles were manufactured by various major American firms; elsewhere, the Italian companies, Breda and Beretta, also busied themselves with the production of this gun to meet the needs of the Italian, Danish and Indonesian Services.

Private industry in the United States – Winchester in this case – did not dally in providing a 'sister' to the Garand in the form of a light, 15-round carbine, which used low power .30 calibre ammunition. This carbine was called the US M1 and enjoyed swift popularity with the Allies (in fact it is still so popular in present-day Europe that the German company ERMA manufactures an exact replica in .22 LR calibre). It eventually replaced the automatic pistol carried by NCOs and specially assigned troops, and came in four different versions: (a) MI, semi-automatic carbine with a fixed wooden stock and pistol grip; (b) M1A1, semi-automatic carbine with folding lightweight metal stock; (c) M2, automatic carbine, firing in bursts, with wooden stock as in the M1; (d) M3, automatic carbine, firing in bursts, with wooden stock and equipped for fitting an infra-red sight.

From 1943 onwards a so-called 'half-moon' clip with a 30-round capacity was manufactured for use with all guns of this type. This carbine broke all production records for World War II, with a total in excess of 4,000,000.

The irksome idea that they no longer had the finest rifle in the world was brought home to the German troops during the campaign in North Africa, when they came up against the 8-round Garand and the 15-round US M1 in service with the American forces. Once more the German Africa Korps were outclassed by superior fire-power. And the same thing happened to the Japanese in the war in the Pacific.

Technicians and experts east of the Rhine took swift action. From the end of 1941 they lined up their first generation of semi-automatic rifles, gas-operated with the Walther GEW 41 (W). Despite its inferior performance as compared with its Russian and American counterparts, it went into service for a limited period of time, in order to make it clear to the Axis troops that the old Mauser's days were now numbered. It used the old German 7.92mm service cartridge with a 10-round fixed magazine.

The Japanese reacted differently. True to their age-old tradition of plagiarism, they copied the American Garand no sooner than it had appeared on the Pacific front, but they never managed to manufacture it in sufficient quantities.

The Americans were encouraged by the early successes of the Garand and issued it as the standard rifle to their combat divisions; to do this they set in motion one of those full-scale production programmes, which only they have the know-how and the means to mount. What is more, they did the same, simultaneously, with their automatic 1911 AC Model pistol, their Thompson sub-machine-gun, their 15-round US M1 carbines and their Browning machine-guns. In no time the American soldier, equipped with automatic weapons and backed up by an efficient logistic system, had at his finger-tips a staggering fire-power which remained supreme throughout the war years.

Things did not go quite this smoothly behind the Russian front, though. Although the arms factories were transferred to the east of the Urals, this did not make up for the fact that Russia had lost the most industrialized areas of her territory, and production suffered as a result. Russians still urgently needed to manufacture large quantities of arms, however, if they were to equip the im-

The American Springfield 1903 A3 rifle, adopted in this version in May 1942.

The Soviet Mossine-Nagant 1938 carbine.

The Soviet semi-automatic experimental Simonov rifle chambered for the 7.62mm rimmed round.

The standard Soviet semi-automatic Tokarev 1940 rifle.

The semi-automatic Mondragon rifle, manufactured by SIG.

The American semi-automatic US-M1 15-round service carbine.

The American semi-automatic US-M1A1 carbine with folded stock.

The German semi-automatic Walther Gew. 41 service rifle.

The Soviet semi-automatic Simonov SKS carbine with bayonet folded.

The French semi-automatic MAS 1949 rifle.

pressive manpower being sent to the front. Unable to continue with the production of the 1940 Model Tokarev rifle on a sufficiently large scale, they concentrated their efforts round production of the 1891/30 Mossine Nagant rifle. This was a simpler weapon and when all was said and done it was a fair match for the Mauser 98K. In addition, they strengthened the fire-power of their infantry divisions by issuing them with PPsh 41 sub-machine-guns. These were relatively inexpensive to manufacture, and with their 71-round drum magazine constituted extremely effective combat weapons.

In 1943 the Germans introduced a new generation of G.43 Model semi-automatic rifles, manufactured by Walther and Mauser, and these were considerable improvements over their predecessors. But the production capacity was still inadequate, and these rifles were distributed in limited numbers among the sharpshooters in the various fighting units.

The G.43 was a logical progression from the GEW 41; the bolt mechanism remained unaltered, but the gas-operated system adopted was that incorporated in the Russian 1940 Model Tokarev. The fixed magazine was replaced by an interchangeable 10-round clip; this could be loaded from the top using two 5-round loading clips. This weapon was still in use with the Czech army several years after peace had been signed in 1945.

With the FG.42 and the Mkb.42, MP.43 and MP.44, all precursors of the modern assault rifle, the war brought Germany to its knees just when it had had the last word (though a little late in the day) in the field of weaponry.

By the time the war ended the situation had taken great strides forward as far as the infantryman's combat equipment was concerned. A 1940 platoon faced with a platoon equipped à la 1945 would have been not unlike an African tribe armed with bows and arrows faced with the sharp-shooting rifles of European colonialists. Tactically speaking, the Garand M1 semi-automatic rifle and the US M1 carbine – both American weapons – scored top marks. On the technical level, the new ideas found by German engineers were unanimously appreciated by their enemies, who were to take full advantage of them at a later stage.

The Germans suffered intensive bombing raids in the industrial zones east of the Rhine and lost a significant proportion of their production potential. They were thus unable to manufacture enough of these new models to equip all their infantry divisions.

As the assault rifle slowly crept into the picture, with its ability to fire in bursts or single shot, the automatic rifle gradually slipped into the background.

The post-war semi-automatic rifle

During the post-war period people's interest in guns gradually dwindled; they had after all held the limelight throughout the war.

The Russians and the English, armed with a classic combination of repeating rifles, sub-machine-guns and light machine-guns, found themselves face to face with a vast wasteland of equipment which was technically obsolete. The nationally manufactured arms stocks of other countries were either destroyed or dispersed. Generally speaking these nations were equipped by their allies and had to accept their armaments standards.

Once the sweet taste of victory had faded, the Allied General Staffs lost no time in trying to draw the appropriate lessons from the war they had just waged, and each individual General Staff made its own proposals on the question of the military rifle.

The Russians developed a new type of infantry ammunition, a 7.62 × 39mm rimless short cartridge (the Mossine cartridge was rimmed). They adopted two separate weapons to use it, together with a light machine-gun. These two weapons are the SKS Model, 10-round Simonov carbine, and the 30-round AK-47 assault rifle, both incorporating a gas-operated system. These are still in use in the people's democracies. They have also been used in local troublespots and conflicts which have cropped up throughout the world since the end of World War II.

The SKS Simonov carbine is a comparatively light weapon, and does not deliver full automatic fire.

France in turn decided to equip her army with a more modern rifle than its now obsolete MAS 36. The Manufacture d'Armes de Saint-Etienne (not to be confused with the Manufacture d'Armes et de Cycles de Saint Etienne, which is now called Manufrance) designed and manufactured the 1949 Model MAS. It was officially adopted in 1949, and showed a good deal of ingenuity by being quick to disassemble, and thus easy to clean and service.

This gun made up the range of weapons used by the French in Indochina and Algeria in particular. It served alongside the MAS 36 and the M1 Garand and US M1 carbine, which remained as the standard issue for the French army until 1960. In this year all the American rifles and other infantry weapons left over from the war stocks or supplied in the immediate post-war period were withdrawn from service.

In 1956 the MAS 49 semi-automatic rifle was given something of a face-lift when it was fitted with a muzzle brake and its sights had their positions modified; previously they had been positioned on the left of the 49 Model to allow for the use of grenades, and now they were moved to the centre of the barrel. Its official name was changed to the MAS 49/56 model. This gun is still the regulation rifle of the French army, which is the only army among the members of NATO which is not equipped with assault rifles.

Basing their ideas on the SKS Simonov carbine, armament experts in Czechoslovakia produced, in 1952, their 52 Model semi-automatic rifle, which used 7.62mm Czech ammunition. In order to standardize things in the Communist bloc, this gun was modified in 1957 to use the standard Soviet 7.62 × 39mm round. The rifle was called the 52/57. But production of it was brought to an abrupt halt, and replaced by that of the Czech VZ 58 assault rifle.

Across the Atlantic we should mention the non-regulation semi-automatic carbines used in the US Army.

The Armalite AR 7 Explorer, is an extremely lightweight (1.130kg) gun which can be completely field stripped without tools; when taken apart all the components fit inside the hollow stock, made of laminated fibre-glass. Although designed for sporting purposes, this gun has been ordered in a limited number by the US Air Force as part of the flight-crews' survival kit; it is known as just the AR 5. The eight .22 LR rounds in the interchangeable clip may be fired in the semi-automatic position in less than 4.5 seconds.

The American semi-automatic
Armalite Explorer AR-7 carbine.

The Algerian War: legionnaires on
patrol equipped with M1 carbines.

The American semi-automatic M1, so-called Garand, rifle.

The Czech semi-automatic 52–57 rifle.

The American semi-automatic Universal 1000 carbine.

The American Universal Enforcer 3000 carbine-pistol.

The American semi-automatic (so-called sporting) Armalite AR-180 Sporter carbine.

The French 1915 machine rifle by Ribeyrolle, Sutter and Chauchat, known as the Chauchat.

The Universal 1000 and (Teflon finished) 1020 semi-automatic carbine is a modernized adaptation of the famous standard-issue US M1 carbine. It uses the same .30 M1 ammunition in a smaller 5-round interchangeable clip. There are variants of this model in different calibres.

The Universal Enforcer 3000 carbine pistol is derived from the regulation US M1 carbine. It comes without a stock, has a pistol-grip and a short barrel. It is fed by interchangeable 5-, 15- or 30-round .30 M1 clips.

These weapons are designed for use by the police forces rather than the army.

Likewise at the commercial level, certain firms make 'sporting' rifles using the .308 Winchester cartridge, its civilian equivalent of the NATO 7.62mm cartridge, (the Swiss firm, SIG, has an AMT model and CETME has an Auto Sport model), or the .223 (5.56 × 45mm) cartridge (Armalite AR-180 Sporter model). Basically these are guns deriving from existing assault rifles, called different names and modified in such a way that they are only semi-automatic.

The automatic or assault rifle

The automatic rifle is the logical development of the light machine-gun. It is lighter and more compact, however, and usually uses a more compact and smaller type of ammunition.

As in the semi-automatic rifle, feeding the first round into the chamber is a manual operation; the other rounds contained in the clip or magazine are then fed and fired automatically, so long as the finger presses the trigger. A mechanical device called 'selector' makes it possible to achieve full automatic fire, or semi-automatic fire, or in some cases to fire a predetermined number of rounds in a burst.

The forerunners of the assault rifle

There is no doubt that the light machine-gun should be regarded as the first attempt by the General Staff to increase the soldier's individual fire-power, and also as the direct forebear of the assault rifle as we know it today.

The Allies used this weapon in both world wars. During World War I the French had pinned their hopes on the Chauchat 1915 Model light machine-gun, which used the 8mm rounds of the Lebel rifle. The troops in the US expeditionary force had virtually no portable automatic weapons, with the exception of 353 Lewis gun. This, for better or for worse, was all the US Army had when it entered the war. They were therefore equipped either with Chauchat 1915 light machine-guns, or, at a later stage, with a variant of this model, the CSRG, which used the standard American .30-06 cartridge. Total numbers of these guns supplied by France were 15,988 and 19,341 respectively.

But like the Chauchat, the Lewis was too heavy and unreliable. John Moses Browning, undisputed Master of the automatic weapon, could not let this chance to try out his ingenious creative talent slip through his fingers. In the latter part of 1917 he designed his famous BAR rifle — the Browning Automatic Rifle, using a gas-operated action, which was hurriedly put into production by the Winches-ter Repeating Arms Co. This weapon proved its effectiveness in the later stages of the war, and during this period production totalled more than 85,000. It was later manufactured by Colt, who called it the Colt Monitor, and by the Belgian Fabrique Nationale at Herstal. It was also used by the US Marines during World War II in recapturing the Pacific islands. Somewhat lighter than its counterparts (8.300kg), and with an interchangeable 20-round clip adapted to shot-by-shot or continuous fire, the BAR foreshadowed the modern assault rifle.

The development of the assault rifle

Not one of the parties to the war understood the significance that should have been drawn from the Browning Automatic Rifle; the French and the English had their new weapons in the form of medium and lightweight machine-guns; the Italians, and later on the Americans and Germans, concentrated on the sub-machine-gun.

In the latter part of World War II none of the jousting armies sported any kind of relatively lightweight automatic weapon with a high fire-power. However, the fire-power factor became crucial for a completely new form of fighting force: airborne troops. In Germany the Luftwaffe which controlled such troop movements brought into service a revolutionary gun, on a limited scale: the FG.42 automatic rifle, with the standard 7.9mm cartridge, capable of individual or continuous fire.

But the most important innovation, technically speaking, of the war in this field, introduced by German arms experts, was undoubtedly the automatic rifle which appeared on the scene in 1942. It started off life as the Mkb 42 and was later called the Sturmgewehr.

Hugo Schmeisser revised and put right one or two minor faults, and it became, by turns, the MP.43, the MP.43/1, the MP.44 and the Stg-44.

Designed as a very heavy-duty, gas-operated carbine, using 7.9 × 33mm ammunition (new standard short cartridge), it was both semi-automatic and automatic. The breech-block and most of the main parts were made of stamped and spot-welded sheet metal. Production was considerably helped by these features, and although Germany was crumbling industrially, a monthly production of 5000 rifles was maintained.

The Sturmgewehr was tested out with a barrel bent at 40° (Stg-44 V Model) and at 90° (Stg-44 P Model), theoretically to enable the crews of armoured vehicles to defend themselves against clambering enemy infantry. The special ammunition used contained a spherical bullet. Both these weapons were turned down by the Waffenamt (Arms Bureau), and only a very few prototype models have survived.

The impressive fire-power of the Sturmgewehr, together with its fairly reasonable accuracy when fired continuously obtained by using relatively low power rifle ammunition, put the Wehrmacht troops back at the top of the list again as far as individual fire-power was concerned. But the Sturmgewehr arrived too late in the day to equip all the German fighting forces, although it represented the first successful marriage between the rifle and the sub-machine-gun. Being neither exactly a rifle nor a sub-machine-gun, its acceptance did not come easily among certain members of the German High Command

The French MAS 49/56 semi-automatic rifle.

The American BAR 1918 automatic rifle.

The German MP-43 (Sturmgewehr) assault rifle.

The experimental German Stg 44(V) assault rifle with the barrel bent at 40°

The Italian Beretta BM 59 Mk Ital assault rifle. Cross-section showing mechanism.

The Italian Beretta BM 59 Alpini assault rifle.

Italian 'Alpini' equipped with the Italian Beretta BM 59 Mark Ital assault rifle.

The FAL assault rifle by the Fabrique Nationale Belge with a 7.62mm NATO calibre.

A Belgian parachutist training with the FAL Para assault rifle.

who, in their reactionary way, stopped it being put into production. Furthermore, it was certainly no simple matter to perfect an entirely new and fairly complicated weapon which called on advanced technological skills, especially in time of war. This is borne out by the various modifications undergone by the Mkb 42 until peace was declared in 1945. One such modification was of major importance. It led to the manufacture of the variant Stg-45M, completed by Mauser in 1945. The new mechanism did away with the gas-operated system and used instead a delayed blowback system, controlled by breech-lock rollers. This ingenious solution was destined for great success subsequently.

The modern assault rifle

Once the war was over, the Western powers formed the North Atlantic Treaty Organization (NATO) and decided to standardize their weaponry.

Accordingly the British, with Belgian and French backing, proposed to their allies a new, reduced power type of ammunition; this was a .280 or 7mm cartridge with a relatively flat trajectory, for use by the troops. Prototype models of automatic assault rifles had been studied for this new cartridge.

The new defence organization was, in practical terms, headed by the United States, and they were sitting on large stock-piles of .30-06 calibre ammunition; what was more, they had the huge means necessary to manufacture it. As a result they beat about the bush for a while when it came to the decision to adopt the new British ammunition, and ended up by prescribing their own experimental cartridge, known thereafter as the .30 NATO (7.62mm). This is virtually the same as the old .30-06, but the case has been very slightly shortened. The difference in power is negligible, and both rounds weigh practically the same. The Americans thus designed the new NATO ammunition with the same power as a traditional offensive military cartridge. Because of this, continuous fire from an individual rifle becomes very inaccurate and the gun itself, which is lighter than a light machine-gun, is subject to almost excessive mechanical stress. The reason given by the experts in America to justify this degree of power was that it was necessary to equip infantry machine-guns, using the same ammunition, with long-range fire-power. All the NATO members accepted the new standardization. But France, which was likewise a NATO member, could see no good reason for adopting a cartridge which was no better than the 7.5mm round used by the MAS 36 rifle, and kept the latter in service. This enabled the French to use their existing stocks and production means, and they continued to base their armament policy on this calibre until quite recently. But it is worth noting that all the automatic weapons manufactured in France are equipped with two barrels, one for use with the 7.5mm French ammunition, and the other for the .30 NATO cartridge.

As we have seen in the case of the SKS Simonov carbine, it was considerably prior to the setting-up of NATO that the Russians had adopted a new standardized cartridge for their automatic weapons. This was the 7.62 × 39mm rimless M 43, an excellent compromise between the Sturmgewehr's 7.9mm Kurz, and the overpowered .30 NATO — according to certain ballistics experts. Of course the members of the Warsaw Pact (the East's response to NATO) practically all adopted the new Russian cartridge. Countries under Communist influence, such as the People's Republic of China, North Korea, North Vietnam and so on, which were supplied by Russian arms factories, were obliged to follow suit.

Shortly after the SKS Simonov carbine went into service, the first Soviet assault rifle appeared: this was the AK-47 Kalashnikov (Avtomat Kalashnikov), the brainchild of Michaël T. Kalashnikov, a young sergeant in the Soviet Tank Corps, who had managed to put together all the positive features of modern weapons. Using the gas-operated system, the AK-47 is a tough rifle with a good degree of accuracy when fired continuously. It is one of the best-designed of the modern assault rifles, and one of the few which work without failure, no matter what the climatic conditions may be: desert, arctic, salt spray at sea and so on. It is manufactured in various forms in most countries behind the Iron Curtain, and even as far afield as North Korea and the People's Republic of China. Finland manufactures its own slightly different version of the AK-47 under licence.

There is a light machine-gun version of the AK-47 as well, which is heavier and has a larger clip capacity, although the Russians also have a weapon designed specifically for this type of use called the RPD.

Once the members of NATO had agreed upon their new standard ammuntion, the next task was to choose a standard type of infantry rifle.

The British held by their .280 calibre prototype, and the Belgians chambered their new light automatic rifle to use the 7.62mm NATO cartridge.

The Italians proposed a modified version of the Garand rifle, developed by Beretta; and the Americans, who had been experimenting with two prototypes since 1944 — one derived from the Garand and the other from the Browning Automatic Rifle — proposed the former to their allies. But this rifle did not have any edge over its European counterparts, and in the end each country settled for its own model.

The Beretta rifle was laboriously brought to perfection as the years passed. It was a good buy (being essentially a converted Garand) and enjoyed a certain amount of success in many parts of the world.

The success of the Belgian FAL light assault rifle made by the Fabrique Nationale at Herstal came overnight. At the present time it is without doubt the most widely used assault rifle in all parts of the world, except in the Soviet satellite countries. It has been adopted by numerous countries: Argentina, Australia, Austria, Belgium, Brazil, Burundi, Cambodia, Canada, Chile, the Dominican Republic, Ecuador, Great Britain, India, Indonesia, Ireland, Israel, Kuwait, Liberia, Libya, Luxembourg, Morocco, Mozambique, Muscat and Oman, New Zealand, Paraguay, Peru, Portugal, Qatar, Ruanda, South Africa, Syria Thailand, Venezuela and so on. It was also used for a time by West Germany.

As well as the Fabrique Nationale, other factories went into production under licence, in particular in Argentina, Austria, Canada, Great Britain, India and South Africa. The US Army put it through a whole series of highly sophisticated tests, with the ulterior motive of only ever using an American-made weapon, although this could not in fact come about until they had tested all foreign materials.

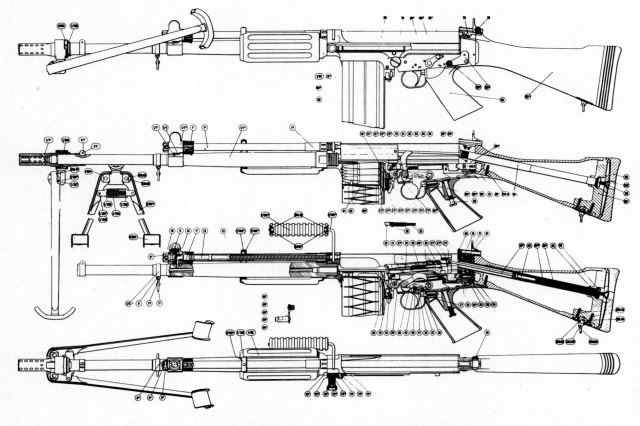

Assembly plan of the FAL assault rifle, light machine-gun version.

The standard Czech Vz-58 assault rifle.

The American Armalite AR-10 assault rifle with the 7.62mm NATO calibre, manufactured by the Artillerie Inrichtingen in the Netherlands.

The Cal Para light assault carbine, made by the Fabrique Nationale Belge in .223 (5.56mm) calibre, shown with the stock folded.

The American sub-machine-gun derived from the Armalite AR-18.

The Spanish CETME assault rifle.

The SIG SG 510 assault rifle. Cut-away showing the internal mechanism.

Before Czechoslovakia toppled in to the other side of the Iron Curtain, Czech arms designers had produced their own assault rifle, the VZ-52, which used a 7.62mm round, unlike the NATO and USSR ammunition. When Czechoslovakia joined the East the VZ-52 was standardized to use the M 43 7.62 × 39mm cartridge and in 1957 became known as the VZ-52/57. The year after, the new VZ-58 assault rifle appeared. It is hardly worth mentioning that this was the Czech version of the Soviet AK-47, despite various alterations being made to it: although they both use the same ammunition, the clips are not interchangeable. Stamped sheet metal was used more widely in the Czech model, the selector is a different shape and the front sight also differs.

In 1957 the United States officially replaced the Garand by its modified successor the M 14, which used the .30 NATO cartridge. But this new rifle did not enter service until 1962, because of production problems. In spite of a stubborn effort by the Pentagon it was clear that the M 14 was outclassed by the Russian AK-47 weapons issued to the Vietcong, and it was withdrawn; the operational units were then issued with an entirely newly conceived rifle, the AR-15, which used .223 (5.56mm) ammunition.

The AR-10 rifle is the 7.62mm NATO version of the US Army regulation AR-15 or M 16 carbine, originally known as the .223 AR-15. The Armalite AR-10 was manufactured for a time by the Inrichtingen Ordnance Factory in Holland under various contract agreements, while Colt bought the licence for the manufacture of the AR-15 on behalf of the US government. The automatic AR-10 rifle is not standard-issue in the US Army. This new rifle requires the most advanced production techniques. But the original feature of the AR-15 or M 16 lies in the fact that it fires small calibre rounds with a high initial velocity. The bullet has a very flat trajectory and the impact is extremely powerful and destructive. In addition this rifle can be perfectly controlled when fired continuously.

Rifle and rounds together are remarkably compact when compared with the present extremely tough but heavy Russian equipment. Despite the usual production problems, the new rifle was a thorough success with the American GI and his Far Eastern allies. Although the M 16 design is a controversial one, even in the United States, the techniques which it embodies are nonetheless widely esteemed for all its comparative fragility, and despite the fact that it overheats when fired full automatic and needs constant servicing.

Firms competing with the Colt company were not long to follow its lead.

Beretta proposed a new gas-operated model called the AR 70/.223, and the Fabrique Nationale at Herstal has just marketed a more lightweight version of the FAL rifle, called the Light Assault Carbine or CAL, which uses .223 (5.56mm) rounds.

The American inventor of the AR-15, who has changed companies in the meantime, has also just put on the market a whole new weapon system using the .223 calibre, consisting of the AR-18 assault rifle, the AR-180 sporting carbine, which is solely semi-automatic, and a sub-machine-gun version of his AR-18 rifle.

But unlike the results of twenty years ago, weapons using the gas-operated action are not the only runners in the race. After the 1945 Armistice one of Mauser's technical staff, a certain M. Vorgrimler, emigrated to Spain; in his pocket he had the drawings for the Stg-45 Sturmgewehr, with its delayed blowback system and roller bolt locking device. To begin with he worked on his rifle at the Centro Estudios Tecnicos de Materiales Especiales and adapted it to a type of Spanish ammunition very akin to the 7.62mm NATO cartridge, but with a lighter bullet.

The final model of this military rifle is now used by the Spanish army. It is known as the CETME rifle and is available on the international arms market, using the normal 7.62mm NATO cartridge.

This roller locking system is also used in France with the AA-52 machine-gun, and the Swiss use it for all their SIG rifles and machine guns with a 7.5mm (Swiss) calibre and a 7.62mm NATO calibre. And we should not forget the few models chambered for the 7.62mm Soviet cartridge, rightly known for its toughness and accuracy.

SIG has also followed the trend towards smaller calibres, and is currently proposing its lightweight SG 530 .223 calibre assault rifle, which is a simplified version of the SG 510, a rifle using the 7.62mm NATO cartridge. This gun can be fitted at will with an interchangeable wooden stock or an extendable retractable-type steel wire stock. We should mention that it uses the gas-operated action which would suggest that the delayed blowback system using locking rollers is not without its disadvantages.

When West Germany was once more authorized to manufacture its own armaments in 1957, the Heckler und Koch company in Oberndorf purchased the CETME patents. It further improved this rifle, which became the regulation issue of the Bundeswehr, and was known as the G 3 rifle. The roller locking system did away with certain problems raised by the gas system, and with the help of a dynamic business organization this weapon was an instant hit and is the standard issue at the present time in twenty-six countries.

This rifle is likewise .223 (5.56mm) calibre and is called the HK 33. The originality of its mechanism poses serious competition to gas-operated counterparts, even though the latter have the advantage of many years of testing in various climatic conditions round the world.

The future of the military rifle

The assault rifle has virtually outclassed the semi-automatic rifles and carbines which, during the last war, had in turn usurped the faithful old repeating bolt action rifle, and relegated it to the show-case. The assault rifle has certain tactical advantages: high fire-power and rate of fire can only be points in its favour among the military, and in the years to come it will probably elbow its predecessors right out of the running in most national armies.

In the next twenty years will the assault rifle adopt the gas-operated system or the delayed-blowback system? It will be up to the General Staffs to decide, on the basis of the technical requirements of specifications to come; but it is likely that the two rival systems will co-exist for some time in military circles.

The Swiss SIG SG 530 assault
rifle.

The German Heckler and Koch G3
A3 assault rifle with the 7.62mm
NATO calibre.

The German Heckler and Koch HK
33 assault rifle with the .223
(5.56mm) calibre.

Left: Fedayin equipped with
Kalashnikov rifles.
Right: an Indian soldier with a
standard Enfield rifle.

From left to right: an Israeli sold
equipped with a heavy-d
Belgian FAL rifle; a Biafran sold
and his Kalashnikov AK 47 assa
rifle; and an American Milit
Policeman with an Armalite M
and a Colt automatic pistol at
h

Left: a motley assortment of
Mauser Gew. 98s side by side with
the modern assault rifle and the old
Beretta.
Right: a scene from the Spanish
Civil War in Barcelona; men
belonging to the workers' militia in
operation behind armoured
screens. The man at top left is
carrying an 'El tigre' carbine,
which is a copy of the 1892
Winchester.

From left to right: Isra
commando unit on the Syri
front; the foreground shows
Uzi sub-machine-gun and a F/
light assaut rifle; Australian a
American soldiers
reconnaissance on the Mekor
equipped with FAL rifle

Taiwan soldiers in training
equipped with the Chiang Kai-
Shek rifle, a Chinese copy of the
standard German Mauser Gew.
1898.

A Chad rebel equipped with th
Italian 91–36 service rifl

Military rifles: technical data

Heckler and Koch, type G3

Country	West Germany
Type	assault rifle
Designation	Heckler and Koch, G3
Variants	G3 A2, A3, A4 etc
Calibre	7.62mm NATO (7.62 × 51mm) NB. there is a conversion unit to .22 LR
Weight	from 4.250–4.500kg
Length	barrel, 45cm; overall 102cm; with stock folded on the G3 A4: 80cm
Fire rate	500–600rpm, 20-round magazine; semi-automatic or automatic fire controlled by three-position selector: 'S' safety; 'E' semi-automatic fire; 'F' full automatic fire
Remarks	newcomers to the arms market, Heckler and Koch have managed to put themselves on a par with the 'great' names in the industry with modern designed arms manufactured by thoroughly sound industrial means. The G3 has been adopted by Colombia, Denmark, the Dominican Republic, Norway, Pakistan, Portugal, Saudi Arabia, Sweden and West Germany. It comes in several variants, the most common being the G3 A3 with a plastic stock and the G3 A4 with a metal telescopic stock.

Heckler and Koch HK 33

Country	West Germany
Type	light assault rifle
Designation	Heckler and Koch, HK 33
Calibre	.223 (5.56 × 45mm) NB. there is a conversion unit to .22 LR
Weight	3.350–3.450kg depending on the stock
Length	barrel 39cm; overall 92cm; stock folded (HK 33 A1) 75cm
Fire rate	600–650rpm, 20- and 40-round clips, fire selector with 3 positions, identical to the G3
Remarks	direct derivative of the G3 for use with .223 rounds, this light assault rifle is more compact and lighter than the G3

Fabrique Nationale CAL
top: normal model
below: model for airborne troops

Country	Belgium
Type	light assault carbine
Designation	Fabrique Nationale de Herstal, CAL
Calibre	.223 (5.56 × 45mm)
Weight	with light alloy clip: 3.310kg
Length	overall 98cm; barrel 47cm
Fire rate	850rpm; clip capacity: 20 rounds; semi-automatic fire and 3-round bursts and full automatic fire; 4 selector positions: S,1,3, and A
Remarks	the current tendency to use small calibres led to the F.N. Belge offering in late 1967 a new range of assault weapons chambering the .223 round. The CAL, made by the F.N., is available in two versions, as illustrated here

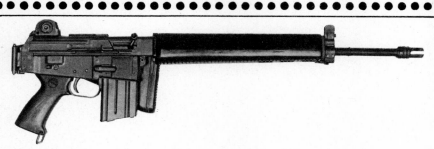

FN Belge FAL
left: with reinforced barrel and biped
right: normal model

Country	Belgium
Type	assault rifle
Designation	Fabrique Nationale de Herstal, FAL
Variants	normal, light machine gun, and 'para' with extendable stock
Calibre	NATO 7.62mm
Weight	4.100kg in normal version
Length	overall 100cm, barrel 53.5cm
Fire rate	650–700rpm, 20-round clip. Semi-automatic fire or full automatic by 3-position selector placed on left side of receiver
Remarks	for years the FAL has been the most common military rifle in the advanced countries. It is still standard equipment in many armies

Armalite AR-18

Country	United States
Type	light assault rifle
Designation	Armalite, AR-18
Calibre	.223 (5.56 × 45mm)
Weight	3.040kg
Length	overall, stock extended 96.5cm; stock folded 73cm; barrel 47.6cm
Fire rate	750rpm, 20-round clip; semi-automatic and full automatic fire by 3-position selector
Remarks	the Armalite AR-18 was brought out to replace the AR-15 (M 16 standard issue for the US Army), just as its manufacturer hopes to replace the 7.62mm NATO AR-10 by the new AR-16. The US army has still not made its final decision. In the version depicted this weapon is designed to fire 55, 62 and 75mm rifle grenades; it is also offered with a short barrel and a sub-machine-gun-type front grip. In addition it is offered on the civilian market as the AR-180, with semi-automatic fire only

Beretta BM 59 Mark ITAL

Country	Italy
Type	assault rifle
Designation	Beretta BM 59, Mark ITAL
Calibre	7.62mm NATO
Weight	4.410kg
Length	overall 110cm; barrel 49cm
Fire rate	800 rpm, 20-round clip, semi-automatic and full automatic fire by 2-position selector
Remarks	derived from the Garand M1 rifle, but capable of full automatic fire, this rifle comes in various versions: the Mark ITAL, shown here, the data of which appear above, is fitted with a biped

and grenade-launcher. The ITAL Alpini is identical to the Mark ITAL but has an extendable metal stock; the ITAL Paracadutisti is likewise equipped with a metal stock but is made lighter by the absence of the grenade-launcher; it is designed for airborne troops; the Mark I is a simplified version of the Mark ITAL without biped or grenade-launcher. The Mark IV has a wooden stock and a reinforced barrel, and is designed as a light machine-gun

Beretta AR 70/223

Country	Italy
Type	light assault rifle
Designation	Beretta 70/223, SC (light carbine with extendable and detachable stock), AR (light assault rifle) and LM (light machine-gun)
Calibre	.223 (5.56 × 45mm)
Weight	3.430kg (AR model)
Length	overall 94cm; barrel 45cm (AR model)
Fire rate	630 rpm, 30-round clip; semi-automatic or automatic fire by 3-position rotating selector: S, safety, L, semi-automatic, and A, full automatic
Remarks	the 70/223 is one of the latest products of the Gardone factory and calls widely on advanced metal stamping and high resistance plastic casting techniques

STGW 57

Country	Switzerland
Type	heavy assault rifle
Designation	SIG of Rheinfall, STGW 57
Calibre	7.50mm Swiss (model 11)
Weight	5.700kg
Length	overall 110cm, barrel 58.5cm
Fire rate	600 rpm, 6- or 20-round clips, semi-automatic or full automatic fire by 3-position selector
Remarks	the Swiss army is gradually replacing its Rubin-Schmidt rifles with the STGW 57, designed and made by SIG of Rheinfall. This gun also comes in the PE 57 variant as a sporting gun, with semi-automatic fire only

SIG SG 510–4

Country	Switzerland
Type	assault rifle
Designation	SIG, SG 510
Variants	510–1, 510–2, 510–4 and 510–3
Calibre	7.62mm NATO (for the 510–1, 510–2 and 510–4), .30 US M1 (7.72mm Short) for the 510–3
Weight	4.250kg (510–4)
Length	overall 101.5cm, barrel 50.5cm
Fire rate	450–620 rpm depending on type, 5-, 10- or 20-round clips, 3-position selector for full automatic or semi-automatic fire

Remarks the SG 510 comes in 4 military versions: 510–1, normal production in 7.62mm NATO calibre with plastic stock and biped; 510–2, lighter, same calibre, wooden stock, no biped or carrying handle; 510–3, light assault rifle in 7.62mm Short calibre (ammunition used by US M1 carbine) without biped or carrying handle, equipped with wooden stock; 510–4, like the 510–1 but fitted with wooden stock and telescopic sight; and a sporting version with no fire selector (just semi-automatic fire) known as the AMT

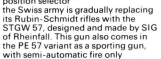

VZ-58

Country	Czechoslovakia
Type	light assault rifle
Designation	Czech State Arsenal, VZ-58
Calibre	7.62 × 39mm Soviet
Weight	3.950kg
Length	overall 84cm; stock folded 63.5cm; barrel 40cm
Fire rate	700–800 rpm, 30-round clip, semi-automatic or full automatic fire by 2-position selector, placed on right of receiver, above the grip
Remarks	directly derived from the famous Soviet Kalashnikov, the VZ-58 is also made with a wooden stock; it equips the Czech army

Kalashnikov AK-47

Country	USSR
Type	light assault rifle
Designation	USSR State Arsenal, Kalashnikov AK-47
Calibre	7.62 × 39mm Soviet
Weight	4.000kg
Length	overall 87cm with wooden stock; 85cm with metal stock, barrel 41.5cm
Fire rate	600 rpm, 30-round clips, 3-position selector for semi-automatic and full automatic fire

Remarks standard equipment in the Russian army, the AK-47 is carried by many Eastern bloc countries, whether supplied by the USSR or manufactured by the respective State Arsenals under different references such as: type 58 in North Korea; type 56 in Red China; MPI-K in East Germany; and the M-62 in Finland

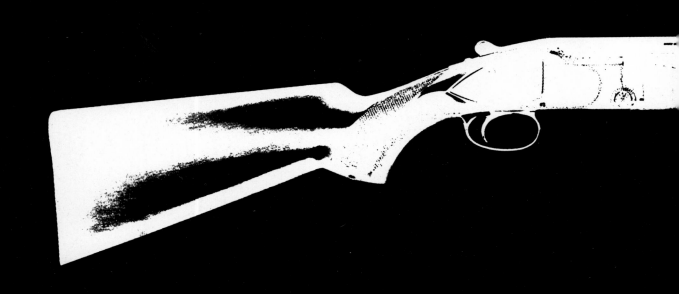

5
sporting
guns

The development of the sporting gun

Firearms using lead shot started to come into use in a big way in the sixteenth century, especially in small game shooting.

For many years these same smooth-bore guns had been used at random for any number of purposes. Affecting the accuracy and the power of the bullet, the rifling of these guns singled out the smooth-bore as well-suited for sporting use. The effectiveness of lead shot in the case of a moving and usually small target is unrivalled, and the relatively short range (which is the inevitable drawback in this sort of weapon) is in fact not a drawback at all.

The choice whether to have a rifled or smooth barrel depends on the type and size of the game to be hunted, and both sorts of barrel have developed side by side, but in their respective ways. Smooth-bore guns started from scratch, so to speak, whereas the rifled barrel followed the development of military weapons very closely.

Of all the guns currently in use, with the exception of those issued to the military, the shotgun is by far the most common throughout the world, and particularly in France.

Hunting, which is a necessity in fewer and fewer parts of the world, has taken most countries by storm as a pastime. It tends to be as widespread as the numbers of game, local tradition and national legislation will permit.

The same guns have also tended to become instruments used in leisure activities which spare the animal kingdom: clay-pigeon shooting (or moving-target shooting, at clay objects) for shotguns, running deer for rifles and carbines, both subject to various codes drawn up by an International Association.

In rural areas they are also used for self-protection in many cases.

It is easy to market these guns, and the clientele is enormous. Although where craftsmanship is involved all the skill of the gunsmith's trade is called upon, actual production of the guns does not require heavy machinery and large investment. This is why there is no shortage of production. Apart from certain underdeveloped countries, there are few other countries, even among those with little industry, which do not have their own production units.

In the Western world this trade is often plied in traditional places, chosen originally for the top-quality metals produced in the region, and the conditions in which they are produced: sulphurless coal, very pure iron ore, good hard water and a tradition of craftsmanship. In many cases, when they are not manufactured in one and the same factory, sporting guns and military weapons are made in the same small area. One can think of Saint-Etienne in France, Liège in Belgium, Brescia in Italy, Birmingham in England, Tula in Russia, and so on. World War II gave rise to some fundamental changes in the design, techniques and use of portable military weapons. Completely new types came into being, and traditional models just vanished into thin air. Effectiveness and power were both conspicuously increased.

The changes made to sporting guns in the immediate post-war period were not so spectacular. Game was becoming more of a rarity, but it was no less vulnerable than before. In addition legislators in most countries were seeing to it that Bills were passed controlling the manufacture and use of firearms, and limiting the destructive power of sporting guns. Thus the French reduced the capacity of automatic repeating weapons to three rounds, while a 12 gauge Breda, including a magazine extension holding seven shot shells, was made in Italy.

Technological progress, which had been boosted by the arms industry during military production, thrived off the way the sporting gun developed.

As far as ammunition was concerned, the use of slower types of powder made it possible to fire heavier charges in weapons with a specific gauge: these charges were called magnum or half-magnum. As a result of improvements in the quality and consistency of powders and percussion caps, and the use of new materials for the heads and cases, all types of sporting shells became more foolproof, more reliable and more uniform. The ammunition for rifles profited from the switch-over from military ammunition, especially the small calibre round with a high initial velocity. What was more, the war upset the distribution of the types of sporting gun in use.

Second only to the United States in sporting gun sales, Europe suffered occupation by foreign armies in most areas. One of the major constant concerns of the occupying Chiefs of Staff was to confiscate all the sporting weapons owned by the civilian population in question. This is what happened in nearly every case. Most of the weapons requisitioned in this way were destroyed, lost or made off with by the occupying forces. Large numbers of sporting guns vanished without trace as a result, especially the older models (apart from those already considered as collectors' pieces). In fact, when summoned to hand over his armoury, the hunter usually did so with great reluctance. And if he decided to risk it, and keep back some of his guns, he obviously chose to sacrifice the oldest models, or those of the poorest quality. Those which remained with their rightful owners frequently deteriorated, sometimes to the point of being unusable; the main reason for this was the fact that they often had to be hidden away in very unsuitable places. Thus the overall number of usable sporting guns dropped considerably.

As we mentioned at the beginning of this chapter, sporting guns are divided in to two main categories: shotguns, for use with lead shot; rifles or carbines, for big-game shooting.

Within these two categories, sporting guns can be subdivided further into several types, depending on the sort of mechanisms used, the barrels, and so on.

Shotguns

Guns with external hammers

Some shotguns which were still in use up to 1939 have completely disappeared. The few rare examples belong to collectors, or are unearthed from time to time in dusty attics. Unlike percussion guns, or those incorporating the Lefaucheux pin-fire system, centre-fire guns with external hammers have managed to hold their own. More than a century after the appearance of the first Anson and Deeley Hammerless gun, there is still a demand for this type. True, their mechanism is currently adapted to the most modern

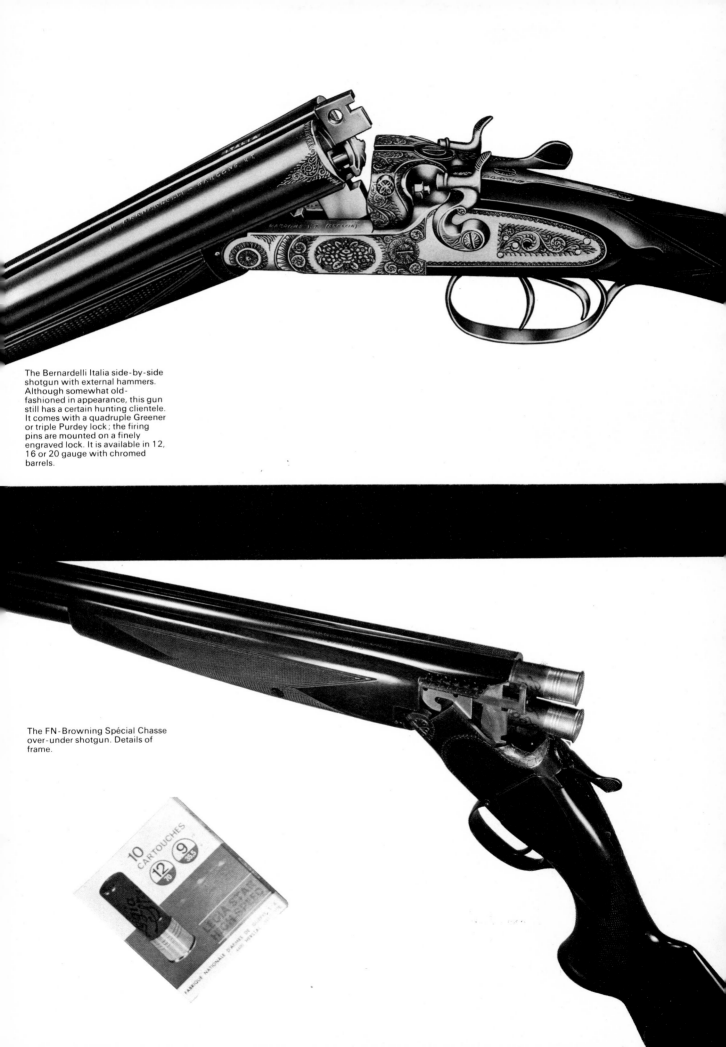

The Bernardelli Italia side-by-side shotgun with external hammers. Although somewhat old-fashioned in appearance, this gun still has a certain hunting clientele. It comes with a quadruple Greener or triple Purdey lock; the firing pins are mounted on a finely engraved lock. It is available in 12, 16 or 20 gauge with chromed barrels.

The FN-Browning Spécial Chasse over-under shotgun. Details of frame.

A Belgian single-barrel gun with the Leclerc system, produced in the pre-war period. The conical breech bolt of this gun was controlled by a side lever.

The Winchester 840 single-barrel shotgun.

The FN-Browning Spécial Chasse over-under shotgun.

The single-barrel Ithaca 66
Blockbuster for slug shells.

The Miroku 12-gauge 800 W
over-under shotgun

The Franchi 12-gauge over-under
shotgun.

The FN-Browning Spécial Chasse over-under shotgun. Detail of the engraving on the frame and lever. Here the engraving is de luxe, copper-plate type D5, Louis XVI style against a background of scroll engraving (see note 11).

The Winchester 101 over-under shotgun. Here we see the ball-trap version.

The Krieghoff Teck over-under shotgun. This model with a Kersten lock is only made in 12 gauge, with English-style stock or pistol grip stock.

types of ammunition. In the old days people chose them mainly because of the quality of their locks which were popular for the fact that the trigger could be subtly adjusted. Those models on the market today are made above all to meet somewhat specialized demands, at low prices.

This category includes, for example:

Among single-barrelled guns: Spain: the AYA from Eibar; United States: Stevens, Winchester 840 with its top-lever locking catch, Savage; France: the Sylvia by Bergeron; Belgium; the Verreres with its lateral under-lever.

Though they are slightly different, this category also includes the 66 Buckbuster made by Ithaca in the United States; here the cocking-lever-cum-trigger-guard, which controls a Martini action, gives it the look of a repeating rifle.

Among double-barrelled guns, usually with a Greener lock system and cross-locks: Spain: the AYA; Italy: Bernadelli's Italia and other models which are hand-made; USSR: the TOZ-66.

Guns with the Gras mechanism

Another anachronistic survivor is the Gras system, now a century old. This system makes it possible to make single-barrelled carbines of small calibre — .22 Long Rifle, 9mm rim-fire, 12mm (or 410 short) and 14mm (.32) — at low cost; these guns are very popular for small-game shooting. They are made in various parts of the world, but mainly in France: e.g. Voere and Anschütz in Germany, Manufrance, Gaucher, and Bergeron in Saint-Etienne, Manuarm at Veauches in the Loire and so on.

So-called 'Hammerless' guns

The bulk of current shotguns is of the so-called 'hammerless' type. They are almost all based on very well-established and old models. But those using these guns have tended to change their taste under the influence, among other things, of the shoot and the rifle-range. These activities have favoured the over-and-under and autoloading shotguns — both of which were seldom used hitherto — and affected the popularity of the gun with double barrels juxtaposed, which used to be more fashionable.

This change is to some extent a result of the last war. It was in effect the huge post-war demand which opened up this branch of the arms industry. The manufacture of sporting guns became a big business and gave rise to ever more efficient and automated production techniques which required less and less real contribution from the gunsmith. This had already been the way of things for some time in the United States.

But this process of mechanization has its pros and cons. On the plus side, it allows the use of special, high resistance types of steel which cannot be worked by hand; it involves ways of producing top-quality (though mass-produced) interchangeable parts; it calls into play the use of light alloys which require very advanced and highly complex processing methods. The result is top-quality, high resistance firearms which are easy to repair and comparatively cheaper than before. They are also easier to service, thanks to the widespread use of chromium plating inside the barrels and on the various component parts, even the rockers and levers. Barrels have also been made in stainless steel.

On the minus side, this mechanization tends to deper-sonalize the firearm. When mass-produced, guns are all the same. It becomes very hard and extremely costly to have a gun tailored to the shape and size of the user, and any hunter will tell you how important it is to feel that your gun fits you. The highly skilled craft of the gunsmith is becoming rarer and rarer. As this disappears, so do certain age-old techniques and secrets. It has become very difficult and often well-nigh impossible to manufacture and above all repair a set of Holland and Holland ejectors, with their fine quality and delicate tooling. This has in fact meant the death of a whole range of so-called 'twelve-carat' guns which called upon the skills of the gunsmith.

Over-and-under shotguns

This development does partly explain the increased production of shotguns which, in a mechanical sense, are easier to manufacture. At the present time this type of shotgun is without doubt the most popular. It is made in many countries, is quick and easy to aim, and is an undeniably handsome object.

In the United States, Savage have even manufactured a model with external hammers and a side-lever locking system.

But nearly all the other models include the Anson system, whereby the gun is loaded by 'dropping down' the barrels. The major difference between these drop-down models is usually the type of locking and percussion systems adopted by the manufacturer.

Despite its trusty age, the Browning Superposé, made by the Fabrique Nationale at Herstal, remains one of the old favourites, thanks to its good resistance to wear and tear, its cross-locking system and top-lever. With helical spring percussion and hammer ejectors, this gun, in its various forms, is an extremely dependable weapon. Engraved models of it are among the finest examples of the art.

The Falconet, by Franchi of Italy, is the same type of gun, made with a light alloy frame better suited to game shooting, because of its lightness.

Several Italian models (Fabarm, Bolognini etc.) employ the same system, as do the French Trap-type Bergeron with ejectors, the Czech Brno with direct percussion, the Japanese Miroku, with a double-leaf spring percussion system.

The heavy though soundly-made Russian Baikal includes a safety mechanism operated by hammer interceptors, which reduces the element of risk.

The American firms Winchester and Savage also make models in this category.

The Spanish Fernand Special with its top-lever but also incorporating a double locking system comes with an original lock; and the French Super-Odegaard, with or without ejector, is a handsome gun, thanks to its dropped hinge.

The Greener locking system, with the top-lever, has been adopted by the Spanish AYA, by one of the Italian Bolognini models, by Bergeron in France, where the meticulous machine-finishing of the guns guarantees that the parts are interchangeable, and by the Italian Astor and

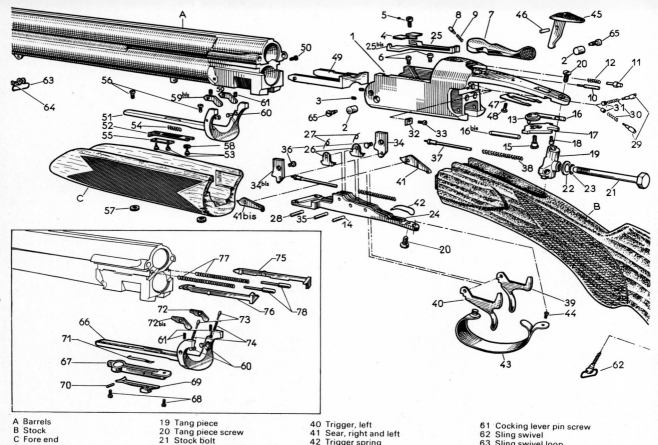

A Barrels	19 Tang piece	40 Trigger, left	61 Cocking lever pin screw
B Stock	20 Tang piece screw	41 Sear, right and left	62 Sling swivel
C Fore end	21 Stock bolt	42 Trigger spring	63 Sling swivel loop
1 Action	22 Stock bolt washer	43 Trigger guard	64 Sling swivel screw
2 Action pin	23 Locking washer	44 Trigger guard screw	65 Cocking lever bearing
3 Action pin retaining pin	24 Trigger plate	45 Safety	66 Fore end bracket for an ejector gun
4 Cocking rods guide	25 Cocking rod, right and left	46 Safety pin	67 Fore end catch
5 Guide screw	26 Cocking lever	47 Safety spring	68 Fore end catch locking screw
6 Floor plate screws	27 Cocking lever spring	48 Safety return spring screw	69 Fore end latch
7 Top lever	28 Cocking lever pin	49 Extractor	70 Fore end latch pin
8 Top lever retaining plunger	29 Striker	50 Extractor bearing screw	71 Fore end latch spring
9 Top lever retaining spring	30 Striker spring	51 Fore end bracket	72 Ejector hammer, right and left
10 Top lever guide rod	31 Striker spring bushing	52 Fore end catch	73 Hammer plunger
11 Locking bolt	32 Striker block	53 Fore end catch guide screw	74 Hammer plunger spring
12 Locking bolt spring	33 Striker block screw	54 Fore end catch spring	75 Ejector right
13 Bolt actuator	34 Hammer, right and left	55 Spring location plate	76 Ejector left
14 Trigger pin	35 Hammer pin	56 Screw for above	77 Ejector spring
15 Top lever screw	36 Hammer pivot	57 Bushing for above	78 Ejector plunger
16 Bolt	37 Hammer spring guide	58 Washer for above	
17 Bolt link	38 Hammer spring	59 Cocking lever, right and left	
18 Bolt link guide screw	39 Trigger, right	60 Cocking lever pin	

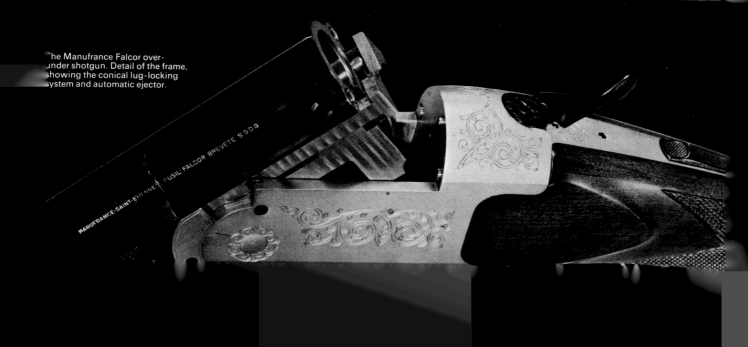

The Manufrance Falcor over-under shotgun. Detail of the frame, showing the conical lug-locking system and automatic ejector.

Firing system:
Because of the special design of this gun, firing pins (56 and 57) strike the shell primers in line with the axis of the barrel.

Cocking system: The drop-down system of the barrel causes the movement of the extractor (46) and the cocking of the firing pins via parts 89, 48, 49 and 85.

Locking system:
When the lever (29) is opened, this causes the retraction of the lower firing pin and the breech bolt (28) by means of the puller (33).

Ejection system: The drop-down mechanism of the barrel pivots the ejector-sear (12), releasing the striker (7), which strikes the extractor (4b), and expels the shell.

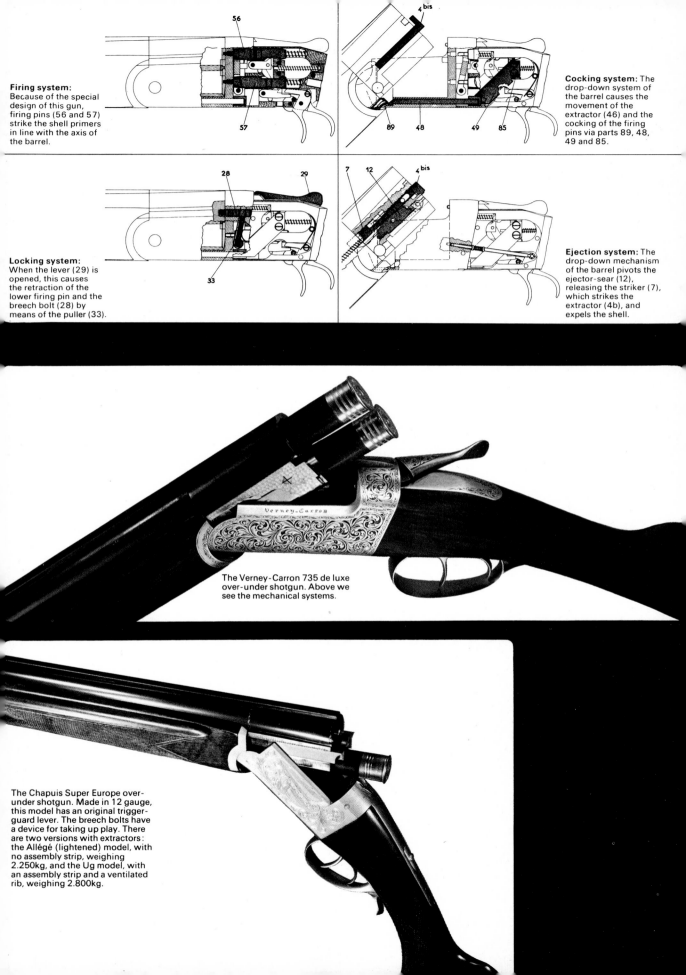

The Verney-Carron 735 de luxe over-under shotgun. Above we see the mechanical systems.

The Chapuis Super Europe over-under shotgun. Made in 12 gauge, this model has an original trigger-guard lever. The breech bolts have a device for taking up play. There are two versions with extractors: the Allégé (lightened) model, with no assembly strip, weighing 2.250kg, and the Ug model, with an assembly strip and a ventilated rib, weighing 2.800kg.

Eagle in Brescia. The Winchester 101, Savage 440 and Ithaca, along with the Italian Salvinelli and Delfino, and the German Wischo use the Purdey locking system, as do Picard Fayolle at Saint-Etienne, who also include an effective direct percussion system.

Three models which are among the commonest and most popular in France because of their quality and soundness, have a lug-locking system with top-lever: these are the Falcor by Manufrance, the Italian Beretta and the Sagittaire by Verney-Carron, in which the direct and parallel percussion device is placed in a removable lock.

Still using a top-lever locking system, but with a catch on the upper barrel, the French Guichard model is manufactured under licence by several companies.

The famous Czech firm of Brno makes an extremely original and interesting model known as the ZH, which has a top-lever Herstem locking device, sliding bolt head, and interchangeable barrels, whether they be smoothbore or rifled.

The H. Krieghoff Company has likewise adopted this locking system for some of its firearms. The engraving on the frame of the best custom-made guns has earned a name for itself way beyond the West German borders.

The Kerner catch-locking system has been adopted by the Italian firms of Pedersoli and Baronchelli, using direct percussion.

There are still a fair number of other over-under guns with the Anson system; among them are models by the French firm of Darne, and the German firm of Voere (the latter with mixed, smoothbore and rifled barrels); also, models by the Italian firms of Sabatti and Peli, ESA, and a noteworthy model by the French firm of Chapuis, with a Greener locking system operated by the cocking-lever, which takes up any play, and direct percussion.

Mention should also be made of a cocking-lever double-bolt Purdey system of opening and loading, the French Super-Martin which has its percussion mechanism on the trigger-guard plate, and the French small calibre Sidna over-under gun, which comes in several different models, with its cocking-lever opening system and independent loading.

An example of the new economical methods in operation in this day and age is supplied by the gun manufactured in Japan by the SKB Arms Company — the largest in the country — following the specifications of BSA Guns Ltd of Great Britain, under whose trademark it is sold.

For closely related reasons, the following guns can be singled out in this large sporting family:

The Browning made at Herstal, already described, which, together with its intrinsic qualities, scores highly for having been one of the first guns of this type to be designed and developed by the brilliant inventor himself;

The Merkel, famous for its excellent quality and the place it has secured for itself since 1905 in major gun collections and the gunsmith's trade. It is made in East Germany, and has a Kersten double-catch locking system, manually dismountable Holland and Holland lateral lock-plates, and ejectors; it is a first-rate sporting gun.

The Purdey; and at this juncture in our discussion, we should add a special word about this 'British institution', embodied by James Purdey and Sons Ltd. The guns made by this company were, are, and will continue to be, the dream of generations of hunters with an eye for quality and beauty.

We were received in the 'Temple' in Audley Street, London, by the Hon. Richard Beaumont, chairman of the famous British firm, gunsmiths 'By Appointment' to the Court of St James since 1763 — under the watchful scrutiny of the ancient Purdey dynasty. In the so-called (and extremely Victorian) Long Room, where the Board of Directors holds its meetings, we were told that when you order a Purdey, this does not necessarily mean that the gun will be delivered to the purchaser within the minimum period of eighteen months; first and foremost the management must examine the customer's application. Once this is done, the gun is 'made-to-measure', taking the specific measurements of the future purchaser into account. All guns and carbines are put through elaborate inspections at every stage of the production, and finally handed to the Chairman in person who tries each individual gun himself at the Purdey Stand in the London suburb of Greenford. Only with the seal of approval 'from the top' confirmed, may the client lay his hands on his new gun, in exchange for a minimum charge of £3,062 ($7,350). You don't get quality for nothing! But included in this high price is the fact that a Purdey may be handed down from generation to generation, and still remain as good as new.

There is another gun which deserves special mention for its originality. Using the modern technology of light alloys, the French firm of Bretton has developed its Baby model with two sliding locks, and made it the lightest 12-bore sporting gun in the world. Its independent barrels can be dismounted by hand in a flash, which affords a valuable selection of different types of cartridge, and different ballistic features.

Among the wide range of over-under shotguns, the Italian firm of Perazzi is currently manufacturing an excellently finished model which is being imported to the United States by Ithaca and called the Ithaca-Perazzi Light Game.

United States: The Hi-Standard Model 10-B automatic repeating rifle. This is a 12-gauge shotgun with a 5-round capacity, but it is extremely short (27in.) and is used primarily by the policeman rather than the hunter. Optional extras are an adaptor for tear-gas grenades and a detachable spotlight whose beam corresponds to the scatter of the shot.

Single-barrelled semi-automatic repeating guns, known as 'Autoloaders'

There are many more over-under guns than we have room to mention here, but there can be no doubt that over the last thirty years this type has gone through some eye-catching changes, and given birth to the repeating sporting gun.

The famous Browning model has been virtually synonymous with it since 1905; with its long recoil and bolt movement, and 5-round magazine, this product of the Fabrique Nationale at Herstal in Belgium is known the whole world over. With the years it has earned a name for reliability and solid workmanship. Its basic design is still the original one, and the only compromise it has made, in various optional versions, has been with a view to modern taste, using special light alloys.

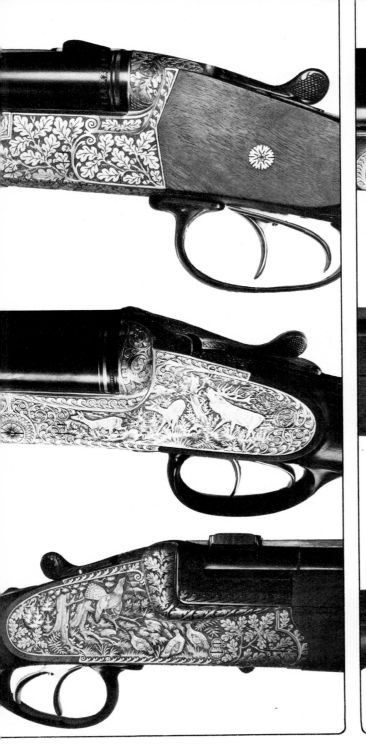
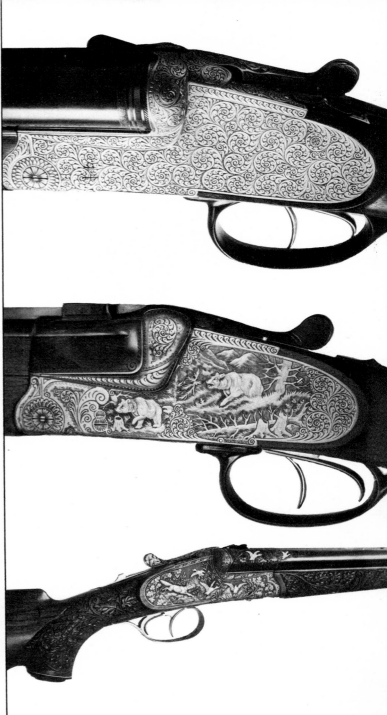

Examples of quality engraving on Krieghoff frames.

The Perazzi over-under shotgun.

The Winchester 1400 autoloader.

The Hi-Standard Supermatic gas-operated autoloader.

The Hi-Standard 10 B autoloader (see note 12).

The Beretta A 300 standard model autoloader.

Bolt release catch

Sliding breech

Barrel

Fore end cap

Front sling swivel

Wooden fore end

Cocking piece

Frame

Trigger guard

Safety

Trigger

Stock

Rear sling swivel

The Manufrance Perfex automatic rifle.

'Perfex' Shotgun Parts List

921 Barrel
A Receiver
B Magazine tube
C Wooden fore end
D Butt-stock

1 Magazine cap
2 Valve
3 Valve spring
4 Valve stop
5 Valve ball spring
6 Action bar
7 Locking block
8 Butt-stock screw
9 Butt-stock screw washer
10 Bolt operating plate
11 Firing pin
12 Firing pin reaction spring
13 Firing pin stop pin
14 Extractor
15 Extractor push-rod
16 Bolt handle
17 Bolt
18 Clips
19 Bolt operating pin
20 Damper
21 Safety catch
22 Safety catch ratchet

23 Safety spring
24 Safety pin
25 Carrier
26 Carrier operator
27 Carrier push-rod
28 Carrier spring
29 Carrier pin
30 Hammer
31 Hammer push-rod
32 Hammer spring
33 Hammer pin
34 Damper spring
35 Carrier latch spring
36 Damper pin
37 Carrier latch spring screw
38 Sear
39 Trigger
40 Sear pin
41 Trigger pin
42 Trigger spring
43 Automatic safety
44 Safety push-rod
45 Safety spring
46 Safety rivet
47 Trigger-guard pin
48 Hollow axles
49 Right link
50 Left link

51 Sear-links pin
52 Links-trigger pin
53 Stock mounting stud
54 Ejector guide
55 Ejector guide rivet
56 Magazine tube screw
57 Cap stop-ball
58 Stop-ball spring
59 Carrier latch
60 Carrier latch spring
61 Carrier latch spring screw
62 Carrier latch pin screw
63 Carrier latch push-rod
64 Automatic safety operator
65 Trigger guard
66 Magazine follower
67 Magazine spring
68 Separator
69 Separator pin
70 Reaction spring
71 Action bar securing washer
72 Piston
73 Piston ring
74 Rubber stoppers
75 Cartridge stop
76 Extractor spring
77 Valve wrench

The American companies of Savage, Winchester and Remington had also been making similar models for some time, using the same principle, and achieving more or less the same quality.

When World War II was over, an addition was made to this significant though, in Europe, not very widespread group: this was an important, original, locally-produced gun. It satisfied a revived interest from hunters in this type of gun, an interest probably aroused by automatic weapons used in the war.

The Italian Breda is a light gun with a long recoil and bolt movement, and its contribution to an already well-proven system lies in its cunning design, which enables one to dismount the gun by hand, without any need for tools: the thorough chromium plating of the various component parts makes this gun virtually rustproof. The Italian arms industry is especially dynamic, and offers a wide variety of other such guns.

But the new technological knowledge and experience acquired from the wartime production of weapons had the effect of sharpening the wits of Mother Invention, and the public was confronted with a fair range of new systems, some successful, others less so.

The fixed-barrel Winchester was made by binding a thin steel tube with high-intensity fibre-glass, with a floating chamber system. This system involves a short recoil which releases a non-fixed bolt, but it has not proved entirely satisfactory. On the other hand, the gas-operated system, already widely used in military weapons, scored high marks.

Winchester is currently manufacturing guns using this system, notably the 1400, Hi-Standard and Supermatic.

In Italy the Beretta A 300, which has undergone several modifications and now been equipped with a self-regulating recoil piston, is fully developed.

The Perfex, made by Manufrance, is a fine gun, renowned for its reliability and light weight; here, expanding gases in a cylinder operate a piston which controls the release mechanism, and the bolt movement is in turn controlled by an adjustable valve.

The Remington 1100 introduces the gases not into but around a cylinder, and exploits their motive energy rather than their expansion. Though heavy, the 1100 is extremely soundly-made and safe.

The last two automatic guns mentioned do not require any adjustment and can use all types of ammunition of their calibre, except the Magnum shot shell, which has too great a power and can only be used in specially adapted guns.

Benelli in Italy have also developed a new system. The release mechanism of the bolt on the fixed-barrel is operated by the movement of an inertial block, held in place by a spring which is adjusted to the pressure. It is completely chromium plated, and can be dismounted by hand without tools; it uses every type of ammunition of the appropriate gauge without any adjustment, but it gives the impression of being heavier and longer than its counterparts.

The Czechs have produced an automatic repeating gun based on the Browning system, and the firm of Verney-Carron in France formerly manufactured various versions of the Franchi automatic rifle under licence.

The Japanese SKB automatic rifle is also a very sound

and modestly priced gun.

Lastly we should mention two novel 9mm rim-fire, smooth-bore carbines with unlocked breech, made by the Italian firms of Marochi and Bernardelli. The latter features a long recoil, and the fixed magazine has been replaced by an interchangeable clip.

All these automatic weapons require the most advanced production methods, use special lightweight alloys and are altogether soundly made, virtually rustproof and easy to service, thanks to the fact that all their component parts may be interchanged.

Slide-action shotguns

Most so-called 'Autoloader' shotguns come in simplified versions, where a single manual movement — i.e. not an automatic system — controls the ejection of the spent shell, introduces the next one to the chamber, and cocks the firing mechanism. These are usually known as 'pump-action' guns, because of the manual movement involved. This type of gun is light, and can use high- or low-power shot shells, which gives it the edge over autoloaders; it has been very popular in the United States for many years, and the European clientele finds its good workmanship and low price doubly attractive.

We might mention in passing that the slide-action shotgun came into being in the USA thanks, naturally enough, to the inventive genius of John Moses Browning.

The 1887 Winchester sporting gun did not have this pump-action, of course; it was one of the rare models to use the cocking-lever made famous by the Winchester Repeating Arms Co. It was a 10- or 12-gauge shotgun and fired ammunition designed especially with it in mind: the 70–150. Its tubular 5-round magazine placed below the barrel gave it considerable firepower and many American stage-coach companies issued their employees with it to safeguard the bullion being transported. Later on, in 1901, they produced a very similar model which came in just the 10-gauge version. Neither of these guns has been manufactured for many years now. New systems have superseded them.

Manufrance's Rapid is an excellent, modestly-priced gun which is currently enjoying wide sales in France and elsewhere.

Most manufacturers of sporting pieces also make a 'pump-action' model, keeping careful watch on high-quality finish and reliability. Worth mentioning among them are: the 870 Wingmaster by Remington, the 1200 Winchester, the Ithaca 37, all illustrated here, and the Beretta RS 200, the Flite-King Hi-Standard and the Marlin 120, all illustrated in the data sheets at the end of this chapter.

Autoloader and slide-action guns are single-barrelled. As a result they have just one constant ballistic performance, and this disadvantage had to be compensated for, for the hunter. Some firms introduced easily and rapidly interchangeable barrels; others, such as Breda, incorporated an easily replaceable detachable, screw-in choke, or a more complicated adjustable choke (like Winchester's Winchoke or the Poly-choke used by Verney-Carron and Franchi on their automatic guns).

The Americans have a repeating sporting gun with a moving bolt, based on rifled-bore guns, in the shape of the Marlin Goose Gun 55 repeating punt-gun. This typically

143

Remington 1100 autoloader.

Franchi autoloaders were formerly made by Verney-Carron, such as the Aquilon (12-gauge) or Zéphir (20-gauge) above and Grand Prix below.

The Bernardelli rim-fire 9mm calibre semi-automatic carbine. This gun is available with a 3-round clip.

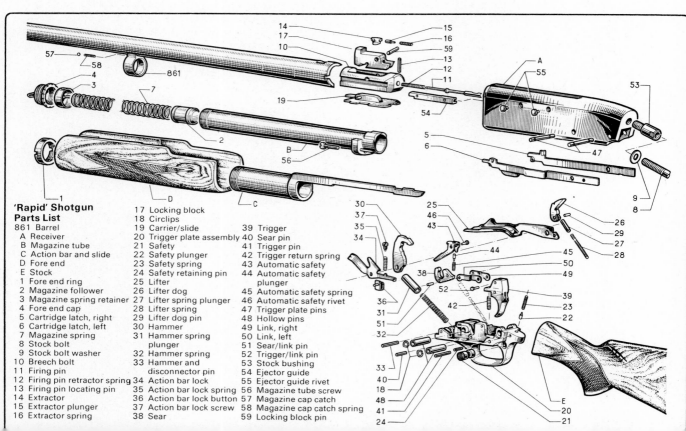

'Rapid' Shotgun Parts List

861 Barrel
A Receiver
B Magazine tube
C Action bar and slide
D Fore end
E Stock
1 Fore end ring
2 Magazine follower
3 Magazine spring retainer
4 Fore end cap
5 Cartridge latch, right
6 Cartridge latch, left
7 Magazine spring
8 Stock bolt
9 Stock bolt washer
10 Breech bolt
11 Firing pin
12 Firing pin retractor spring
13 Firing pin locating pin
14 Extractor
15 Extractor plunger
16 Extractor spring

17 Locking block
18 Circlips
19 Carrier/slide
20 Trigger plate assembly
21 Safety
22 Safety plunger
23 Safety spring
24 Safety retaining pin
25 Lifter
26 Lifter dog
27 Lifter spring plunger
28 Lifter spring
29 Lifter dog pin
30 Hammer
31 Hammer spring plunger
32 Hammer spring
33 Hammer and disconnector pin
34 Action bar lock
35 Action bar lock spring
36 Action bar lock button
37 Action bar lock screw
38 Sear

39 Trigger
40 Sear pin
41 Trigger pin
42 Trigger return spring
43 Automatic safety
44 Automatic safety plunger
45 Automatic safety spring
46 Automatic safety rivet
47 Trigger plate pins
48 Hollow pins
49 Link, right
50 Link, left
51 Sear/link pin
52 Trigger/link pin
53 Stock bushing
54 Ejector guide
55 Ejector guide rivet
56 Magazine tube screw
57 Magazine cap catch
58 Magazine cap catch spring
59 Locking block pin

The Winchester 1887 lever-action repeating shotgun.

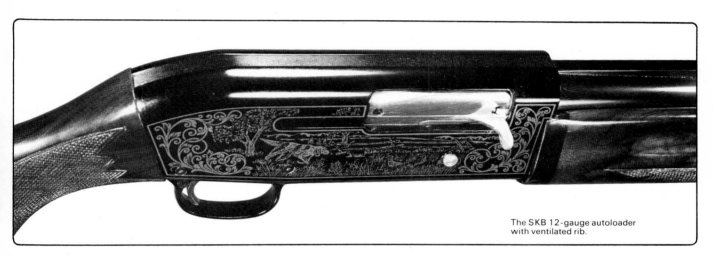

The Remington Wingmaster 870 slide-action shotgun.

The SKB 12-gauge autoloader with ventilated rib.

The Rivolier Père et Fils shotgun with side-by-side barrels.

The 'Long Room' at James Purdey and Sons, London.

Details of engraving and damascening of locks for Purdey shotguns.
These engravings are carried out on request and differ from one gun to the next.

A Purdey De Luxe side-by-side shotgun.

'Drilling' gun with double Purdey locks and external hammers.

Engraving on a Verney-Carron Grand Prix autoloader.

American gun is virtually unknown in Europe; it comes with a 27.5in. (91cm) smooth-bore barrel, and the rounds are fed by an interchangeable 2-round clip (normal 12-gauge, or 12-gauge Magnum).

Side-by-side shotguns

The sweeping craze for over-and-under and autoloader shotguns has by no means meant the disappearance of the good old side-by-side shotguns. This has an especially strong following in Spain and Italy, where production methods have not undergone any dire changes, particularly for popular standard models. Thus the major arms centre of Eibar in Spain offers a wide range of guns, with the superior model rubbing shoulders with the average.

Most of these guns are of the Anson type, in which loading is carried out by dropping the barrels down.

Italian guns are amply represented by the Beretta 424 Series and 451 Series, and the Bernardelli S. Uberto F.S. and Roma 4; the latter has cross-locks; there are also the Ariete and Vulcano Record models by Antonio Zoli, and a score of others.

Manufrance's famous Robust, along with the Etendard and the Helicobloc by Verney-Carron, all French products, is one of the finest side-by-side shotguns produced in the country; a close second to them is the Rivolier, which is less of a name, but offers excellent workmanship nonetheless.

A handful of craftsmen have survived from the heyday of Saint-Etienne, and these few continue to manufacture fine French guns.

The number of models available is impressive, both in Europe and in the United States, where Marlin is marketing its L. C. Smith (12-gauge and 12 Magnum gauge); despite its outwardly thoroughbred appearance, it does not compare with its similarly priced European counterparts.

When they are manufactured by any of the major firms, all these guns profit from the technological advances already alluded to. Whether they be two-, three- or four-bolt Purdey or Greener systems, whether they have the toplever and so on, their quality is undoubtedly higher than their predecessors. In addition the novelty of some guns singles them out.

The Russian MC 11 Series Baikal is equipped with a safety device operated by hammer interceptors, which is a rare phenomenon on sporting guns.

Torsion springs have replaced the traditional springs of the Anson system on Gaucher and Verney-Carron collections, but the Gefar has an adjustable bolt.

Within this wide range there are some guns with ejectors, and some without, some with a single selective trigger, and some without, and any of these models can be counted among the finest that the modern arms industry can offer — for instance, Lebeau-Courally, Merkel, Verney-Carron, AYA, and others.

Holland and Holland side-lock models, which can sometimes be dismounted by hand, are made to measure to the requirements of the user; these guns satisfy two criteria; they manage to carry on the gunsmith's tradition, and at the same time they are among the finest guns manufactured at the present time. English guns are without doubt a cut above models made by AYA, Bayard and Boss, for example; indeed, the English have the last word as far as sporting pieces are concerned, and any hunting enthusiast nurtures the dream of owning one, one day; but the top rung belongs to just three firms: Holland and Holland, Purdey and Westley-Richards.

Other models with side-by-side barrels — most of them French — are more modest, but interesting nevertheless for the fact that their design is less traditional.

High on the list comes Manufrance's Idéal. Here, the lever system, which operates the loading mechanism, has been adopted by the Italian firm of Lucchini. Bergeron and Gaucher make the Gallia and the Tarzan with locking and loading mechanisms operated by a cocking-lever on the trigger-guard. Bergeron has even marketed a model with loading carried out by a top locking-lever.

A typically French gun, devised by Darne, that inventive genius from Saint-Etienne, includes fixed barrels on a table with a sliding, diagonally-bolted bolt. Charlin adopted this system by hinging the bolt on a shaft.

The SMFM at Saint-Etienne for its part has experimented with an electric firing mechanism; this has theoretical advantages to it, but is handicapped in a practical sense by having to use special ammunition.

Single-barrelled drop-down guns

There is also a whole category of sporting guns with a single barrel which use the drop-down hammerless system. The best example is without doubt the Simplex by Manufrance, with release and loading mechanisms operated by cocking-lever. The same release and loading mechanisms have been retained by the Russians in their IJ-18 E Model, whereas the Beretta uses a loading and release lever placed in front of the trigger-guard on its 412 Series model. The Americans also make very similar models.

'Drilling' guns

There is another category of guns, manufactured mainly in Germany and Central Europe, which represents a transition between the shotgun and the rifle. These are called 'Drillings'; they are Anson-type, drop-down guns, with two smooth-bore side-by-side barrels beneath which there is a third rifled barrel. These have been produced for some time to meet certain legal requirements and certain hunting methods, but they are little known elsewhere. Generally speaking they are not particularly handsome. They are largely made by Merkel, Boss and Krieghoff, all German firms.

We should also mention the mixed gun, which may have over-under or side-by-side barrels, and may have a smooth-bore and a rifled barrel. This type is made, for example, by the Finnish firm of Valmet, which otherwise manufactures traditional over-under models. Probably under the influence of their Central European satellites, the Russians also produce an over-under model: this is known as the MC 5-18; it has an upper rifled 5.6mm barrel and a lower smooth-bore 16-gauge barrel. These models are very popular in the United States, where Ithaca makes its Turkey Model for its devotees. This gun has an upper 12-gauge smooth-bore barrel and a lower .222 calibre rifled barrel equipped with a muzzle-brake — although its purpose is not all that evident at first glance, or even at the second!

Last of all we come to the drop-down guns with side-

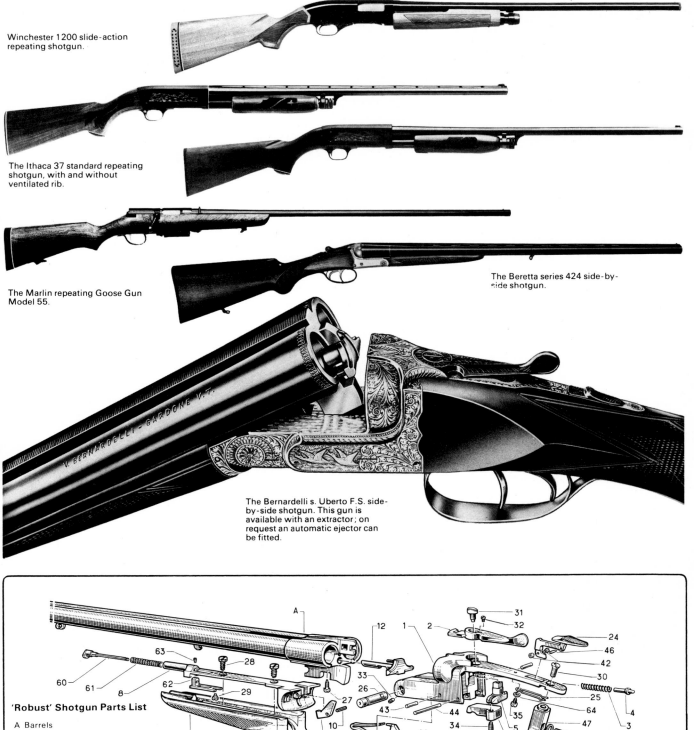

Winchester 1200 slide-action repeating shotgun.

The Ithaca 37 standard repeating shotgun, with and without ventilated rib.

The Marlin repeating Goose Gun Model 55.

The Beretta series 424 side-by-side shotgun.

The Bernardelli s. Uberto F.S. side-by-side shotgun. This gun is available with an extractor; on request an automatic ejector can be fitted.

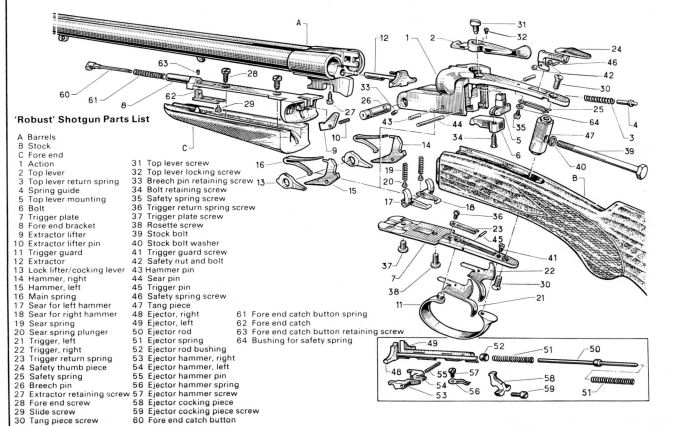

'Robust' Shotgun Parts List

A Barrels
B Stock
C Fore end
1 Action
2 Top lever
3 Top lever return spring
4 Spring guide
5 Top lever mounting
6 Bolt
7 Trigger plate
8 Fore end bracket
9 Extractor lifter
10 Extractor lifter pin
11 Trigger guard
12 Extractor
13 Lock lifter/cocking lever
14 Hammer, right
15 Hammer, left
16 Main spring
17 Sear for left hammer
18 Sear for right hammer
19 Sear spring
20 Sear spring plunger
21 Trigger, left
22 Trigger, right
23 Trigger return spring
24 Safety thumb piece
25 Safety spring
26 Breech pin
27 Extractor retaining screw
28 Fore end screw
29 Slide screw
30 Tang piece screw

31 Top lever screw
32 Top lever locking screw
33 Breech pin retaining screw
34 Bolt retaining screw
35 Safety spring screw
36 Trigger return spring screw
37 Trigger plate screw
38 Rosette screw
39 Stock bolt
40 Stock bolt washer
41 Trigger guard screw
42 Safety nut and bolt
43 Hammer pin
44 Sear pin
45 Trigger pin
46 Safety spring screw
47 Tang piece
48 Ejector, right
49 Ejector, left
50 Ejector rod
51 Ejector spring
52 Ejector rod bushing
53 Ejector hammer, right
54 Ejector hammer, left
55 Ejector hammer pin
56 Ejector hammer spring
57 Ejector hammer screw
58 Ejector cocking piece
59 Ejector cocking piece screw
60 Fore end catch button

61 Fore end catch button spring
62 Fore end catch
63 Fore end catch button retaining screw
64 Bushing for safety spring

Top to bottom:

The Purdey 20-gauge side-by-side shotgun with automatic ejector.

The Purdey Express .470 calibre big game rifle.

The Purdey .404 calibre big game carbine.

The Holland and Holland Royal side-by-side shotgun. The excellent quality of the finish and engraving of this magnificent gun defy comment. The smooth working of the locks and the ejector of this gun with a Purdey double lock make this an exceptional example of the gunsmith's art, although it is unfortunately beyond the reach of many a pocket.

The Verney-Carron Etendard 484
side-by-side shotgun.

An unsigned, old 'drilling'
shotgun. Both upper barrels are 16
gauge, and the lower barrel is .360
Express calibre.

The Krieghoff Trumpf drilling
shotgun, available in 12, 16 and
20 gauge.

The Krieghoff Teck big game rifle.
The hollow stock is used to house
two regular cartridges, a
conversion barrel for firing .22 LR
rounds and 6 .22 LR rounds.

The Ithaca Turkey gun with mixed
superposed barrels.

The Remington 700 DDL .222 calibre Custom Deluxe bolt-action repeating rifle.

The Hämmerli big game rifle, available in various calibres.

Mauser Jagdwaffen big game rifles. Top to bottom: the 2.000 and 4.000 with two triggers; and 66 with single trigger.

Details of the open bolt of the Ruger M-77 rifle.

by-side, or more rarely over-under, rifled barrels, known as Express rifles; these often have large calibres and are more especially designed for African safaris and big-game hunting. In Germany Merkel makes both models, and Winchester offers a small-scale production of a prestige over-under model with a 9.3 × 74mm calibre. The colonial tradition of Great Britain made big game rifles part and parcel of the gunsmith's production, and James Purdey, Holland and Holland and other great British trade names did the tradition proud.

Sporting rifles

In this chapter so far we have discussed certain fairly classic sporting weapons which are capable of firing slug shell. When the use of a solid projectile or bullet becomes really necessary, the hunter usually prefers to use a single-barrelled repeating rifle. These rifles, with rifled barrels, can be generally subdivided into various categories according to the repeating mechanism used: bolt-action repeating rifles, Mauser type; lever action repeating rifles; slide-action repeating rifles; semi-automatic repeating carbines, known as autoloaders.

Bolt-action repeating rifles, Mauser type

The need for a reliable, strong, simple gun, easy to handle in every calibre and under every type of condition, plus the fact that such a gun must comply with legislation prohibiting the use of automatic weapons – all these factors have led practically every manufacturer to retain the Mauser-type bolt action system: this is far and away the most widely used and is manufactured across the globe either with or without adaptation. We cannot mention them all, there being so many different calibres and variants. In the United States, for example, Remington offers its 700 model in seventeen different calibres. Some names crop up more frequently than others, particularly those of the Austrian firm, Mannlicher, the Swiss Hämmerli, the Finnish Sako, the English BSA, the Belgian FN, the German firms Mauser and Walther, the Swedish Husqvarna, the American firms Marlin, Winchester, Remington, the Russian Vostok, the Japanese SKB and a good many more. Every calibre, from the tiny .17 Remington to the mighty .458 Winchester Magnum, figures in the various catalogues and enables the purchaser to choose the gun which is precisely suited to his needs. As far as large calibres are concerned, Purdey produces several models which are made to measure according to the requirements of the future owner.

All currently manufactured carbines have profited from the recent technological advances made, in particular, in the case of military weapons. Some models offer new solutions. The .17 Remington round, with an initial velocity of 1200 metres per second, for which one of the Model 700 carbines is chambered, gives extremely accurate performances for long-distance small game hunting.

In addition, Remington has fitted its carbines with a breech which has multiple breech locks, thus increasing the tightness of the locking mechanism.

Mauser uses a three-part breech, and thus achieves not only a shorter mechanism, but also a more effective locking mechanism, more direct percussion and, most of all, a quite exceptional interchangeability of barrels.

The Birmingham Small Arms company (BSA) in Great Britain, with its Monarch model, pushes the de luxe manufacture of a classic type of gun to the point of perfect hand-polishing of the chamber so as to protect the cases of those reloading their own cartridges.

Mannlicher, retaining its rotating magazine, which suits the use of soft-headed bullets, machines its receiver with such precision that when one works it one has the impression that it is sliding in oil or on ball bearings. Apart from the over-sized breech with its shortened locking mechanism, its S.L. carbine is mounted on a stock made of synthetic material.

In the United States Ruger is currently marketing its M-77 rifle fitted with a very efficient bolt, short or Magnum, which makes it possible to use very powerful ammunition with this gun.

Lever-action repeating carbines

The Mauser repeating system is nevertheless not exclusive, and the Americans in particular have remained faithful to the Browning system adopted by the Winchester Repeating Arms Co. for its 1894 Winchester carbine. This latter continues to enjoy a unique career in the annals of commercial guns with more than 3,000,000 models sold, and the 94, available in three options (calibres .32, .30 × .30 and .44 Magnum) together with the Model 60, has been delighting the shooting enthusiast for almost eighty years. Since 1966, the centenary of the first 1866 Winchester carbine, Winchester Olin International regularly produces commemoration carbines celebrating events and protagonists of American history. The mechanisms of these guns are based on the 1894 Winchester frame, the lever of which has earned the make its prestigious position. There are, for instance, the 66 Centennial, the Golden Spike, the Theodore Roosevelt, the Buffalo Bill, the Lone Star, the Cowboy, the M.R.A. (with long or short barrel), and the Yellow Boy Indian which has recently appeared, and which has been closely followed by the centenary model of the Royal Canadian Mounted Police, the Apache.

Marlin is still producing its lever-action carbines, among which are the 336 C and 336 T, 1895, 444, and so on, as well as the commemorative carbine, Zane Grey Century, dedicated to the memory of the novelist famous for writing American westerns. The success of this type of gun is so huge that Miroku in Japan is currently marketing its ML .22 model in standard and Deluxe engraved versions. The same goes for Germany where Erma, at Dachau, is manufacturing a .22 calibre replica; as is Winchester with its self-copied 9422 model. For some years now the Brescia arms industry in Italy has been making replicas of 1866 and 1873 Winchesters in .22, .38, .357 Magnum and .44-40 calibres. The main manufacturers are Uberti and Euroarms.

Slide-action repeating carbines

There are also several versions of the slide-action system. Devised by J. M. Browning a long time ago, the pump-action .22 LR calibre carbine is still made by the Belgian FN. It is principally the Americans who have remained faithful to this formula, and though the .22 calibre is the

From left to
right:
the Miroku
ML.22
.22 calibre
engraved de
luxe carbine.
The Manufrance
Falcor shotgun
(see note 13).
The BSA
Monarch carbine
(see note 14).

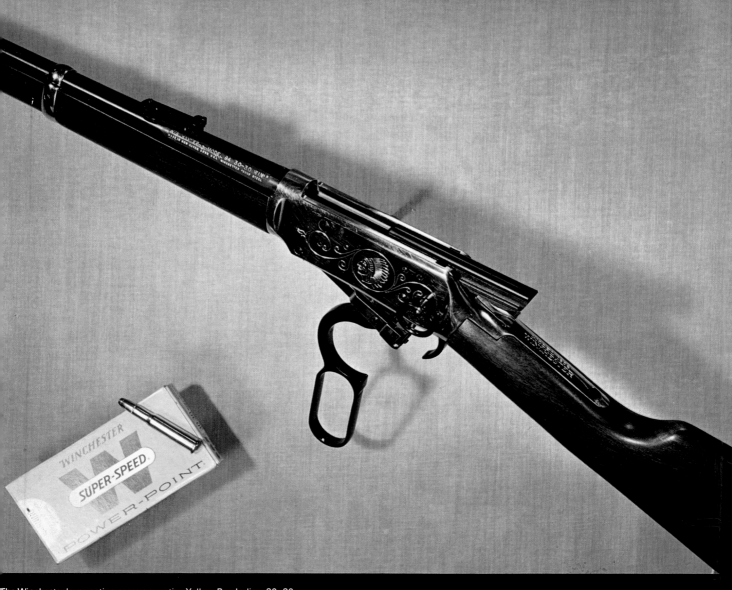

The Winchester lever-action commemorative Yellow Boy Indian .30–30
VCF repeating carbine.

most common, Remington's 760 Gamemaster nonetheless uses rounds as powerful as the .30-06 US Army or the .308 Winchester.

Semi-automatic repeating carbines, known as 'autoloaders'

Automatic repeating guns are, like the Mauser System, particularly well represented in the .22 (LR or Magnum) calibre. In these calibres the possibility of using a system with a non-locked bolt makes for simple and economical production. This is the classic popular gun. It is manufactured all over the world in numerous models and large quantities. Among current models are the Marlin 49 DL carbine, the Ruger 10/22 carbine, the Remington Nylon 66 carbine, the Italian Jager AP-15 carbine, derived from the famous Armalite AR-15, and the Unique Combo carbine. But there are two models which seem rather different, and have certain qualities in common: a Browning carbine by the Fabrique Nationale Belge and one made by Unique, the French firm. These are very sound guns, and fire most types of ammunition of the calibre; they are easily stripped for maintenance, and this operation does not require tools. Large calibre rifled automatic sporting guns are less common. For the most part these are directly derived from military weapons. They are mostly marketed by the Americans, who offer:
— with Winchester and its 100 model, an automatic gas-operated repeating carbine in .243 WCF calibre, and even .308 WCF calibre (NATO 7.62mm);
— with Remington and its 742 model, in five calibres, from the 6mm Remington to the .308 WCF, gas-operated, and with the mechanical parts coated with 'Teflon' thus assuring self-lubrication and protection;
— with Ruger, its .44 Magnum Auto carbine.

In Europe the Fabrique Nationale Belge is marketing its B.A.R. (Browning Automatic Rifle) carbine in seven calibres, from the .243 WCF to the .338 WCF Magnum. For some time now assault rifle manufacturers have been offering semi-automatic versions of these military weapons on which the burst device has been eliminated. This is the case, for example, with the Swiss firm SIG, which is marketing its big-game A.M.T. model, and with Armalite in the United States, with its AR-180 model chambered for the .223 round, both using military ammunition.

Conclusion

All these sporting guns, whether shotguns or rifles, with the exception of rare automatic repeating models, are hallmarked less by the novelty of their systems than by the quality of their manufacture — a factor which has enabled them to keep pace with the current advances in ammunition.

The present-day sporting gun is extremely robust, sound and often very handsome. Its future development will depend on the direction taken not by technical expertise but by legislation. In fact conditions have become such that legislators are deeply concerned and are inevitably being prevailed upon to restrict the power and effectiveness of arms in use.

Winchester lever-action commemorative N.R.A. repeating rifle and carbine. In order to celebrate the centenary of the National Rifle Association, Winchester marketed these two guns whose stocks are decorated with a medallion bearing the emblem of the N.R.A. The rifle has a 66cm barrel, and the carbine a 60cm barrel. Both guns chamber the .30–30 WCF round.

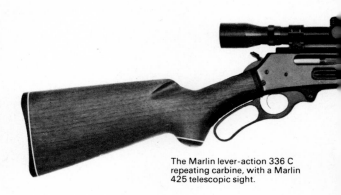

The Marlin lever-action 336 C repeating carbine, with a Marlin 425 telescopic sight.

The Italian Euroarms replica of the Winchester 1873 .44–40 calibre carbine.

The Marlin 49DL .22 LR calibre autoloader.

The Ruger 10/.22 autoloader.

The Remington Nylon 66 carbine.

The Jäger AP 15 carbine.

157

The Winchester 100 autoloader.

The Ruger 44 .44 Magnum calibre autoloader.

The FN-Browning Bar. Battue automatic hunting rifle.

The Unique Combo autoloader.

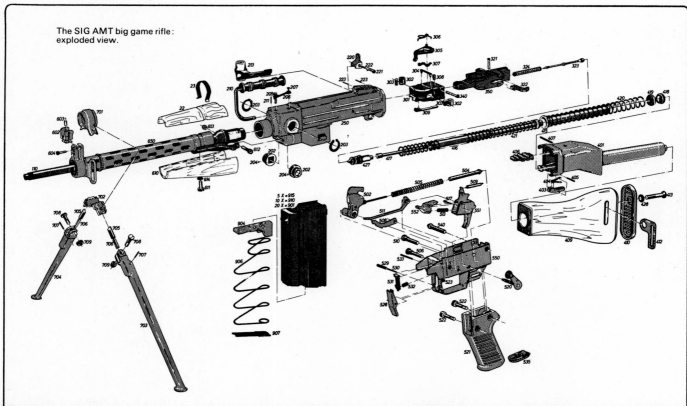

The SIG AMT big game rifle: exploded view.

Sporting guns: technical data

Browning FN. Spécial Chasse
top: 20 Magnum
below: 12 gauge

Country	Belgium
Type	over-under shotgun
Designation	Fabrique Nationale de Herstal. FN Browning, Spécial Chasse
Calibre	20, 20 Magnum, 12, 12 Magnum
Weight	2.800kg for 20 gauge, 3.300 for 12 gauge
Length	barrel: 67cm, 71cm and 76cm (12 gauge only); chamber: 70 or 76cm
Remarks	the different versions are supplied with or without a ventilated rib, upper barrel full choke, lower barrel half- choke. The stock is 'English' or pistol grip, and the gun has a double or selective trigger. With this gun the FN Herstal has achieved one of the high points of top quality mass-produced sporting weapons. The hammers on this gun have a safety catch to prevent untimely percussion in the event of a fall. There are also sporting versions of this model in the shape of the 'Special Skeet' and 'Special Trap'

Winchester 101

Country	United States
Type	over-under shotgun
Designation	Winchester 101
Calibre	12 Magnum, 12, 20 Magnum, 20, 28 and 410
Weight	2.400kg to 3.400kg depending on calibre and barrel length
Length	barrel: 66, 67, 71, 76 and 81cm
Remarks	this model is offered in several versions based on calibre variations, choke and barrel length. There are also Skeet and Trap models. The 101 Trap has double barrels, the lower one being closed at the breech; this is one of those numerous American whims whose actual usefulness is sometimes hard for others to grasp

Beretta SO Series

Country	Italy
Type	over-under shotgun
Designation	Beretta SO series, SO 1, SO 2, SO 3 EL, and SO 3 BELL
Calibre	12 only (12 Magnum to order)
Weight	3.000kg (average)
Length	barrel: 71cm standard, but available in 66, 68, 74 and 76cm (choke on request)
Remarks	the different designations refer to types of finish. All the SO series may be supplied with English or pistol grip stock. On every gun the trigger-pull is adjustable on request and there is a double Purdey lock. There is also an SO 4, a Trap version with 74–76cm barrels, and a Skeet version with 71cm barrels

Bernardelli Orione

Country	Italy
Type	over-under shotgun
Designation	Bernardelli Orione (with ventilated rib)
Calibre	12 gauge only
Weight	3.300 to 3.600kg depending on barrel length
Length	barrels: 71 or 74cm (Trap), 66 to 68cm (Skeet)
Remarks	this model is fitted with automatic extractors or ejectors to order; it has a Purdey double locking mechanism, K.M.O. steel barrels, chromed, three-quarter and full choke

FN-Browning 'automatic' rifle

Country	Belgium
Type	autoloader shotgun
Designation	Fabrique Nationale de Herstal, FN-Browning
Calibre	12 Magnum, 12, 16 and 20
Weight	3.000 to 4.000kg depending on type (barrel, calibre, model)
Length	barrel: 66, 71, 76 and 81cm
Capacity	2 or 4 rounds
Remarks	this is the oldest of the automatic shotguns, and also the most widespread. Its essential quality is its robustness. It comes in 'standard', 'light' and 'extra-light' versions, with or without ventilated rib. The barrels are bored to full choke, 3/4 choke, half choke and 1/4 choke, Skeet and smooth-bores. With interchangeable barrels this gun can be used for a variety of purposes

Ithaca 51 Featherlight
top: with ventilated rib
below: without rib

Country	United States
Type	autoloader shotgun
Designation	Ithaca 51 Featherlight
Calibre	12 only
Weight	3.400kg
Length	barrel: 66–76cm with various chokes: overall, 118–128cm
Capacity	2 rounds, thus three shots, barrel supplied on request with or without ventilated rib
Remarks	in the Ithaca range this is the only 'automatic' weapon which is gas-operated. There is also a de luxe version made with selected woods

Remington 1100

Country	United States
Type	gas-operated autoloader shotgun
Designation	Remington 1100
Calibre	12 Magnum, 12, 16, 20 Magnum, 20, 28 and 410 Magnum
Weight	from 2.350 to 3.400kg, depending on calibre and barrel
Length	barrel: 55.5cm (with slug) to 76cm
Capacity	4 rounds, thus 5 shots; except for Magnum (76mm case) capacity reduced to 4 shots (three rounds in magazine)
Remarks	this is one of the most widely used guns in the USA; offered in several versions, with or without ventilated rib, it has interchangeable barrels in the same calibre

Winchester 1400

Country	United States
Type	gas-operated autoloader shotgun rifle
Designation	Winchester 1400
Calibre	12 Magnum, 12, 20 Magnum and 20
Weight	3.200kg
Length	barrel: 56cm (with slug), 66, 71 and 76cm
Capacity	4 rounds (5 shots) except for Magnum: capacity reduced to 3 + 1 rounds. Thanks to a regulator, all rounds of the same calibre can be used in the same gun (including Magnums)
Remarks	this gun is marketed in 39 different types, with or without ventilated rib, all types of stock, right and left-handed versions, with choked barrel on request, or with adjustable Winchoke

Beretta A 300 de luxe

Country	Italy
Type	gas-operated autoloader shotgun
Designation	Beretta A 300
Calibre	12 and 20
Weight	2.850 to 3.100kg depending on calibre and barrel length
Length	barrel: 62, 67, 71 and 76cm with different chokes
Capacity	3 rounds (4 shots)
Remarks	this gun, gas-operated with a regulator piston, comes in two versions: A 300 normal and A 300 de luxe

Ithaca 37

Country	United States
Type	slide-action shotgun
Designation	Ithaca 37
Calibre	12, 16 and 20
Length	barrel: 66, 71 and 76cm in 12 gauge; 66 and 71cm in 16 and 20 gauge
Capacity	4 rounds (reduced to 2 by special cap)
Remarks	there are several models: 37 D without rib, 37 DV with ventilated rib and selected wood, 37 Standard Deerslayer without ventilated rib, for slug, with special sighting instrument (front and back sights on slide, possibility of mounting Redfield telescopic sight to order). The 37 Supreme is available in Skeet and Trap versions

Marlin 120

Country	United States
Type	slide-action shotgun
Designation	Marlin 120
Calibre	12 and 12 Magnum
Weight	3.100 to 3.400kg
Length	barrel: 66, 71 and 76cm
Capacity	4 rounds in 12 gauge (5 shots) and 3 in 12 Magnum (4 shots)
Remarks	barrels available with this gun are instantly interchangeable; the magazine capacity can be reduced to 2 rounds (3 shots) by a special plug, available to order.

Hi-Standard, Flite King

Country	United States
Type	slide-action shotgun
Designation	Hi-Standard, Flite King
Calibre	12, 20, 28 and 410
Weight	3.200kg
Length	barrel: 66cm (Skeet) and 76cm (Trap)
Capacity	4 rounds
Remarks	very popular in the United States, slide-action shotguns are less so in Europe. This one comes in two versions: the Skeet model (all calibres) with 66cm barrels and the Trap model in 12 gauge only with 76cm barrel (barrels have ventilated ribs in both cases)

Remington 870 Wingmaster

Country	United States
Type	slide-action shotgun
Designation	Remington 870 Wingmaster
Calibre	12, 16, 20, 28 and 410
Weight	2.500 to 3.500kg depending on type
Length	barrel: 45.5cm (police model without rib) to 76cm
Capacity	4 rounds (2 with reducer) in 12, 16, 20 and 28 gauge and 3 rounds in 410 gauge (2 with reducer)
Remarks	like all popular American guns, the 870 Wingmaster comes in many versions. Note that the barrels are interchangeable and that the gun takes all rounds, including Magnums. Apart from the police model, the 870 Wingmaster is supplied with ventilated rib, except where not required on request

Winchester 12

Country	United States
Type	slide-action shotgun
Designation	Winchester 12 'Field'
Calibre	12 only
Weight	from 3.500 to 3.900kg depending on barrel length
Length	overall: 127cm with full-choke barrel of 76cm; 122cm with modified 71cm barrel; 117cm, with improved 66cm smooth-bore barrel
Capacity	6 rounds (2 with reducer)
Remarks	the model 12 is the prestige pump-action rifle in the large Winchester range. The receiver is engraved in three styles ('1 A', '1 B' or '1 C'). To make transportation easier the barrel and magazine are fixed to the receiver by an arrangement which can be speedily dismantled. There is also a Trap model with 76cm barrel and a Skeet model with a 66cm barrel

Beretta RS 200

Country	Italy
Type	slide-action shotgun
Designation	Beretta RS 200
Calibre	12 and 16
Weight	3.000kg
Length	barrel: 67, 71 and 76cm, with or without ventilated rib
Capacity	3 rounds (4 shots)
Remarks	a light gun thanks to the use of light alloy for the mechanism manufacture, the RS 200 is relatively low-priced

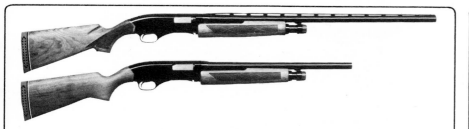

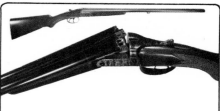

Winchester 1200
below : police model

Country	United States
Type	slide-action shotgun
Designation	Winchester 1200
Calibre	12 Magnum, 12, 16, 20 Magnum and 20
Weight	from 2.500 to 3.500kg depending on model
Length	barrel : 46cm (police model), 56cm (slug), 66, 71, 76cm

Capacity	4 rounds (5 shots)
Remarks	like most sporting arms produced by Winchester, this model comes in many versions, with chokes to order or the adjustable Winchoke, standard or Monte Carlo stock, Skeet and Trap models etc. The 1200 does not have a left-handed model

Manufrance Robust

Country	France
Type	side-by-side shotgun
Designation	Manufrance Robust
Calibre	12 Magnum, 12 and 16
Weight	3.000kg
Length	barrel : 70 and 76cm
Remarks	available in various versions (automatic ejector, Supra rifled barrel, automatic sling, long barrel etc), this is one of the lowest priced shotguns and one of the most sought after in the Manufrance range

Verney-Carron Etendard

Country	France
Type	side-by-side shotgun
Designation	Verney-Carron, Etendard 482, 484 and 489
Calibre	12 and 16
Weight	from 2.600 to 3.000kg depending on model
Length	barrel : 70cm
Remarks	the different models and model-numbers refer to the type of finish, and are all 12 or 16 gauge : Etendard 482 : tapered ribbed barrels, engraved dropdown, extractor ; Etendard 484 : extractor, plume ribbed barrels, frame engraved ; Etendard 489 : automatic ejector, narrow ribbed barrels, finely engraved frame

Beretta Series 451, 451 EELL

Country	Italy
Type	side-by-side shotgun
Designation	Beretta Series 451
Calibre	12 Magnum and 12
Weight	average 2.900kg
Length	barrel : 66, 68, 74 and 76cm (standard 71cm)
Remarks	these guns, the firm's prestige range, are fitted with barrels which are bored to order and all fitted with automatic ejectors. They all originally come with a standard 71cm barrel. They are sold in three versions : 451 E, normal version ; 451 EL, identical to the E but with scroll engraving and selected figured walnut ; 451 EELL, de luxe finish with elaborate signed engraving, gilded triggers and spindles, top quality wood

Bernardelli Roma 4

Country	Italy
Type	side-by-side shotgun
Designation	Bernardelli Roma 4
Calibre	12, 16 and 20
Weight	average : 2.800kg
Length	barrel : 71cm (supplied 1/2 choke right and full choke left)
Remarks	fitted with lock, hammerless, Anson Deeley system, with Purdey lock, the Roma 4 is supplied with extractor or, on request, with automatic ejector. The barrels are always chromed

Beretta Series 424
top : 426 E
bottom : 427 E

Country	Italy
Type	side-by-side shotgun
Designation	Beretta Series 424, 4 variants : 424, 12, 16 or 20 gauge with matt chrome engraved dropdown and extractor ; 424, 12 or 20 gauge, with matt chrome frame, selected wood and extractor ; 426 E with 12 and 20 gauge, with finely engraved dropdown and automatic ejector ; 427 E, with dropdown with false lock plates, de luxe engraving, selected wood, automatic ejector, only available in 12 gauge
Calibre	12, 16 and 20
Weight	average : 2.800kg
Length	barrels : 67, 71 and 76cm with choke to order
Remarks	all the models in this series have nickel-chrome steel barrels and a Purdey triple locking mechanism ; the selector operates regardless of the safety position

Walther KKJ Rifle

Country	Germany
Type	bolt-action repeating rifle
Designation	Walther KKJ
Calibre	.22 LR, .22 Magnum or .22 Hornet
Weight	2.600kg
Length	overall 105cm
Capacity	5 rounds
Remarks	the Walther KKJ is supplied with or without double triggers, and, on request, left-handed stock. The telescopic sight and mounting are extras

F.N. Browning Big Game Rifle

Country	Belgium
Type	bolt-action repeating rifle
Designation	Fabrique Nationale de Herstal, F.N. Browning carbine
Calibre	.222, .222 Magnum, .22–250, .243, .308, .270, .30–06 US Army, 7mm Remington Magnum, .300 WCF Magnum, .308 Norma, .338 WCF Magnum, .375 Holland-Holland and .458 WCF Magnum
Weight	'light' 3.050kg; 'average' 3.200kg; 'heavy' 3.750kg
Length	barrel: standard 56cm, Magnum 61cm
Capacity	varies according to calibre
Remarks	with a Mauser breech, this carbine comes in many models

Ruger M-77

Country	United States
Type	bolt action repeating rifle
Designation	Ruger, M-77
Calibre	with short breech: .22–250, 6mm Remington, .243, .308 6.5mm Magnum, .284 and .350 Remington Magnum. With Magnum breech: .25–06, .270, .30–06 US Army and 7mm Magnum
Weight	average 3.400kg
Length	barrel: 56cm (61cm thickened in .22–250, .25–06 and 7mm Magnum calibres)
Capacity	3 or 5 rounds, depending on calibre
Remarks	equipped with a Mauser action, this carbine has an action of different lengths, depending on the ammunition used, and may be fitted with a telescopic sight (as shown above)

Winchester M/70

Country	United States
Type	bolt-action repeating rifle
Designation	Winchester M/70 (Standard, Magnum, African and Varmint (see remarks))
Calibres	.22–250, .222 Rem., .243 Rem., .270 Win., .30–06, .308 Win., .25–06 (Standard); .264 Win. Mag., 7mm Rem. Mag., .338 Win. Mag., .300 Win. Mag., .375 H. and H. Mag. (Magnum); .458 Win. Mag. (African); .222 Rem., .22–250, .243 Win. (Varmint)
Length	overall: 108cm (Standard, except for .25–06 calibre and African) and 113cm (.25–06 calibre Standard, Magnum and Varmint; barrel: 56cm (Standard, except 25–06 calibre and African), 61cm (Magnum and Varmint), 66cm (Standard .25–06 calibre)
Weight	3.500kg (Standard and Magnum, except .375 H. and H. calibre), 3.900kg (African and Magnum with .375 H. and H. calibre), 4.400kg (Varmint)
Remarks	with the M/70, Winchester 'accommodates' the Mauser breech of the German 98 Gewehr to every calibre. This rifle is also supplied in a 'Target' model, 'International Match' and 'Ultra Match'. Only the Standard, Magnum and African versions are fitted with sighting instruments, the other models using telescopic sights

Husqvarna repeating carbine

Country	Sweden
Type	bolt-action repeating rifle
Designation	Husqvarna 1970 Standard, 1972 Monte Carlo Standard and 1979 Monte Carlo de Luxe (shown here left ro right)
Calibre	.243 WCF, 6.5 × 55mm, .270 WCF, 30–06 US Army, 7mm Rem. Mag. and 9.3 × 62mm
Weight	3.200kg
Length	barrel: 60cm
Capacity	5 rounds or 4 rounds in 7mm Rem. Mag. and 9.3 × 62mm
Remarks	the 1970 Standard is available in all calibres listed; the 1972 Monte Carlo Standard is identical to the above but has a Monte Carlo stock and can use a telescopic sight. The 1979 Monte Carlo de Luxe is only available in .308 WCF, 6.5 × 55mm, .30–06 US Army and 9.3 × 62mm. But it has a de luxe finish, with polished rosewood butt plate

Ithaca 49

Country	United States
Type	single-shot carbine
Designation	Ithaca 49 Saddlegun de Luxe
Calibres	.22 Short, .22 Long and .22 LR
Weight	approx. 2.500kg
Length	overall: 88cm; barrel: 46cm
Remarks	the lever recalls a repeating weapon, but it only controls the Martini-type breech mechanism. This is a fairly cheap gun, used for fun as well as shooting vermin

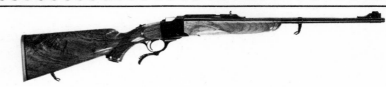

Ruger No 1

Country	United States
Type	single-shot rifle
Designation	Ruger No 1 (Light Sporter, Medium Sporter, Standard Rifle, Special Varminter or Tropical Rifle, depending on fittings)
Calibres	.243 Win., .30–06 and .270 Win. (Light Sporter); 7mm Rem. Mag. and .300 Win. Mag. (Medium Sporter); .22–250, .25–06 .243 Win., 6mm Rem., .270 Win., 7mm Rem. Mag., .300 Win. Mag. (Standard Rifle); .22–250, .25–06, 7mm Rem. Mag. and .300 Win. Mag. (Special Varminter); .375 H. and H. Mag. and .458 Win. Mag. (Tropical Rifle)
Weight	3.300kg (Light and Medium Sporter); 3.630kg (Standard Rifle); 3.750kg (Tropical Rifle with .375 H. and H.); 4.080kg (Special Varminter and Tropical Rifle with .458 Win.)
Length	barrel: 56cm (Light Sporter); 60cm (Special Varminter and Tropical Rifle); 66cm (Medium Sporter and Standard)
Remarks	this is quite popular in the USA. Note that the Standard Rifle and Special Varminter come with sighting instruments and can take telescopic sights too. Breech opening is by means of a lever

Ruger No 3

Country	United States
Type	single-shot rifle
Designation	Ruger No 3
Calibre	.45–70
Weight	2.720kg
Length	barrel: 56cm
Remarks	the breech is controlled by a lever on this robust carbine, which is reasonably priced

Marlin 39 A

Country	United States
Type	lever-action repeating rifle
Designation	Marlin Golden 39 A
Calibre	.22 Short, .22 Long and .22 Long Rifle
Weight	2.400kg approx.
Length	barrel: (Micro Groove) 61cm
Capacity	26 rounds in .22 Short, 21 in .22 Long and 19 in .22 LR
Remarks	Marlin has just updated its old 1891 model. This carbine can be fitted on request with telescopic sights (Marlin)

Marlin 336

Country	United States
Type	lever-action repeating rifle
Designation	Marlin 336 C (pistol grip stock) and Marlin 336 T (English stock)
Calibres	.30–30 Win. (also available in .35 Rem. for the 336 C)
Weight	3.200kg
Length	overall: 98cm; barrel: (Micro Groove) 51cm
Capacity	6 rounds
Remarks	in production for more than 80 years, it was first called the 1893 model; this excellent carbine still enjoys a popular career thanks to its flawless operation and quality finish. The side ejection port makes it easy to mount a telescopic sight. The receiver is drilled and threaded for this purpose

Winchester 94

Country	United States
Type	lever-action repeating carbine
Designation	Winchester 94 (Standard, Magnum and Antique)
Calibres	.30–30 Win. (Standard and Antique); .44 Mag. (Magnum)
Weight	2.800kg (Magnum), 2.900kg (Standard) and 3.200kg (Antique)
Length	overall: 96cm; barrel: 51cm
Capacity	6 rounds in .30–30 Win. and 10 rounds in .44 Magnum
Remarks	since 1894, when this gun was known as the 1894 model, it has been exceptionally popular throughout the world and to date more than 3,500,000 models have been sold. The Antique is a variant of the Standard model with an engraved receiver, saddle ring and brass loader

Winchester 9422

Country	United States
Type	lever-action repeating carbine
Designation	Winchester 9422
Calibre	.22 Short, .22 Long, .22 LR and .22 Magnum
Weight	2.400kg
Length	barrel: 61cm
Capacity	21 rounds in .22 Short, 17 in .22 Long and 15 in .22 LR; 11 rounds in Magnum version
Remarks	when Winchester imitates itself, the result is an excellent .22 calibre repeating carbine. The receiver is greatly inspired by that on the 1894 model. Note that the first Winchester to chamber the .22 round was the 1873 model

Unique X 51 B

Country	France
Type	autoloader rifle
Designation	Manufacture d'Armes des Pyrénées Françaises, Unique, X 51 and X 51 B
Calibre	.22 LR
Weight	X 51: 2.400–2.600kg; X 51 B: 2.700kg
Barrel	X 51: 50 or 60cm; X 51 B: 60cm
Length	X 51: 93 or 103cm; X 51 B: 103cm
Capacity	5 or 10 rounds
Remarks	with these two models the Manufacture d'Armes des Pyrénées Françaises offers two excellent automatic repeating carbines; the only difference between them is the sighting instrumentation and the shape of the stock. They can be fitted with telescopic sights and a bayonet-mounted silencer

Beretta Olympia

Country	Italy
Type	autoloader rifle
Designation	Beretta Olympia
Calibre	.22 LR
Weight	3.700kg
Length	overall 109cm; barrel 60cm
Capacity	one of 5 rounds, the other of 10 rounds
Remarks	although listed in Italy for target shooting, this arm does not lend itself to international competitions. But it is a fine rifle for sporting use, especially when fitted with the Beretta diopter. Note that the trigger can be adjusted by a screw close to it

F.N. Browning B2

Country	Belgium
Type	autoloader rifle
Designation	Fabrique Nationale de Herstal, F.N. Browning A2 and B2
Calibre	.22 Short and .22 LR
Weight	A2 .22 Short: 2.270kg; A2 .22 LR: 2.350kg; B2 .22 short: 2.200kg; B2 .22 Long Rifle: 2.280kg
Length	A2 .22 Short: 94cm; A2 .22 LR: 100cm; B2 .22 Short: 94cm; B2 .22 LR: 100cm barrel, in same order: 49, 56, 48 and 56cm
Capacity	11 rounds in .22 LR and 15 in .22 Short
Remarks	the two models differ only in their sighting instruments and the type of woods used: the A2 has a beechwood hand shield and stock, and graded backsight; the B2 is fitted with a graduated hinged backsight and scored frontsight. Walnut is used

SIG AMT sporting carbine

Country	Switzerland
Type	autoloader rifle
Designation	Société Industrielle Suisse SIG AMT
Calibre	.308 Winchester (7.62 × 51mm NATO)
Weight	with hand shield: 4.330kg; with biped: 4.520kg
Length	overall: 99cm; barrel: 48cm
Capacity	5, 10 or 20 rounds
Remarks	the SIG AMT is no more or less than the civilian version of the SIG SG 510 assault rifle, on which the automatic selector position has been eliminated

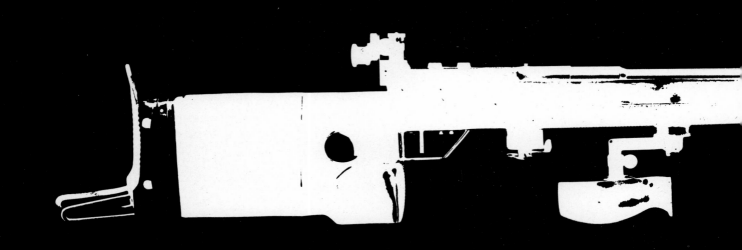

**6
competition
weapons**

The Smith and Wesson 41 automatic target pistol, with 5.5in. (14cm) barrel.

Ruger Mark I Target .22 LR calibre automatic pistol with 17.5cm barrel.

The Hi-Standard 107 automatic pistol which won the 1952 Olympic Games at Helsinki.

Target shooting

Since the day the firearm was born owners have felt the desire to compete with, and pit their wits against, one another, just as had earlier been the case with swordsmen (using blunted weapons) and weapons used to project missiles. The switch from the utilitarian gesture to the sporting one has recurred right down the ages and right across the globe. But these encounters did not preclude a spirit of practicality, and at the same time provided excellent training in the then extremely complicated handling of all these new weapons.

It was not until the end of the nineteenth century that the organization of these matches went beyond local regions and hit the international scene with the organization of the first world championships. It had been necessary to await a period in time when transportation means could bring participants from various countries together, and also when technical knowledge permitted the manufacture of firearms which complied with the same standards. In order to organize such an encounter it was first of all necessary to decide under what conditions it would take place and establish a minimum number of characteristics common to the guns used. Thus it was that the first skeet championship was arranged by Remington at Lordships in Connecticut, USA, in 1880.

Target shooting as we know it today consists in using guns, the nature of which is laid down by a standard and in conditions which are laid down by a ruling. The establishment of these rulings and this standard falls to the international committee of the International Shooting Union. This embraces the various national federations, which are themselves comprised of local organizations, and which set up ranges where their members can come and fire smooth-bore sporting guns or rifled guns.

Thus the Fédération Française de Tir consists of two sections, having in the not too distant past known a period when there was one federation for each shooting discipline. Another federation embraces pigeon shooters who, because they are not allowed to shoot live pigeons (since the law has only permitted this under certain given conditions), now use clay plates called 'ZZs', which have a zigzag trajectory.

Target handgun shooting

For competitions and matches in the various disciplines handguns have characteristics governed by the specifications laid down by the International Shooting Union: barrel length (150mm), weight (less than 1.200kg), length of sighting line, weight of the trigger (the force applied to it for firing), the type of butt, general dimensions, for the standard pistol. Pistol shooting is essentially divided into small calibre (.22 LR) and big bore (over 9mm), and has undergone certain modifications introduced by the ISU in recent years.

The present-day disciplines can be divided in the following way: the standard pistol; Olympic rapid fire; centre-fire competition; free pistol at 50 metres.

Standard pistols

For this 'standard pistol' discipline in .22 calibre the shooting consists of a series of twenty shots precision fire and, at the same target, two series of five shots fired in ten and twenty seconds at 25 metres. Rapid fire involves the use of automatic pistols in this category, and this attracts the greatest number of entrants. The most widely used pistols are manufactured in countries with highly developed arms industries.

The Smith and Wesson .22 Automatic Model 41, together with the Colt Woodsman Sport, Woodsman Target and Match Target, make up the American range along with the Ruger Mark I Target, the Hi-Standard Supermatic and so on. European arms production, which is far more limited than American production in terms of arms for self-defence, is on the contrary well-placed as far as target guns are concerned, and in terms of manufacturing quality of guns used in international competitive shooting surpasses the quality of similar American production.

Under Walther licence, Manurhin offers its .22 LR calibre Sport and Sport-C models with two interchangeable barrel lengths of 20.6cm and 15.5cm. The double action mechanism is borrowed from the Walther PP pistol. The Sport C has the same features as the Sport, but the mechanism is single action and trigger-pull is set at 1.250kg. This gun, which is technically out of date for top level competition use, is more suited for sporting shots than for competitive marksmen.

Also French, the Unique .22 LR calibre D.4 and .22 Short E.4 are excellent guns for sporting shooting, whereas the DES-69 model, with its adjustable butt, micrometric sight and high performance, is a good match for the very best guns in the field.

Hämmerli, in Switzerland, with its three models including the 208, Walther in Germany with its GSP, Browning-FN in Belgium with its three Competition and Concourse models, Beretta in Italy with its 76 model, stand up well against the Russians, whose Margoline MCM is well known.

All these guns fire .22 (5.5mm) calibre rim-fire ammunition and are extremely accurate. They are equipped with sighting instruments which are adjustable for lateral allowances and height, the recoil is very slight and their trigger-pull (the pressure applied to the trigger to release the firing pin) is low, and within the limits laid down by the regulations of sporting bodies which govern pistol shooting. As a general rule this pull (or pressure) is between 100 and 400g for Olympic rapid fire pistol shooting, and between 1000 and 1500g for so-called 'Standard' pistols.

Olympic rapid fire

Automatic pistols are likewise used for Olympic rapid fire; here, at 25 metres, five shots must be fired at five figure targets in four, six and eight seconds successively.

Shortly before the 1936 Berlin Olympic Games a large number of guns of dissimilar quality were manufactured in Germany by Walther, who equipped the German team with the Olympia automatic pistol. This gun walked off with the first five places in its category at the 1936 Olympics. World War II put an end to its career and the Olympia had to make way for military weapons on the production lines at Zella Mehlis. For a gun to be only slightly off target and jump as little as possible when fired, it is generally fitted with a deflector or muzzle brake, and

The Unique DES-69 automatic target pistol.

The Walther Manurhin Sport automatic pistol for sporting use.

The Unique D.4 automatic pistol, for training.

The Hämmerli 208 automatic pistol, left-hand view, and exploded view showing component parts of the 207 Hämmerli rapid-fire pistol.

The Walther Olympia .22 LR calibre automatic pistol.

The Beretta 76 automatic pistol.

The Hämmerli 230 rapid-fire automatic pistol.

The Margoline Vostok MU automatic pistol, .22 LR calibre.

adjustable counterweights which can be set as required; it is in this light that the .22 Short calibre is used, but it is at once a more delicate task to obtain a perfect performance with an automatic pistol using this much less powerful ammunition. Many manufacturers seem to have achieved success in this respect, however.

In the USSR the blind gunsmith Margoline devised and built the Margoline MCU in 1948. Mass production of this gun started in 1951. It is now outclassed by numerous other guns, but is still a worthy entrant in local matches.

The Swiss firm Hämmerli, with its rapid fire pistols, has taken home many a trophy in international competitions:

1954 World Championships at Caracas
1955 Pan-American Games in Mexico
1956 Olympic Games at Melbourne
1958 Asian Games at Tokyo
1961 International Shooting Week at Turin
1962 Central American Games at Kingston, Jamaica
1964 Olympic Games at Tokyo
1965 European Championships at Bucharest
1966 World Championships at Wiesbaden
1967 Asian Championships at Tokyo
1968 Olympic Games in Mexico
1969 European Championships at Pilsen
1970 World Championships at Phoenix, Arizona (USA)

It was inconceivable that these technically perfect pistols might be improved. But very recently everyone was forced to eat their words by the expert from Lenzburg with his new 230 model which will, as of now, take over from the 210 model. It goes without saying that a few teething troubles, as with any new gun, have meant that it has not gone straight to the top of its class, but we can wager that before long its name will be being broadcast in competition results. Since 1957 the Hungarians have been using the Lampagyar V-57-44. And for some time the Italians have had the new Beretta automatic pistol with the trigger set to 200g and drilled gas-ports. In the United States the Hi-Standard company has been marketing its Olympic I.S.U. model.

But the most salient fact to emerge in recent years, as far as competition guns are concerned, is the return of Walther; with their O.S.P. model it looks very much as if they are keen to resume the lead in a sector of production where they excelled before the last war.

For all this, the advanced technology of competition guns is more or less irrelevant, as one might guess, in the hands of the novice. It is only in the hands of our present-day champions that staggering scores are scored, and first place can be decided literally by just one point, as the results of the Olympic Games in Munich in 1972 will testify:

Rapid fire honours list for pistol

Medal	Name	Nationality	Points
Gold	Joseph Zapedzki	Poland	595*
Silver	Ladislav Falta	Czechoslovakia	594
Bronze	Victor Torshin	USSR	593

*New Olympic record

The Italian, Giovanni Liveranzi, 1970 world champion and holder of the world record with 598 points, could manage no more than an admirable sixth place with 591 points. The first British entrant, J. Cooke, took nineteenth place with 585 points, and the first Frenchman, J. Haumann,

was classed twenty-eighth with 582 points.

In the Women's events France has a real champion in the person of Madame Gisèle Lecourtier, whose record reads as follows:

1966 bronze medal in the French championships
1967 silver medal in the French championships
1968 gold medal in the French championships
1969 silver medal in the European championships and gold medal in the French championships
1970 gold medal in the French championships

She has become the all-round French record-holder with:
Pistol 10 metres: 376/400 points
Standard pistol: 546/600 points
Centre-fire competition: 577/600 points

The centre-fire competition

The large calibre centre-fire competition, which consists of precision firing at 25 metres followed by rapid fire at moving figure targets which disappear every ten seconds, can be entered with both revolvers and pistols. The guns used are for the most part derived from self-defence models which are more refined, better finished, fitted with micrometrically adjustable sights, and quite frequently made with a .22 calibre, because the centre-fire event is still fought over in this calibre in some organizations. This applies to Smith and Wesson's K-22, K32, and K-38 Master Piece, and Colt's .38 and .22 calibre Officers Model Match and .357 Magnum Police Python, with its easily identifiable ventilated rib. Some automatic pistols are particularly sought after by marksmen: from Smith and Wesson: the model 41 in .22 LR or .22 Short calibres, and the .38 mid range or wad cutter 52/.38 Master Automatic; from Colt: the Gold Cup National Match and Gold Cup National Match Mk IV with a .45 ACP or .38 mid range or wad cutter calibre. These 5-round guns are direct derivatives of the Colt Government Model of 1911 A1, a standard issue for the US army; from Hi-Standard: the Victor with a .22 LR calibre, available with two barrel lengths: 4.5 and 5.5in. (11.5cm and 14cm) with discharge adjustable between 910g and 1020g.

Faced with the predominance of these American models on their own markets, European manufacturers have been trying hard to match them. But despite their efforts, the American quality as far as revolvers are concerned has not been equalled by Brno, of Czechoslovakia, with its ZKR 590 revolver, the German firms Arminius, with its .38 calibre HW 38 and .22 calibre HW 9, and Rohm with its .22 calibre Target model, Korth and Saver with their SR 3 model, and the Spanish firm, Gabilondo, with its .22 calibre Llama XXIX with ventilated rib and .38 calibre Llama XXIII with muzzle brake.

The same does not apply to large calibre automatic match pistols. In this category Beretta, in Italy, offers a converted version of its 952 Standard model with a 15cm barrel chambered for 9mm Parabellum, referred to as the 952 Special.

With the SIG P-210-6 Sport, a long-barrelled variant in 7.65mm or 9mm Parabellum calibre and micrometric sights, the Swiss have produced a high performance gun for large calibre competition.

In France the military shooting teams usually use the MAB P.15 M1 automatic pistol, directly derived from the 15-round MAB P.15 pistol.

The V–57–44 .22 Short calibre rapid-fire pistol.

The FN-Browning Concours 150 .22 LR calibre automatic pistol. With a 15cm barrel this pistol complies with the ISU rulings and is an ideal gun for the newcomer to competition shooting.

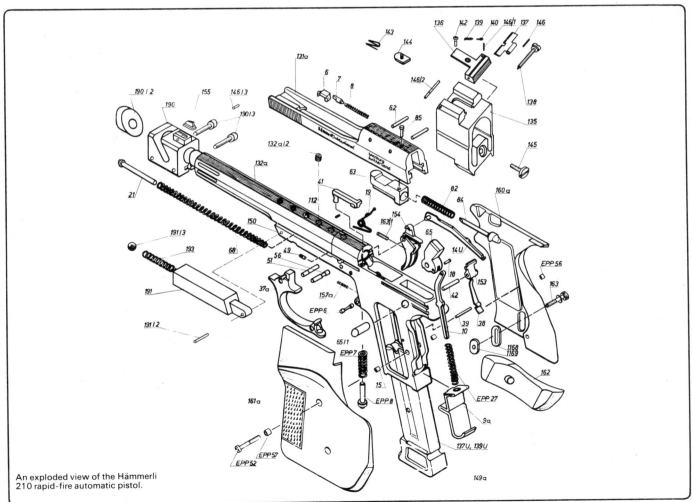

An exploded view of the Hämmerli 210 rapid-fire automatic pistol.

Smith and Wesson K-32
Masterpiece .32 calibre target
revolver.

The Hi-Standard Olympic ISU .22
Short calibre automatic pistol,
complying with ISU rapid-fire
regulations.

The Colt New Police Python
revolver with 6in. and 4in. barrel.

The Rumanian champion,
Atanasiu, clearly demonstrates the
modern firing position.

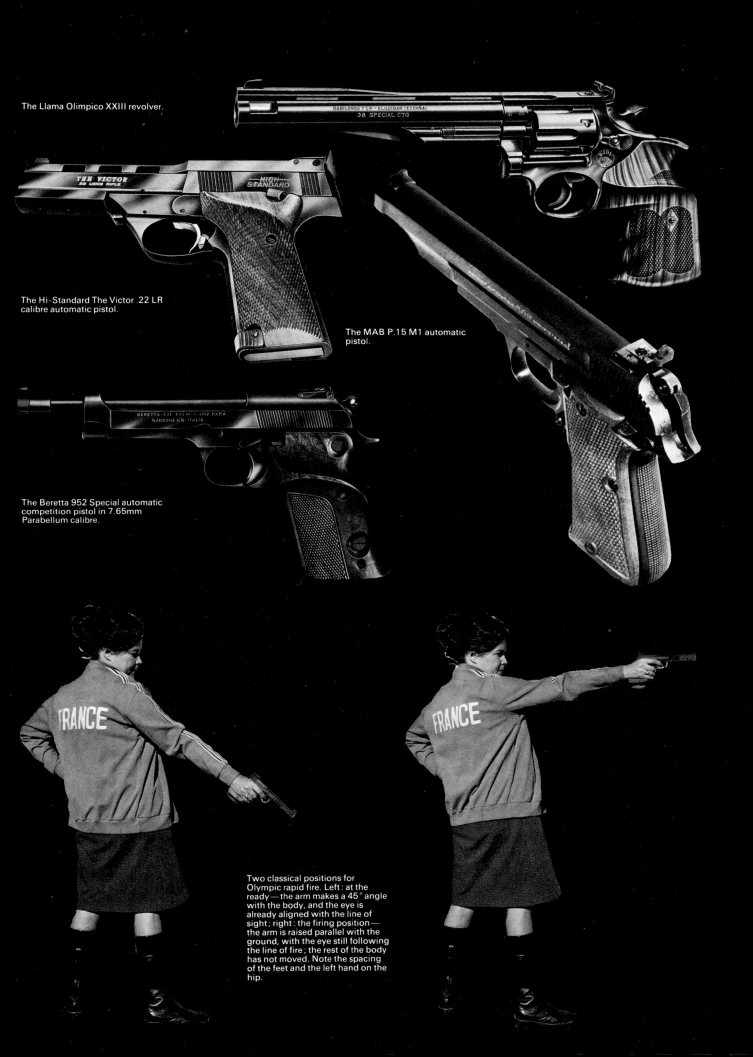

The Llama Olimpico XXIII revolver.

The Hi-Standard The Victor .22 LR calibre automatic pistol.

The MAB P.15 M1 automatic pistol.

The Beretta 952 Special automatic competition pistol in 7.65mm Parabellum calibre.

Two classical positions for Olympic rapid fire. Left: at the ready—the arm makes a 45° angle with the body, and the eye is already aligned with the line of sight; right: the firing position— the arm is raised parallel with the ground, with the eye still following the line of fire; the rest of the body has not moved. Note the spacing of the feet and the left hand on the hip.

The Toz 35 single-shot free pistol.

The SIG P–210–5 Sport automatic pistol.

The new Hämmerli 150 free pistol, replacing the 107 model.

The Hämmerli one-round 120 single-shot .22 LR calibre sporting pistol.

Falta, the Czech champion, holding his Hämmerli 208 pistol.

Free pistol at 50 metres

Europeans have come into their own in a less well-known category, but one where, as for the carbine, we find the best Target pistol performances: the free pistol at 50 metres in .22 LR calibre. For this event the Americans import European pistols.

In the Vostok series, the TOZ-35 Soviet pistol has been highly developed by the famous Toula gunsmiths in close cooperation with the engineer Efime Haidurov, Russian champion, and several times world and European champion. This gun enabled the Soviet shooting team to take first prize in team placing at the world championships at Wiesbaden, where V. Stolypine was placed first with 556/600 points. A special feature of this gun is the low barrel position over the hand, along with an extremely short trigger-pull mounted on the trigger guard, a trigger with a multilateral adjustable accelerator controlling the position and axis, and a centre of gravity at the trigger.

The Hämmerli 107 and 150 also feature an orthopaedic grip and possible trigger-pull adjustment. The 'gunsmith by appointment to world champions', as the famous Swiss firm is rightly called, is tending to abandon production of its old 107 model in favour of the new 150 pistol, which is more modern in both shape and design, and has a conspicuously futuristic line which makes it extremely comfortable to hold and will, without doubt, produce even better scores as a result. Both the Hämmerli models have the Martini action which has been dropped for rifles, but is retained here because it is laterally compact. Special mention should be made of the French Grolleau pistol which, with an electric firing system, attempted to offer an original solution to the tricky problem posed by this pistol's trigger mechanism.

All these highly specialized guns make it possible to chalk up remarkable scores at the international competition level. The results obtained in this event at the 1972 Olympic Games in Munich give ample evidence of this.

Free Pistol at 50 metres

Medal	Name	Nationality	Points
Gold	Ragnar Skanaker	Sweden	567*
Silver	Dan Iuga	Rumania	562
Bronze	Rudolf Bollinger	Austria	560

*New Olympic Record

In the United States, in particular, there are certain shooting events and disciplines which are not recognized by the International Shooting Union (ISU), but which are nonetheless engaged in at the national level. In this instance typically American models of double or single action revolvers by Ruger, Iver Johnson, and Harrington and Richardson are used, or the Remington .221 calibre Fireball XP 100 single shot pistol with the spiral breech bolt, or again the Thompson Center Contender which offers a choice of twenty-seven interchangeable barrels with different calibres, all of which can be mounted on the same frame. Hämmerli for its part has just brought out its 120 single-shot model with a .22 LR calibre. This gun has been designed more as a training model for match shooting than as an actual match model. But it does offer some remarkable qualities for a relatively modest price. In terms of accessories it can be fitted with a telescopic sight and a tubular metal stock.

Competition shotgun shoting

The committee of the F.F.T. (Fédération Française de Tir — French Shooting Federation) issues the various rulings governing smooth-bore shooting, use of shot, clay-pigeon shooting using 'plates', 'clay-birds' or 'clay pigeons' which are at once tough and brittle, and in so doing follows two methods: trap and skeet shooting. The regulation dimensions of the layout reflect the Anglo-Saxon origins of this sport which has been enjoyed in the United States for more than seventy years, although in France it was almost an unknown quantity in those days.

a) *The 'ball trap'*, which is sometimes simplified to just 'trap', consists of a device placed at ground-level which contains several smaller devices which project the disks in such a way that at a distance of 9.10 metres from their point of departure their trajectory follows a path at a height of between 1.83m and 3.66m. The distance reached by the disk or pigeon projected must not exceed 80 metres or drop below 50 metres. Five firing positions are set up radially from where the disks or pigeons are launched. At 14.56 metres from the point of launching they must be 2.73 metres apart at the centre. They are 10 metres long, and divided into metres. With each object launched the competitors move from one firing position to the next and, when instructed, take aim at the disks as they are launched at an angle which covers 90°.

b) *The skeet* consists of firing at disks launched from two huts, one high (3.05 metres) and the other low (1.07 metres), standing 38.58 metres from one another. The two trajectories coincide at a height of 4.57 metres. A semicircle is marked out, its diameter being the straight line joining the two huts, and divided into seven firing positions placed 8.13 metres apart, with an eighth position in the middle, between the two huts. The disks are launched at a rate of between 0 and 3 seconds and the competitor must hit 25, in twos, from each firing position successively. In this way the trajectories are varied and conditions are much more akin to hunting conditions. The rules specify the use of smooth-bore 2-round double-barrelled sporting guns, or pump-action or automatic repeating guns with a calibre not in excess of 12 gauge, firing shot shells containing not more than 36g of shot for the trap and 32g for the skeet, and not exceeding No 8 in the international series, that is, with a diameter of 2.25mm. Michel Carrega who returned to France with the silver medal at the Munich Games, says of the ball trap:

'At the present time the ball trap is a sport which is on the up and up because game is becoming rarer and rarer due to the ever-increasing number of hunters, roads and motorways. Nowadays, in fact, game has little hope of escaping from the trappings of modern society. But there's plenty of clay about. The ball trap gives any individual a sort of physical and mental equilibrium because he has to obtain perfect control of all his movements.

'What is more, handling a gun in a competition or when training gives a sense of responsibility and teaches people to be extremely thoughtful, and these qualities are visibly echoed in the person's daily life. A good shot always drives his car very well, and rarely turns irritable. Today,

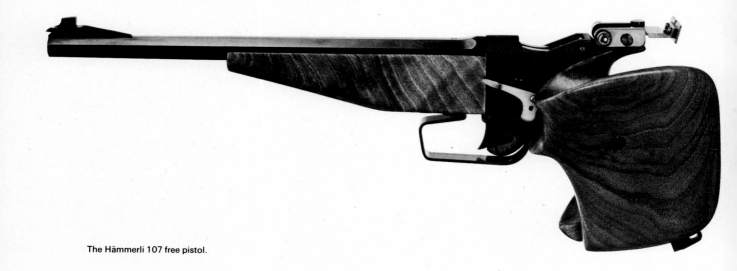

The Hämmerli 107 free pistol.

1105a
1106
1107
41X8
1104a

1103c

M2 X4
S1.5X6

1202
1212
1207
1211a
1214
B.S. 32X7
1117
1154/1

1209
1210
1206
1202
1203/4/5
1208
1213
1208
1201
1118
1119
1115
1120
1122
1121
M26X4
1156

42X25 aL

M4X5   1215

1171
M3X10
1150
1151
1152
1153
1131
1130
M3X6
1112
M2X5
1123a
1133
1134
1135
1136
M4X25
1148
1142
1146
1163

1110

EPP.56
1233
M3X10

M5X30

1101

1147
1120

1132
1156

1129
1125
1138
1138
M2
1127

1155   41x6

1137

1234

42X9
1161
1162a
1160a

1231
1167a
M4X14

1141

1114a
1116a
M3X6
1115
1178
1157
1159
1158
43X8

452X10

1232
1230
1168
1169

102062

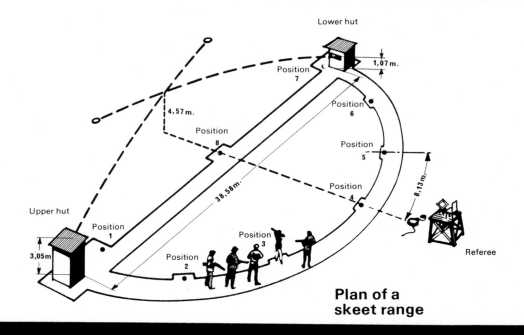

Lower hut

Position
7

1,07 m.

Position
6

4,57 m.

Position
8

Position
5

8,13 m.

38,58m.

Position
4

Upper hut

Position
1

Position
3

3,05m

Position
2

Referee

**Plan of a
skeet range**

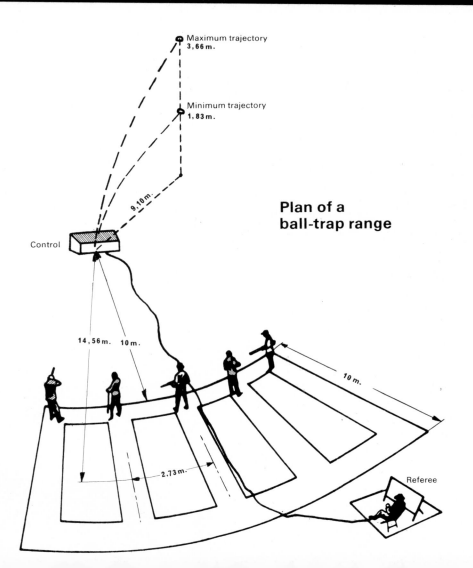

Maximum trajectory
3,66 m.

Minimum trajectory
1,83 m.

9,10 m.

**Plan of a
ball-trap range**

Control

14,56 m.   10 m.

10 m.

2,73 m.

Referee

with life being so hectic, I quite sincerely believe that shooting enables us to get to know ourselves better and possibly helps us to get rid of some of the shortcomings which are common to all of us.'

Competition shotguns

For the majority of gun-owners and competitors these guns were for a long time the same ones they used when hunting. As far back as 1874 Remington had brought out a trap gun with double side-by-side barrels and, among an admittedly very small circle of people, live pigeon shooting was carried on with particularly carefully made guns. Since then, the sport has spread like wildfire and become commonplace, encouraging manufacturers to bring out guns designed especially for this purpose, which are consequently considered to be competition guns, even if other uses are not altogether unthinkable for them.

Mechanically speaking they are hallmarked by a low rate of wear and tear; this is their primary quality because their task is to fire heavily charged ammunition at a rate and in quantities rarely experienced when hunting. They are basically similar to sporting guns, but differ in certain essential features: the skeet gun is kept light, but the trap gun is usually fairly heavy, weighing between 3 and 3.500kg. Fitted with straighter and less dropping stocks, they often have a 'Monte Carlo', a pistol grip and a honeycombed recoil-reducing butt plate. The barrels are surmounted by a wide ventilated rib, which frequently has an intermediate foresight.

The quest for optimum ballistic performance has led, where the trap is concerned, to fitting them with 76cm barrels, with full choke on both barrels. The skeet, on the other hand, requires a more manageable gun, quick to bring to the shoulder and aim, and because the disks are launched nearer, the barrels are shorter, between 65 and 66cm, with either 'improved' or 'full' choke.

The guns most frequently are over-unders. This does not mean that side-by-side models are completely overlooked, however, and although automatics are very little used, the Americans have always had a weak spot for slide-action repeating guns. This sport has been carried on for a very long time in the United States, and the Americans obviously have a very wide range of competition guns at their disposal.

With several variants, Remington offers its 1100 model automatic rifle with long or short barrels, for trap or skeet, a ventilated rib, Monte Carlo stock, and on request it can be fitted with a Cutts compensator, which partly suppresses the kick. Its 870 Wingmaster slide-action repeating model has the same features and exists in a left-handed version.

Winchester publishes a very full catalogue which includes many over-under models, including the Super Grade Trap with ejectors, a single trigger operated by inertia, a wide ventilated rib, and a weight of 3.700kg. As far as the 101 model is concerned, the Special Trap and the Special Skeet only differ in barrel length, and both are fitted with an intermediate foresight. The range is completed with the automatic 1400 Mark II Skeet and Mark II Trap, with a special Monte Carlo stock and a very efficient trigger. A rare thing for an automatic gun is that, upon special order, there is an ejection window on the left, designed for the left-handed. Lastly, of course, Winchester offers a pump-action model, the 1200 with trap or

skeet barrels and an improved trigger. The American range does not stop here however. It is very well-stocked and includes, among others, Savage, Stevens and Mossberg. Special mention should be made of the Ithaca range; as well as its own production of hunting and competition guns, it offers in collaboration with the great Italian expert its Ithaca-Perazzi Combination Trap or Skeet. In addition, under its own trade name and in Japan it manufactures the Ithaca-SKB.

The Japanese have likewise become known in the field by their collaboration with BSA in Great Britain, offering an over-under model (the 600 Trap weighing 3.600kg, with a 76cm barrel, full choke on both barrels), and the 600 Skeet (with shorter and lighter barrels). Both are fitted with a wide ventilated rib, and share in common an original and unique trigger-pull being selectable by means of a push button on the trigger. Miroku, the Japanese manufacturer, offers its sporting model in two competition versions, trap or skeet, the two types – 800 and 800 W – differing with regard to the ventilated rib width.

European production has not lagged behind, and for several years now the various gunsmiths have been marketing models which are almost invariably derived from existing sporting models. Browning FN of course occupies a dominant position with its over-under model. More than sixty years old, this had all the qualities required to satisfy even the most demanding owner, and is now offered for match shooting as the Browning 105 Special Skeet and Browning 105 Special Trap. It was incidentally with the latter that Michel Carrega carried off his silver medal at the 1972 Olympic Games in Munich, as well as a host of other international prizes.

Increased demand has given rise to many other guns. Without attempting to name them all, let us mention, for example, the Italian Perazzi guns with special competition-designed models, and Beretta with its over-under, side-by-side, slide-action and autoloader models. The famous Gardone manufacturer, who enabled Angelo Scalzone to beat the Olympic trap record (199/200) at Munich, offers the S 58 model with a Bochler Antinit barrel, wide ventilated rib, intermediate foresight, single selective trigger, stock with a Monte Carlo – and the skeet model has a sharply dropping stock. The same types of guns are available with Purdey locks and triple breech bolt locking mechanisms, are referred to as the SO 4 Trap or SO 4 Skeet, and currently represent a fairly rare type of gun.

The single-barrel drop-down model for the trap, which is very common in the United States and virtually unknown in France, has nevertheless been taken up in Europe by the British.

The German firm Merkel and Krieghoff, whose 32 Skeet and Trap models are engraved and carved and represent decorative masterpieces; and the Finnish firm Valmet are not alone, despite the exceptional quality of their products. In the Baikal range the Russians offer two excellent superposed models: the IJ-25(T) Trap and the IJ-25(SK) Skeet. With the Baikal MC 8-03 they offer the choice of a pair of trap barrels and a pair of skeet barrels which can be fitted on the same frame.

In France, with its Falcor model, Manufrance offers a similar solution designed to satisfy the requirements of the person who wants to use one and the same gun for all match events, and for hunting as well, either for financial reasons or because the habit of always using the same gun results in a feeling of considerable confidence in it. Verney-Carron, in association with the great Italian firm Franchi, offers the latter's range of automatic guns on which a whole series of interchangeable barrels can be fitted, some of which are designed for trap or skeet, with or without the standard or ventilated Poly Choke which gives seven settings. Nearly all French manufacturers offer competition guns which are heavier, reinforced versions of sporting guns and have improved selective triggers. All these guns are the result of special gun-foundry methods, and their barrels are selected with a view to obtaining both optimum grouping and the most regular and consistent cone of dispersion possible. This latter condition is absolutely vital if the competitor is to be certain of breaking the disk at the given firing distance. Modern techniques of barrel forging and boring have, here too, come to the aid of owners and competitors by supplying them with guns whose qualities are beyond the wildest dreams of their fathers and grandfathers before them.

The last events as far as competitive shooting and hunting with shotguns is concerned is the 'Rabbit', which consists in shooting at larger, heavier clay disks, which move along an 18-metre belt; and 'sporting clays', where competitors fire at disks which are launched at random in conditions reminiscent of the field.

Target rifle shooting (rifled bore)

Using the rules of the International Shooting Union (ISU), the target shooting section of the Fédération Française de Tir (FFT) controls competition shooting with so-called rifled bore guns. This category embraces more disciplines than those covered by smooth-bore shooting events. Even the method of classing competitors is different. In both the trap and skeet events they are divided into four categories depending on their performances, and given handicaps. These categories do not exist for target shooting, where the only criteria are age and sex: cadets, juniors, seniors, adults (men and women).

There are two major foci: handgun shooting, which we dealt with at the beginning of this chapter, and rifle shooting. This latter is subdivided into several disciplines: .22 LR calibre 60-round English match, prone position at 50 metres; .22 LR calibre 60-round English match, prone, standing and kneeling (20 rounds in each position) at 50 metres; big bore at 300 metres.

In each discipline the firing conditions are specified by rules and regulations applying to the target, the gun and the ammunition, as well as the firing time. For the .22 LR calibre carbine at 50 metres, there are two categories: standard carbine and free carbine. The features of these guns are such that the person able to afford a more elaborate model has an advantage; standardization of these features in the standard gun is aimed, as far as is possible, at sorting out the competitors on the basis of their worth alone, and at making the event open to the greatest possible number of entrants. The so-called 'free' event, on the other hand, where the specifications are less rigid – apart from those governing the calibre – permits a

shooting élite to mark up maximum performances. Adhering to the ISU standards, the .22 LR standard carbine must have a stock with a maximum width of 6cm, a distance of 8cm maximum between the axis of the barrel and its lowest part in front of the trigger guard, a butt plate which cannot be adjusted by more than 3cm; its foresight must not have a tunnel more than 5cm in length; it must not have two triggers, or sights incorporating optical lenses, and must not weigh more than 5kg, and so on and so forth. The specifications are thus very precise.

Rifles

The 'standard' rifle

This is the most sought-after gun fired from the shoulder, and offers the largest number of models. It is obviously manufactured mainly in countries where there have always been large shooting fraternities and where shooting is more than an abstract idea. The field is dominated by the United States, Switzerland, Germany and the USSR. In France, nonetheless, Bergeron manufactures a standard gun in three variants, with a Mauser-type bolt with a bilateral locking mechanism and adjustable percussion: one of these variants is fitted with a trigger of the Hämmerli type. The addition of a Hämmerli palm-rest and rail and a hooked butt plate can change it into a 'free' gun. Another French manufacturer, Unique (Manufacture d'Armes des Pyrénées Françaises) markets a competition model T.66 Match complying with the ISU norms, with adjustable trigger-pull, adjustable butt plate, and heavy barrel. This is one of the rare French guns which is also designed for left-handed users, with a cocking lever on the left.

Similar guns are also made by Sako in Finland with its P.54 model, Husqvarna in Sweden, Valmet in Finland with its Lion Standard ISU, and BSA in England. There are also the Swedish firms Carl Gustaf, and Schultz and Larsen.

On the borderline as far as competition guns are concerned, the T-Bolt model by Browning FN, a light training carbine, with its cross-pin bolt, is one of the few guns not to have a spiral breech bolt, a type which has superseded the Martini system in more or less every corner of the industry. It is a pity that this excellent carbine has sights of only mediocre quality.

Then we come to the great experts in the field with, in Switzerland, Hämmerli, whose manufacturing quality and jealous care paid to the finish and adjustment are universally respected, and which offers the additional service of making special models to order. Other major European masters of the art are the Russians, whose carbines have a following throughout the world with the TOZ-8-M and TOZ-12 light training models and the ISU standard CM-2 and Ural models. With the latter, Russian champions took second place at the 1969 world championships in Wiesbaden, the same year that the gun came on the market.

As usual, of course, the Americans have access to a large range of these guns. Among other firms, Remington offers its 40 XB Rangemaster with Mauser action, non-slip butt plate, wide trigger, Redfield Olympic sights and aiming aperture, and its 540 Match, equipped with a very precise trigger adjustable for extremely rapid fire, plus a stock which is adjustable lengthwise. Winchester offers a remarkable 52 model Target in two variants, one with a standard barrel, the other with a heavy barrel. The gun is

A training session at the Aix-en-Provence Ball-trap Club, with Michel Carrega in the foreground.

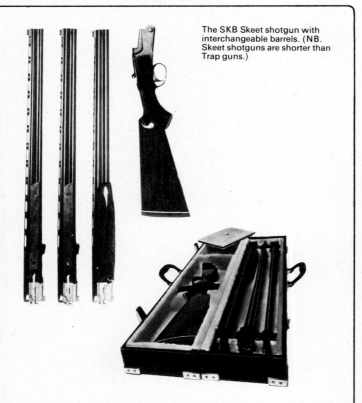

The SKB Skeet shotgun with interchangeable barrels. (NB. Skeet shotguns are shorter than Trap guns.)

Two champions: Michel Carrega and his FN-Browning Special Trap over-under shotgun.

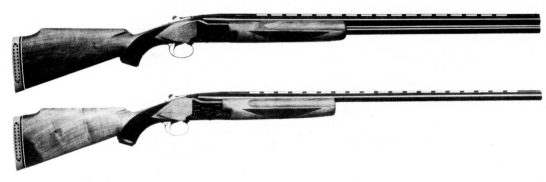

Winchester 101 shotguns. Above: the over-under Trap type with Monte Carlo stock. Below: the single-barrel Trap version with Monte Carlo stock.

Winchester 1400 shotguns. Above: the Trap UT, with Monte Carlo stock, only made in 12 gauge. Below: Skeet model with normal stock, available in 12 and 20 gauge.

The Remington 870 Wingmaster pump-action model.

Winchester pump-action 1200 guns. Above: Trap model with Monte Carlo stock, only available in 12 gauge. Below: Skeet model with normal stock, available in 12 and 20 gauge.

A signed Purdey-London single-barrel trap gun.

FN Belge Browning 105 over-under shotguns. Above: the Special Skeet; below: the Special Trap.

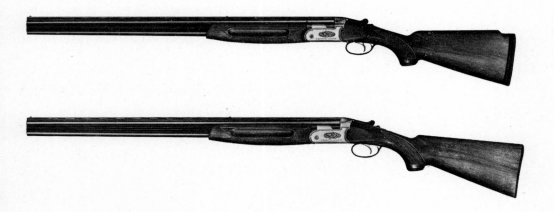

Beretta S 58 over-under shotguns. Above: Trap model with Monte Carlo stock; below: Skeet model with normal stock.

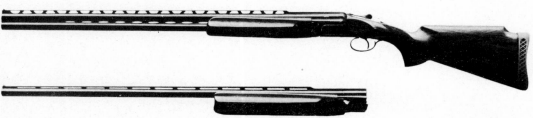

The Perazzi shotgun with interchangeable barrels.

Ithaca de luxe single-barrel Trap guns. Above: 4E model; below: 5E model.

Miroku 800 W over-under shotgun with 76cm barrels for trap.

The Beretta SO 4 Trap over-under shotgun.

Over-under Ithaca shotguns. From top to bottom: Competition 1 Trap, Competition 1 Skeet, and MX-8 Trap.

The Browning FN T-Bolt .22 LR carbine.

The Soviet Standard Ural .22 LR calibre competition carbine.

The Winchester 52 D Target .22 LR calibre competition carbine.

The Walther ISU Special .22 LR calibre carbine.

Walther KK carbines (KleinKaliber: small calibre). In the range offered by Carl Walther we have shown three carbines. From top to bottom: the KK ISU for lying position, the KK ISU, moving target model, and the KK Match.

The Winchester 70 Target rifle for
300-metre events.

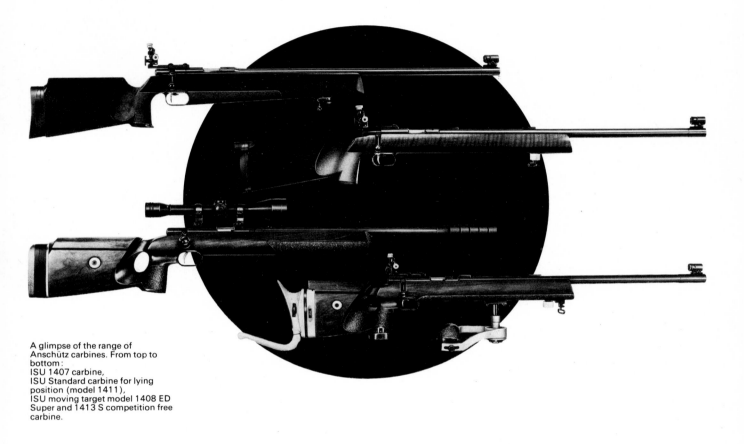

A glimpse of the range of
Anschütz carbines. From top to
bottom:
ISU 1407 carbine,
ISU Standard carbine for lying
position (model 1411),
ISU moving target model 1408 ED
Super and 1413 S competition free
carbine.

The Hämmerli 506 .22 LR calibre
'free' carbine.

The Taifoun 'free' carbine, made in
the USSR.

supplied without sighting instruments, and can, at will, fit a telescopic sight or a dioptre, depending on the discipline involved. Mossberg and Savage complete the American list. The latter also markets Anschütz German carbines in the United States.

For the Germans are in fact top of the league in this field. Carl Walther has achieved very impressive results with the ISU Spezial and ISU Standard weighing 5.5kg, and supplied, on request, either with the so-called 'Olympia' classic stock or with a modern square stock, and a trigger which can be instantly adjusted between 150–500g.

Anschütz carbines won five out of six medals, and broke all Olympic records at Munich in 1972: Ho Jun Li, of North Korea, scored an incredible 599/600 (a new world record) in the English 60-round match in the prone position at 50 metres, and won the gold medal; the American John Writer won the gold medal in the 3-position English match at 50 metres with a score of 1166 points (a new world record). Such was the honours list at the 1972 Munich Olympics. Is there any further need to sing the praises of this famous German firm? The 1402 and 1403 models, weighing 2.600 and 3.500kg respectively, are more specifically designed for beginners, cadets and juniors. The 1407 ISU Standard is equipped with a bolt with a double locking mechanism by means of lugs of the Match 54 type, has a very sound trigger-pull (which is both very short and very rapid), and also comes in left-handed models. Anschütz fits it out with a whole range of accessories which make it the most out-and-out complete competition gun. In the prone position this gun has a special 1411 S stock.

The 'free' carbine

As its name indicates, the 'free' carbine is not bound by any specifications, except for calibre, and the fact that it must not have sights incorporating optical lenses. There is no weight limit; it can have an all-round adjustable butt plate, an orthopaedic stock, and palm-rest, and so on. This type of gun certainly features the most handsome models in the field of precision firing offered by the present-day arms business. There are .22 LR calibre carbines in which the actual dispersion at 50 metres does not exceed the diameter of the bullet itself. They may sometimes look a little grotesque to the layman, but then they require tremendous mastery of the very elaborate technique of precision firing.

The 1413 Anschütz, weighing 7kg, with a Match 54 type bolt known as the Super Match, is its most highly developed model. In this category, which is more restricted than the preceding one, it goes side by side with Walther's KKM Match, Remington's free carbine (a model derived from the 40 XB with trigger set to 56g), and the Valmet Free Lion Match. In the same category we also find Hämmerli, with its 506 model, and Winchester with its 52 International Match Rifle with stock made of laminated wood and designed to be fitted with a Kenyon or ISU Kenyon double set trigger, as well as the Russians, whose Taifoun carbine enabled their champions to carry off the silver medal, for team performance, at the Wiesbaden world championships in the 3-position 50 and 300 metre events. The Taifoun is available in three calibres: the Taifoun 1 in 7.62mm Soviet calibre; the Taifoun 2 in 6.5mm calibre; the Taifoun 3 in .22 LR calibre.

A model with a toggle-type trigger mechanism permits adjustment between 20 and 1500g. The normal trigger model can be adjusted for a pull of between 300 and 1500g. The maximum weight of the gun is roughly 8kg.

There is another event, for small calibres: the moving target. A dummy running deer or boar offers a moving target across the line of fire which the competitor must hit, using a carbine with a telescopic sight.

The heavy carbine, for 300 metre events

Lastly we come to the 'standard' carbine at 300 metres. Little used in France because of the lack of ranges suited to this event, and because of the cost of large calibre ammunition, it is widely enjoyed in Central Europe and the United States.

The expert hands of Anschütz of course offer the Grunel-Anschütz with a bossed match trigger, in 7.62mm calibre, which also features on the Hämmerli Tanner with spiral-breech bolt manufactured in several calibres (see technical data at end of this chapter), and on the Soviet Taifoun 1, and 2, with 7.62mm Soviet and 6.5mm calibres respectively, while, in the United States, Winchester, among others, offers its 70 Target, 70 Ultra Match and 70 International Match with .308 WCF (7.62mm NATO) and .30-06 Springfield calibres for the first two models, and just .308 WCF calibre for the 70 International Match. These three guns come without any sights and can be fitted at will with a telescopic sight or dioptre.

Some guns are especially designed for mixed competitions, such as the present-day winter all-round event in which, of course, the Soviet Vostok Biathlon carbine, with 6.5mm and 7.62mm calibres, meets the various requirements dictated by climatic conditions: it is light, its mechanism is snow-proof, and it is designed to be moved quickly from the carrying position to the firing position. Sight adjustment and magazine loading have been designed to be carried out as simply as possible by cold and swollen hands.

Competition weapons: technical data

Browning FN International ISU

Country	Belgium
Type	Standard ISU automatic match pistol
Designation	Browning FN, International ISU
Calibre	.22 LR
Weight	1.325kg empty, with counterweight overall, 298mm; barrel, 150mm
Length	
Capacity	10 rounds
Remarks	latest of the line of Browning automatic match pistols, this model has not yet shown its paces in competitions. But we wager it will come high up the list

Smith and Wesson 41 EFS

left: with heavy barrel and line of sight adjustable lengthwise
right: the 41 with 20cm barrel

Country	United States
Type	automatic match pistol
Designation	Smith and Wesson, 41 and variants
Calibre	.22 LR or Short, to order
Weight	41, 1.080 or 1.230kg with muzzle brake; 41HB, 1.250kg; 41 EFS 1.250kg
Length	barrel 5in. (12.7cm) and 7 in. (20cm) with muzzle brake for model 41; 5.5in. (14cm) for model 41 EFS; 5.5in. (14cm) for model 41 HB. Overall 21.5cm and 30.5cm with muzzle brake

for model 41; 23cm for model 41 HB; 23cm for 41 EFS

Capacity	10 rounds
Remarks	Smith and Wesson offers for match use the model 41, available with various options using the same frame and single-action lock. It is also possible to change from one barrel to another by simple replacement, and a conversion kit is also supplied on request for changing from .22 LR to .22 Short, as well as an Olympic counterweight which is adjustable and is fitted on the 7¾in. barrel. Line of sight lengths vary from 19.7cm (model 41) to 24.4cm (41 EFS)

Unique DES 69

Country	France
Type	Standard ISU automatic match pistol
Designation	Manufacture d'Armes des Pyrénées Françaises, Unique DES 69
Calibre	.22 LR
Weight	1.000kg; trigger: 1.000kg for standard match and 1.360kg for ISU centre-fire training in .22 calibre
Length	overall 27cm, barrel 15cm, line of sight 22cm
Capacity	10 rounds
Remarks	having supplied the T.66 Match carbine for match use, the MAPF has scored another success with its competition pistol, which was marketed in 1969. Note that it is available for left-handers as the 521 DES .22 LR

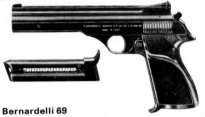

Bernardelli 69

Country	Italy
Type	Standard ISU automatic match pistol
Designation	Bernardelli, 69
Calibre	.22 LR
Weight (ca.)	1.070kg
Length	overall 22.8cm; barrel 15cm; line of sight 17.9cm
Capacity	10 rounds
Remarks	for some years the Gardone firm of Vincenzo Bernardelli has been making its model 69 Standard ISU match model. Relatively low-priced, this is an ideal gun for beginners and training for ISU Standard events, rather than a fully-fledged match pistol

Hämmerli 208
engraved and damascened

Country	Switzerland
Type	Standard ISU automatic match pistol
Designation	Hämmerli standard ISU 208 pistol, known as the International
Calibre	.22 LR
Weight (ca.)	0.915kg
Length	overall 25cm; barrel 15cm; line of sight 29.8cm
Capacity	8 rounds
Remarks	the 208 is one of the best in the Hämmerli range. The 211, mentioned in this chapter, is similar but has a conventional grip with no hand-rest

Walther OSP (left) and GSP (right)

Country	West Germany
Type	'rapid fire' automatic pistol (OSP), and 'precision' pistol (GSP)
Designation	Walther, OSP and GSP
Calibre	GSP: .22 LR; .32 S. and W. Long Wadcutter; OSP: .22 Short
Weight (ca.)	1.270kg; 1.400kg; 1.200kg
Length	all overall 30cm; barrels all 11.5cm; line of sight 22cm, 22cm, 26cm
Capacity	5 rounds for all three versions

Remarks	worthy successors of the pre-war Olympia, these new Walther models are adapted to all Olympic events. Features in common are: detachable lock, clip in front of trigger guard acting as counterweight, barrel low set, reducing effect of slant. Trigger of GSP models adjustable from 1.000 to 1.360kg; that of OSP between 200 and 300g

Beretta 80

Country	Italy
Type	Olympic rapid-fire automatic pistol
Designation	Beretta, 80
Calibre	.22 Short
Weight	1.050kg
Length	overall, 30.5cm; barrel, 17cm; line of sight 21cm
Capacity	6 rounds
Remarks	made recently with meticulous care on a small scale, this pistol, made with the best steel available, has not yet earned the place it merits in competitions

Hämmerli 230

Country Switzerland
Type Olympic rapid-fire automatic match pistol
Designation Hämmerli 230
Calibre .22 Short
Weight (*ca.*) 1.240kg
Length overall 29.5cm; barrel, 20.5cm; line of sight 25.3cm
Capacity 5 rounds. Trigger adjustable between 150–300g
Remarks destined to replace the 'old' 210 Hämmerli, with its brilliant honours list, this new Hämmerli model has benefited from all the usual qualities of this make

Smith and Wesson 52 Master Auto

Country United States
Type 'precision big bore' automatic match pistol
Designation Smith and Wesson, 52 Master Automatic
Calibre .38 Smith and Wesson midrange wadcutter
Weight (*ca.*) 1.160kg
Length overall 22cm; barrel 12.7cm (5in.); line of sight 17.5cm
Remarks derived from the Smith and Wesson 39 with double action, this automatic pistol is a top level competitor for all round large calibre events

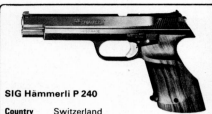

SIG Hämmerli P 240

Country Switzerland
Type Standard ISU big bore centre-fire automatic match pistol
Designation SIG Hämmerli P 240
Calibre .38 Special (Wadcutter)
Weight 1.170kg
Length overall 25.2cm; barrel 15cm; line of sight 21cm
Capacity 5 rounds
Remarks designed and made by the two pastmasters of Swiss precision, this top class automatic pistol can be converted to .22 LR calibre by means of an optional kit, thus making it eligible for Standard ISU events. The clip capacity in this case is 10 rounds and the weight increases to 1.270kg. The trigger can be set between 1.000 and 1.400kg

Colt Python

Country United States
Type single or double action revolver
Designation Colt New Police Python
Calibre .357 Magnum
Weight (*ca.*) 1.100kg (with 4in. barrel)
Length 2.5in. (6.2cm), 4in. (10cm) and 6in. (15.2cm)
Capacity 6 rounds
Remarks one of the latest in the Colt range, the Python has been on the market since 1955 and is undoubtedly the most handsome Colt currently available. Its finish and careful workmanship make it a good match for the Smith and Wesson K 38 Masterpiece

Weight 1.100kg and 1.200kg loaded, depending on barrel length
Length overall: 28cm with 6in. (15cm) barrel, and 34cm with 8in. (21cm) barrel
Remarks There is also the 48 K-22 Masterpiece MRF with .22 Magnum calibre in different lengths: 28cm with 4in. barrel (10cm), 28cm with 6in. barrel (15cm) and 34cm with 8in. (21cm) barrel; weight: 1.030, 1.130 and 1.220kg depending on barrel length; the 16 K-32 Masterpiece with .32 S and W Long and .32 S and W Wadcutter with a total length of 28cm with a 6in. (15cm) barrel weighing 1.000kg loaded; models 14 K-38 and 14 SA K-38 Masterpiece, single action, .38 S and W Special and .38 Special Mid-Range calibres with total lengths of 28cm with 6in. (15cm) barrel, weighing 1.100kg loaded and 34cm with an 8in. (21cm) barrel, weighing 1.200kg loaded. All these guns are made on the same frame with double action lock except for 14 SA K-38 Masterpiece which has a single action lock

Smith and Wesson 17 K-22 Masterpiece

Country United States
Type revolver designed for precision fire
Designation Smith and Wesson 17 K-22 Masterpiece
Calibres .22 Short, .22 Long and .22 LR

Ruger Old Army

Country United States
Type competition percussion revolver
Designation Ruger, Old Army
Calibre .44
Weight (*ca.*) 1.300kg
Length overall 34cm, barrel 19cm
Remarks faced with the rigidity of most national rules concerning firearms, many enthusiasts in the USA organize 'black powder' matches, with old guns or their replicas. The Ruger company has just brought out the Old Army percussion model, designed for such use, with a micrometric sight. The lock is naturally single action

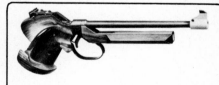

Hämmerli 150

Country Switzerland
Type free pistol
Designation Hämmerli, 150
Calibre .22 LR
Weight 1.200kg, 1.400kg with counterweight
Length overall 39cm; barrel 28.7cm; line of sight 37cm
Remarks this is a new Hämmerli pistol, designed to replace the highly successful 107 model. It retains the 107's Martini breech, but the barrel is set much lower, to avoid slant, and the hold has been considerably improved. Trigger can be set between 5 and 100g

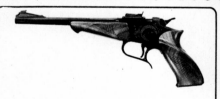

Thompson Center Contender

Country United States
Type single-shot pistol
Designation Thompson-Center, Contender
Calibre from .17 Hornet to .44 Magnum; 27 calibres available
Weight (*ca.*) from 1.200 to 1.400kg depending on barrel
Length varies according to barrel
Remarks this is a sporting rather than a match model. Calibre changeover by means of barrel change

Anschütz 1411

Country	West Germany
Type	match carbine for international prone events
Designation	Anschütz, 1411
Calibre	.22 LR
Weight	5.400kg
Length	overall 116cm; barrel 69cm
Remarks	this gun won the gold medal at the Munich Olympics in the prone event. The carbine shown here has a special stock

Anschütz Super Match 1413

Country	West Germany
Type	match carbine for 'free' events
Designation	Anschütz, Super Match 1413
Calibre	.22 LR
Weight	7.000kg
Length	overall 114–117cm; barrel 69cm
Remarks	in accordance with ISU rules, this gun is specially designed for 'free' events at the highest level

Winchester 52 IMR

Country	United States
Type	match carbine for international 'free' events
Designation	Winchester, 52 International Match Rifle
Calibre	.22 LR
Weight	6.100kg
Length	overall 113cm; barrel 71cm
Remarks	this model is widely used in the USA above all, and has not been readily accepted in Europe, because of the indisputable supremacy of Anschütz models in this field

Unique T.66 Match

Country	France
Type	standard ISU competition carbine
Designation	Manufacture d'Armes des Pyrénées Françaises, Unique T.66 Match
Calibre	.22 LR
Weight (*ca.*)	4.800kg
Length	overall 110cm; barrel 65cm (heavy barrel)
Remarks	thanks to the MAPF, France now has a Standard ISU carbine for competition use which can match the best international makes. The trigger can be set between 150 and 2000g by means of three adjustment devices

Husqvarna 1999 Sporter

Country	Sweden
Type	moving target big bore match rifle
Designation	Husqvarna, 1999 Sporter
Calibre	.222 Remington or 6.5mm Remington Magnum
Weight (*ca.*)	4.400kg
Length	overall 110cm; barrel 72cm
Capacity	3-rounds with .222 Remington and 2 rounds with 6.5mm Remington Magnum
Remarks	There is a 1998 variant of this gun which is supplied with a polished and treated stock. On the 1999 model the stock is made of untreated wood so as to fit exactly the contours of the user

Hämmerli Tanner

Country	Switzerland
Type	300 metre event rifle
Designation	Hämmerli, Tanner
Calibre	7.5mm Swiss, 7.62mm NATO (.308 WCF), 6.5 × 5.5mm or 30-06 Army
Weight (*ca.*)	7.300kg
Length	overall 129cm; barrel 75cm
Remarks	this carbine by Hämmerli, a make whose reputation in the field is beyond reproach, is one of the best in the world in its category. 2-stage trigger adjustable up to 150g

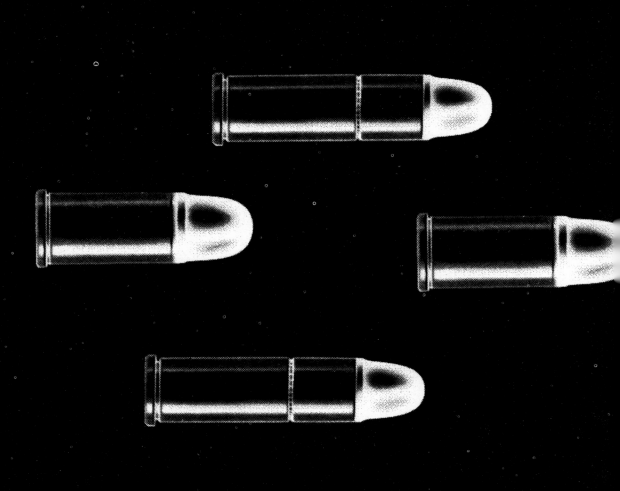

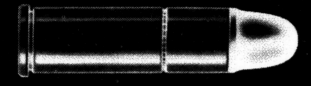

7
types of ammunition

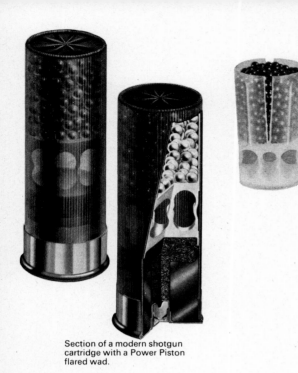

Section of a modern shotgun cartridge with a Power Piston flared wad.

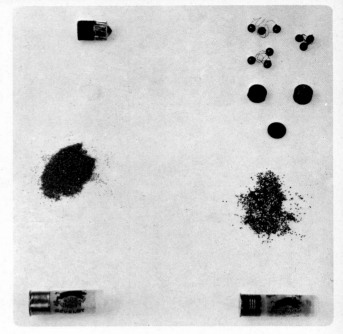

Gévelot cartridges for wild-boar hunting; type: wild-boar Supervix. Left: Brenneke type bullet; right: with connected buck-shot. Shooting big game with buck-shot has been prohibited since 1 July 1973 in France.

Equivalent shot numbers

	Game	Shot	Remarks
	Hare	4 – 5	The hare is very lively and a much sought-after game. Use powerful charges.
	Pheasant	5, 6, 7.5	At the start of the season, the pheasant is easier game, requiring medium charges and chokes. Later it becomes more aggressive and wilder, which requires it being shot at greater distances.
	Quail	7.5, 8, 9	Average barrel length and choke for these birds, which are nearly always hunted with dogs.
	Wood-pigeon	6 – 7.5	Distances can vary greatly with these fast-flying and wary birds. Most common gun is the .12 bore with intermediate chokes.
	Woodcock	8 – 9	Very rapid fire, generally at close quarters. Fine shot so as not to maim the Queen of the Woods.
	Partridge	7.5 – 8	This fowl, worthy of respect as it is, falls easily when winged. Light average-length guns, easy to handle and with medium choke, are the best suited.
	Waterfowl (sitting)	6 – 7.5	At 25yds No. 6 shot will down any waterfowl. Some hunters prefer the denser cone of dispersion of No. 7.5 shot for shooting these swift birds.
	Waterfowl (in flight)	4 – 5	Distances will be considerable and the game flies past high. The hunter needs to have all his wits about him. A .12 bore is necessary with 76mm Mag. cartridges.
	Skeet	9 – 9.5	Short barrels, low choke, will be needed for this exciting sport.
	Trap	7.5 – 8	The 'pigeons' are launched at very close quarters. This target is most like the so-called 'going-away' bird.

Suggestions for charges and ranges

Diameter (mm)	France	Germany	Britain	Belgium	USA
5,00	0000	4/0	AA	3/0	0
4,75	000	3/0	-	2/0	BBB
4,50	00	2/0	A	0	BB
4,30	-	-	-	-	-
4,25	0	0	BBB	1	-
4,10	-	-	-	-	-
4,00	1		BB	2	1
3,90	-	-	-	-	-
3,65	-	-	1	-	-
3,50	3	3	2	4	3
3,30	-	-	-	-	-
3,25	4	4	3	5	4
3,10	-	-	-	-	-
3,00	5	5	4	Gr.6	5
2,90	-	-	-	-	-
2,85	-	-	41/2	-	-
2,80	-	-	5	-	6
2,75	6	6	51/2	Kl.6	-
2,70	-	-	-	-	-
2,50	7	7	61/2	-	7
2,40	71/2	-	7	7	71/2
2,30	-	-	-	-	-
2,25	8	8	8	8	8
2,10	81/2	-	-	-	-
2,00	9	9	9	9	9
1,90	-	-	-	-	-
1,75	10	10	10	10	10
1,70	-	-	-	11	-
1,50	11	11	12	11	11

General data

Without its ammunition the firearm is a complex and totally unusable gadget.

For more than a century ammunition has been made in the form of a cartridge or, in other words, a case which contains three essential things:

1. the primer
2. the powder charge
3. the bullet.

Cartridges can be classified according to the type of priming: some are called centre-fire: the priming charge is placed in a (firing) cap in the centre of the base of the cartridge; the gun's hammer crushes it against the so-called anvil, which is part either of the case (Berdan type) or of the primer cap (Boxer type); others are called rim-fire; the priming charge is contained in the actual rim of the case; here, the hammer presses it against the face of the breech.

Groove-headed cartridges, therefore, cannot incorporate the rim-fire system; this is the oldest system, and although it is simpler and cheaper, it can only be used with relatively low pressures; this is because the case must have, so to speak, paradoxical qualities: malleability for compression; resistance for air-tightness. It is used for some small, low or average velocity calibres with lightweight bullets. The most common is the .22 L.R.

Cartridges can likewise be classified according to the type of projectile: bullet for rifles and handguns, or variously sized lead-shot for shotguns. The shotgun can sometimes use the bullet in the form of a slug, but one would be unlikely to come across a rifle using lead shot. It has, in fact, become quite standard practice to divide them into shot shells for shotguns and cartridges for rifles.

Shot shells for shotguns

Shot shell is easily identifiable by the case, which is more often than not made of metal only at the base. This is not an absolute rule, since Gévelot made a 12-gauge shot shell entirely of aluminium, which was fairly successful. Other materials, such as paper or plastic, make for a tight seal, either by crimping or rolling, which is still efficient where firing of the powder is concerned and sufficiently soft not to hamper the passage of the shot and wad.

This shot shell has an important component: the wad; the very nature of the shot demands a certain degree of waterproofing and a certain thrust between it and the charge. Since the work of General Fournier, everyone has become aware of the importance of this component for the high performance of a shot shell.

The use of plastics for the manufacture of flared wads, which were known in theory before but impossible to make, represents a major step forward. These give much better waterproofing for the powder's combustion gases, and thus avoid the formation of shot clusters which are caused by the shot partly melting, and also produce a more regular muzzle velocity. In addition they improve the evenness of the cone of dispersion by stopping the shot from becoming deformed by friction against the wall of the barrels.

The other parts of the cartridge have also been improved. The use of plastic for the case, instead of the traditional cardboard, was introduced for better waterproofing. Nevertheless it posed some intricate problems: first, it was necessary to find a mechanically resistant type of plastic which would remain soft in spite of large temperature variations (the ammunition being fit for use in any climatic conditions); the case must not stick in the chamber, so it had to be scored; and the rolling or crimping must open, without tearing. All these problems have been resolved by the various manufacturers.

And yet not everybody is satisfied. These plastic cases are inorganic, thus indestructable, and this has given rise to considerable opposition: they are ugly litter in hunting country; and there have been cases of animals suffering or even dying as a result of swallowing these empty plastic cases.

The last war saw huge advances being made in explosives, and consequently in the field of powder. The range made available to the gun owner by this specialized industry has widened, and it is possible to make a perfect match between the calibre and the weight of the shot. Increased combustion has made it possible to increase the charge to Magnum size, which is now common (46g for a 12 gauge). Fulminate compounds are also safer, more sensitive and more uniform, and they are now in airtight primers.

The result of all this is that a sporting cartridge can now remain immersed in water for several hours, and still be fired in an autoloader. This is a major advance, when one thinks that until quite recently this type of ammunition was regarded as particularly easy to spoil and extremely sensitive to damp.

Generally speaking there has been a tendency towards heavy charges. All modern guns have a 70mm (2.75in.) chamber. The cartridge cases are longer and thus more easily sealed by rolling; this does not decrease the actual charge and consequently improves the consistency of the cone of dispersion by doing away with the obturators (shutters). The use of split obturators had produced similar results.

It has been possible to standardize sporting ammunition thanks to an international agreement. This standardization refers mainly to the diameters and their max./min. tolerances (18.02mm–18.04mm for a 12 bore), guns and chambers. It guarantees a good ballistic performance, regardless of the origins of the gun and the ammunition used. It also covers the dimensions of the rims and tends to avoid percussion failures caused by the use of thin rimmed cartridges in barrels with grooves which are too deep.

As the performance of shotguns depends not only on the type of ammunition used but also on the vibration rate and reboring of their barrels, advances made both with present-day ammunition and with gun manufacture give the hunter or sportsman a particularly effective weapon. It might be made still more effective by the use of even heavier charges or more revolutionary techniques, such as self-propelled charges. It is unlikely, however, that things will take such a path without coming up against opposition from legislators who, not without reason, believe that the present destructive potential of the conventional modern gun is more than adequate.

Bullets for centre-fire revolvers

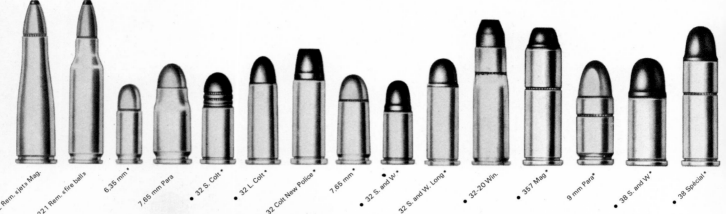

- 22 Rem. «Jet» Mag.
- 221 Rem. «fire ball»
- 6.35 mm *
- 7.65 mm Para
- 32 S. Colt *
- 32 L. Colt *
- 32 Colt New Police *
- 7.65 mm *
- 32 S. and W.*
- 32 S. and W. Long *
- 32-20 Win.
- 357 Mag.*
- 9 mm Para*
- 38 S. and W.*
- 38 Spécial *

Bullets for centre-fire carbines

- 218 Bee
- 22 Hornet
- 222 Rem.
- 222 Rem. Mag.
- 22-250 Rem.
- 223 Rem. (5.56 mm)
- 6 mm Rem.
- 243 Win.
- 244 Rem.

- 30-30 Win.
- 30 Rem.
- 30-40 Krag*
- 30-06 Springfield*
- 300 Sav.
- 300 H. and H. Mag.
- 300 Win. Mag.
- 303 Sav.
- 303 British*
- 308 Win. (7.62 mm OTAN)*
- 8 mm Mauser*
- 32 Rem.
- 32 Win. Special

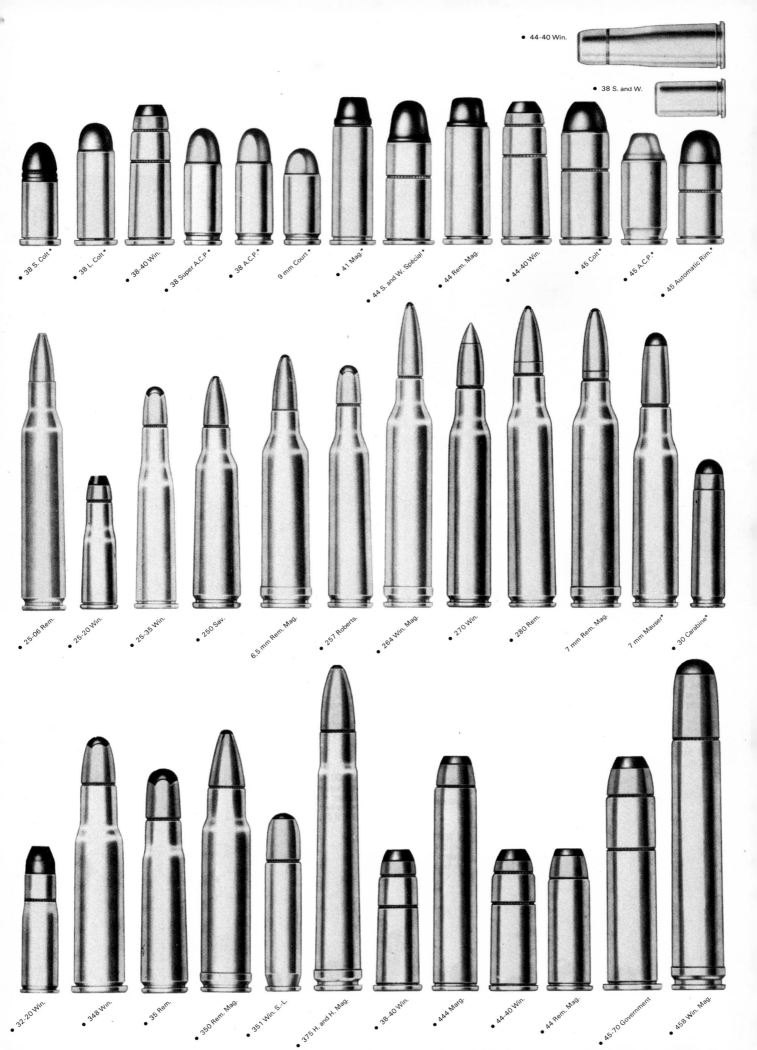

● 44-40 Win.

● 38 S. and W.

● 38 S. Colt *

● 38 L. Colt *

● 38-40 Win.

● 38 Super A.C.P. *

● 38 A.C.P. *

● 9 mm Court *

● 41 Mag. *

● 44 S. and W. Spécial *

● 44 Rem. Mag.

● 44-40 Win.

● 45 Colt *

● 45 A.C.P. *

● 45 Automatic Rim. *

● 25-06 Rem.

● 25-20 Win.

● 25-35 Win.

● 250 Sav.

● 6.5 mm Rem. Mag.

● 257 Roberts.

● 264 Win. Mag.

● 270 Win.

● 280 Rem.

● 7 mm Rem. Mag.

● 7 mm Mauser *

● 30 Carabine *

● 32-20 Win.

● 348 Win.

● 35 Rem.

● 350 Rem. Mag.

● 351 Win. S.-L.

● 375 H. and H. Mag.

● 38-40 Win.

● 444 Marg.

● 44-40 Win.

● 44 Rem. Mag.

● 45-70 Government

● 458 Win. Mag.

Cartridges for rifles

The metal case is more specifically reserved for smaller calibre rifles. Here the muzzle velocity and pressure are higher and the single bullet renders wadding superfluous. The powder industry has supplied products which have made it possible to increase muzzle velocities, while metallurgical progress has produced cases and bullets with improved mechanical features.

Rim-fire is still used for one of the most common calibres, especially with competition models, the .22 (or 5.5mm) which has been improved to .22 Magnum. While the average muzzle velocity varies from 350—400 metres per second, Remington now makes a 5mm Magnum with an initial velocity of up to 645 metres per second. This tendency towards very high velocity small calibres is also evident in the range of centre-fire metallic cartridges, either with grooved or rimmed head, ranging from the .17 Remington (5mm) to the .577 Nitro-Express (14mm).

Together with the .30 × 30 WCF, or other British .303s which have been around for some time, there has appeared ammunition giving remarkable performances:

.17 Remington, 5mm	with 1225 m/s muzzle velocity
.222 Remington Magnum	with 1006 m/s muzzle velocity
.22—250	with 1161 m/s muzzle velocity
.223 Remington	with 1006 m/s muzzle velocity
6mm Remington	with 1079 m/s muzzle velocity
.225 Winchester	with 1100 m/s muzzle velocity
and many others.	

The small calibre range, from 5mm to 6.5mm, with very high velocity, and the medium calibre range from 6.5mm to 8mm with lower velocities but heavier bullets, are particularly well stocked. Large calibre ammunition has also obtained remarkable performances: with 835 m/s a .375 H. and H. Magnum produces, at the muzzle, kinetic energy of 622kgm and, with 649 m/s a .458 Winchester Magnum produces 710kgm. These are powerful enough to fell any animal. Handgun ammunition had developed in the same direction too. The .221 Remington 'Fire Ball' (5.5mm) has a muzzle velocity of 807 m/s; the .357 Magnum (9mm) produces 116kgm at the muzzle. There are also the .41 Magnum with 150kgm and the .44 Remington Magnum with 159kgm.

The competitor is little concerned with what becomes of his bullet once it has passed through the target. But the hunter or the soldier have different problems. Having chosen a bullet or cartridge based on the volume of the projectile and its velocity and energy on impact, they are looking for its effectiveness. Velocities exceeding 450 m/s prohibit the use of lead bullets, which are virtually confined to the .22 calibre, and call for bullets made of a lead core sheathed in harder metal (soft steel or, more often, a copper and zinc alloy).

The Hague agreements, which are still in force, forbid fragmenting bullets for use as military ammunition. Ammunition is thus usually fitted with jacketed heads, so-called because their conical head is entirely covered with the envelope. They have high penetration potential, and virtually never become deformed.

Hunters, concerned only with knocking their prey down by the impact of the shot and wounding it as seriously as possible, have at their disposal a whole range of so-called 'soft-pointed' bullets with the conical head not covered by the envelope. They have less penetration, deform on impact, and being curbed more sharply transform most of their kinetic energy into lethal power.

In order to reconcile the aerodynamic shape with the volume required for the right velocity, accuracy and deformation necessary for effectiveness, manufacturers have devised many types of bullets: round-headed, flat, pointed and semi-pointed; hollow-headed, jacketed or not, with a careful eye on deformation, or fragmentation as the case may be. The hunter can thus find the calibre and ammunition perfectly suited to the animals which he is after. The competitive shot, on the other hand, is concerned only with the ballistic properties. Basic to his requirements are the accuracy and consistency of the ammunition. Generally speaking they all look much alike, but are made with the best available material and undergo a whole series of tests at every stage of production, a factor which considerably increases their price.

Winchester reports that every day a million of its rounds are fired throughout the world. Such a figure from just one manufacturer makes the mind boggle and gives some idea of what is at stake in the munitions industry, which requires highly developed machinery, and is quite closely allied with the chemical industry which supplies the explosives. Besides the American giants, Winchester and Remington, Weatherby, in the USA, also manufactures ammunition with cases imported from Sweden. The Swedish firm, Norma, is one of the best in the world. In Europe we should mention in passing ICI and Kynoch in Great Britain, Léon Braun and Fiocchi in Italy, Sellier and Bellot in Czechoslovakia, FN and Coppal in Belgium, RWS, DWM in Germany, Gévelot, Cartoucherie Française, MGK, Cartoucherie Nationale and Rey in France, Sako in Finland, and lastly Vostok in the USSR.

As well as supplying finished ammunition for smooth- and rifled-bore guns, the industry also supplies the component parts. Many enthusiasts load their own cartridges, and more often reload them, especially when expensive ammunition for competition practice is involved.

The future of ammunition

The future of ammunition, apart from that made for military use which is subject to different criteria, will probably like the future of guns be dictated by the future of gun legislation. For reasons based on protection and safety, such legislation will tend to curb technical progress and generally apply more rules and regulations.

Bullets for centre-fire revolvers and pistols

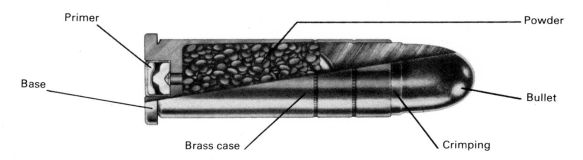

Primer

Powder

Base

Bullet

Brass case

Crimping

Type of heads

Lead
Currently used head for all types of shooting.

Wad cutter
Lead head for competition shooting.

Jacketed point bullet
Gives better penetration than lead head, with the point protected by armour plating which does not foul.

Gas check bullet
The cap keeps the gases behind the head.

Jacketed bullet
For automatic pistols.

¾ -jacketed hollow point bullet
Made in .38 Special calibre to make handguns more effective.

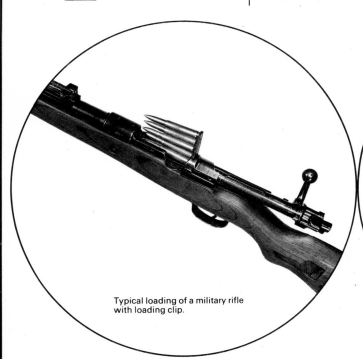

Typical loading of a military rifle with loading clip.

The range of .22 ammunition offered by Gévelot.

Rim-fire bullets

.22 Calibre 'Hi-Speed' and 'High Velocity' with OR head

22 Short   22 Long   22 Long Rifle   22 W.R.F.

.22 Calibre Standard

2 Short   22 Short Gallery   22 Long Rifle   22 Winchester automatic

.22 Calibre Long Rifle Match

22 Long Rifle   22 Shot Cartridge   22 Short

5mm Remington Magnum

5 mm Rem. Mag.

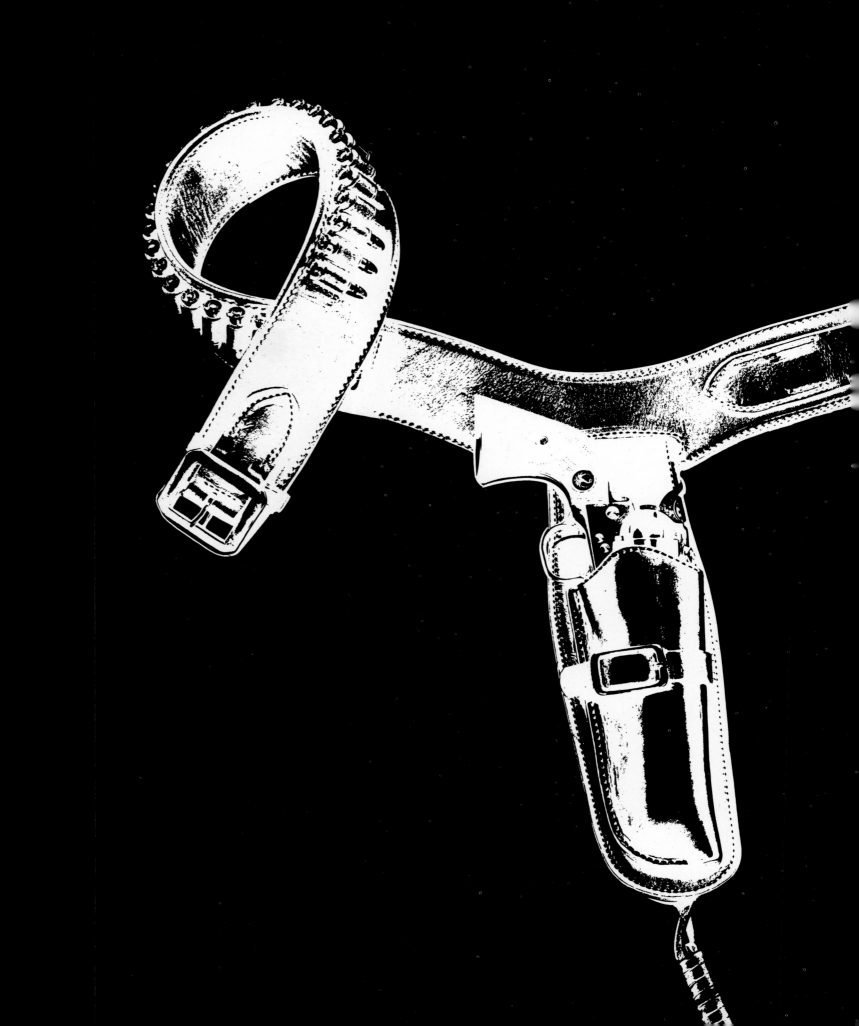

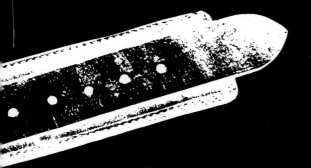

8
accessories

If we were to list under this heading *all* the different things which are associated with the use of firearms, it would be an extremely long list.

Some of these things apply directly to the gun itself; their usual purpose is to make the gun suit its owner or user as closely as possible, or else to modify the features or performance of the gun to some extent. Others have to do with ammunition.

Accessories are often manufactured by the actual maker of the gun, but throughout the world there are specialized firms which supply these 'optional extras' directly to the manufacturers.

Orthopaedic grips and adjustable stocks

In order to suit the gun to the shape and size of its owner, in the case of a hand-gun, wooden or plastic so-called anatomical or orthopaedic stock-plates or grips are offered as alternatives to replace the original parts. Similarly, the rifle may be fitted with butt plates which may be adjustable and made of foam rubber, to reduce the kick. These come in many varieties, of differing thicknesses and quality. The angle of the butt may be modified by fitting a rubber shoulder, either sunk into or stuck on to the wooden butt-shoulder. The drop may be varied by the use of cheek-pieces attached with rubber straps.

Sighting gear

If the recoil injures the second-finger, usually placed behind the trigger-guard, a finger-guard may be used. Sighting gear comes high on the list of accessories. There are many types of front- and rearsights, with the Parker company in England and the firm Bo. Mar, Lyman Redfield and Williams in the United States making literally hundreds of models. Manufacturers such as Walther, and Anschütz in Germany, and Unique in France with its 'Micro Match' lens, all offer optional sighting gear for their weapons.

The leaf-sights used on sporting and hunting models are replaced by micrometric dioptric sights on match rifles. These lenses may entail additional accessories such as: an iris diaphragm, diaphragm tunnel frontsight, and filters. The eyeball may be protected by rubber 'blinkers'.

Telescopic sights make it easier to aim the gun and by magnifying the target make it possible to shoot during bad lighting conditions. They are very popular, although their adjustment and use are sometimes complicated. The range is vast, embracing as it does the small .22 carbine telescope, × 10 magnification, with a field from 10—100 metres, to the prism scope, designed for big-game hunting or war-time use; this is a constant sight, waterproofed and in some cases filled with nitrogen to avoid internal condensation, and capable of standing up to the mule-like kick of Holland and Holland .375 Magnum cartridges. Between these extremes there are also scopes with varying focal distances and thus different strengths of magnification; those with a wide field of vision give a more 'panoramic' effect and may or not be equipped with a telemetric (range-finding) device to measure the dis-

tance of the target.

The Germans, Japanese and Americans are perhaps the best-known in the field, with the firms of Hensoldt, Kriegeskorte, Telle and Carl Zeiss in West Germany, Monope in Japan, Buschnell, Discop, Longway, Lyman, Redfield and Weaver in the United States, Vidi in France, and so on and so forth.

American enthusiasts can treat themselves to special butts and adaptable telescopic sights for some revolvers, like the Smith and Wesson Jet Magnum or the Contender by Thompson/Center; this enables long-distance firing with a handgun, which is something Americans are fond of.

In order to pre-adjust (or pre-set) telescopic sights, the Japanese have designed a cunning little device called a 'Scope-Sighter', which is sold in the USA under the Marlin-Veri-Fire mark. It consists in mounting a cross-ruled screen on a properly calibrated rod which is inserted into the muzzle of the barrel; this screen is lit from behind and produces a precise image in the telescopic sight, thus making it possible to adjust the latter in the vertical plane of the barrel's axis.

For night-time operations, the military use telescopic sights which are sensitive to infra-red radiation emitted by the body heat of another human being. These sights are obviously extremely costly and cumbersome, which restricts their use considerably.

In the last few years a new device has appeared for sighting game. This is the British 'Single Point' sight, which is available in various versions: the SP 270 (for day and night use) is mounted at the front end of the barrel rib of a rifle or revolver with the help of plastic supports of different widths (for ribs which are 5—16mm wide); the 220 is adjustable and is attached with collars, like a telescopic sight. In the United States, Weaver makes a similar model, called the 'Qwik Point', for direct sighting. These strong, compact, precision instruments are derived directly from the instruments used in aircraft to aim automatic weapons; they do not magnify the target or increase the field of vision. They project a virtual small red dot over the target, thus representing the point of impact of the bullet. The red dot is visible in broad daylight; by moving the gun it is brought directly over the target (this applies to shotguns and rifles). It can also be used for short-range with revolvers. These are waterproof instruments and virtually foolproof too; what is more, their very principle requires an excellent binocular vision.

Recoil-reducers and chokes

Some guns are improved by the addition of detachable counterweights generally attached to the barrel. This is a frequent modification to pistols (Walther, Colt, Beretta) but rarer in the case of carbines (Anschütz).

The kick and jump of competition guns are minimized by the attachment of recoil-reducers or muzzle brakes: these can be fitted by simply screwing them onto the muzzle, as on the .22 Margoline match pistol, and also to rifles and carbines, as is the case of the Besa brake on the .458 WCF calibre BSA Majestic rifle.

In order to modify the ballistic performance of a shotgun, one modifies the boring of its barrel muzzle or

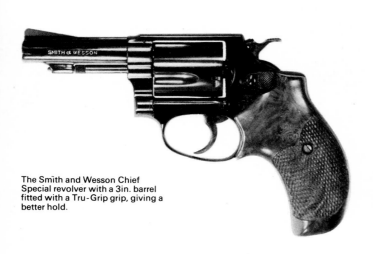

The Smith and Wesson Chief Special revolver with a 3in. barrel fitted with a Tru-Grip grip, giving a better hold.

A Bo-Mar attachment with micrometric adjustment fitted to a Browning GP automatic pistol.

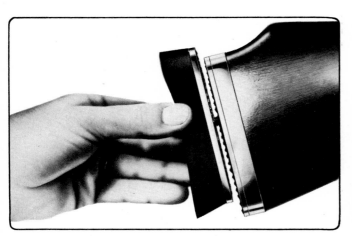

The adjustable butt plate on the Unique T-66 Match rifle.

The micrometric sight fitted to the SIG P 210–5 and P 210–6 automatic pistols.

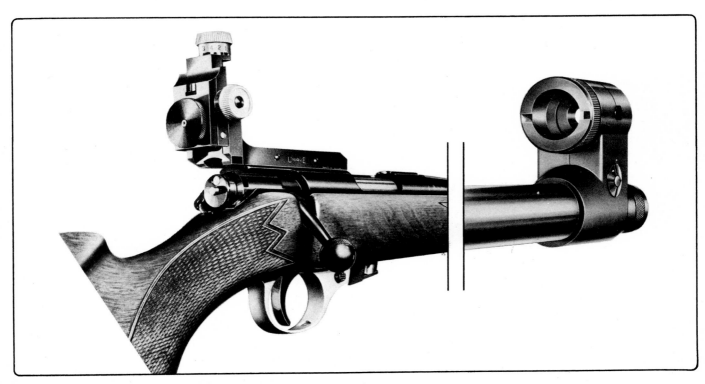

With its new sighting devices and in particular with the Micro Match dioptre, Unique has entered the international class.

The Weaver K 10 telescopic sight with fixed × 10 magnification, fitted to a Browning High Power rifle.

The Lyman high magnification telescopic sight fitted to the Ruger M-77 rifle with quick mounts.

The Weaver V 4.5 telescopic sight with magnification variable between × 1.5 and × 4.5 fixed to the Savage 99 DL rifle.

The Weaver V22-A1 telescopic sight with magnification variable from ×3 to ×6, designed for .22 LR calibre rifles.

Redfield wide-angle variable telescopic sights. Top: magnification from ×3 to ×9; below: magnification from ×2 to ×7.

The Hensolt telescopic sight mounted on the standard Swiss SIG Stgw 57 assault rifle.

Heckler and Koch G3 assault rifle with Hensolt telescopic sight.

Infra-red telescopic sight mounted on a SIG 510–4 assault rifle.

Qwik-Point S1 special sight by Weaver mounted on the Remington 1100 automatic shotgun.

Single Point special sights. Left: the SP 270, fixed on the rib of an over-under; below: intermediate supports; right: the 220.

Poly-Choke adjustable choke mounted to order by Verney-Carron on Franchi autoloader shotguns.

'choke'. This is only possible on single-barrel models:
— by screwing different chokes on to pre-designed thread, as in the case of the Italian automatic Breda, or single-barrel Winchester shotguns which take the three 'Win-chokes': improved cylindrical choke, half- and full-choke, in 12 or 20 gauge;
— by permanently attaching an adjustable poly-choke, which in some cases also acts as a muzzle brake. The Americans have a wide choice here with Cyclone, Emsco, Lyman and Polychoke products. It is incidentally the latter which Verney-Carron and Franchi offer for their series of autoloaders; it is available in two versions: the PCS standard model and the PCV ventilated model, both with seven adjustment positions:

1 Extra Full	Full choke,	Geese, ducks,
2 Full	more than 25m	ball-trap
3 Imp. Mod	Half-choke,	Pheasant,
4 Mod.	20–25m	grouse
5 Imp-Cyl.	Improved bore,	Rabbit
6 Slug	15–20m	Quail
7 Full-open	Cylindrical,	Woodcock,
	10–15m	skeet

In order to improve accuracy by reducing the trigger pull, Sako in Finland, Parker in Great Britain, Mauser in West Germany and many others manufacture double-trigger systems which can be used on certain carbines and rifles.

Silencers

There is quite a lot to be said for reducing or even totally suppressing the report. It should be pointed out, however, that legislation in many countries prohibits the use of such accessories for hunting. Improperly called silencers, these sound-control attachments generally consist of a cylinder with baffle-plates which is screwed to the muzzle of the barrel. Most effective on small calibres, they reduce the noise of a .22 by 50–75 per cent, as long as one does not use supersonic ammunition, where the shock-wave at the muzzle makes more noise than the gas discharge. When the calibre is larger, this system involves too cumbersome silencers. A 9mm Parabellum calibre P-08 already requires a silencer that is larger than the pistol itself. Other systems are used in such cases. For example, in certain military weapons, the barrel, which is drilled with a given number of gauged apertures, is enclosed in a sleeve consisting of a latticed metal coil itself placed within a drilled cylinder. The result is effective but muzzle velocity is reduced. The Sten Mk II S sub-machine-gun was fitted with a silencer; and the Thompson M1A1 and the American M3 sub-machine-gun were also equipped with this accessory for commando operations. A whole branch of arms research has been given over to this problem since World War I: the silent gun.

Miniature-range shooting and calibre conversion

If one wants to practise with a gun in conditions where there are restrictions on noise, distance and danger, in other words on the miniature range, and because cheap ammunition may be a determining factor, there are several solutions, but these are only designed and possible for certain guns and calibres.

One can use plastic or metal cases for firing plastic bullets. These can be reloaded with normal percussion caps, and are made mainly for .38 Special and .44 Magnum calibres in the series of American ammunition, and in 7.65mm and 9mm Parabellum calibres in the series of European ammunition. They are made by RWS in West Germany and Paris Sport in France, in Europe, and also manufactured in the United States by some major manufacturers.

It may also be necessary to use a reducing tube the length of the barrel. This solution is very often used for shotguns and rifles as well as for pistols in 7.65mm and 9mm Parabellum or .45 Colt Auto calibres. In the case of automatic pistols, this tube makes it possible to use 4mm calibre ammunition with a spherical bullet. It also exists in .22 calibre for the P.08, P.38 and .45 Colt Government Model automatic pistols.

When the calibre of the reduced ammunition is the same as that of the gun, a chamber reducer is then necessary. This applies to 5.6 × 52R, .220 Swift or .222 Remington calibres which can take the .22 LR ammunition. The Smith and Wesson Jet Magnum revolver can take chamber reducers enabling it to use .22 Magnum, .22 Hornet and .22 LR ammunition.

Some manufacturers have supplied 'conversion kits'; these consist, in general, of a collection of items which make it possible to change the calibre and hence the gun. The Colt .45 Government Model can thus be turned into the .22 LR calibre by means of 'Conversion Unit 45-22', which is made up of a bolt, a barrel, a terminal bolt sleeve, a recoil spring with guides, a clip stop and a clip. SIG offers a very complete kit making it possible to convert its P.210 automatic pistol with a 9mm Parabellum calibre into a 7.65mm Parabellum and .22 Long and LR calibre gun. The Thompson/Center Arms Contender in the USA offers twenty-seven interchangeable barrels with different calibres, from the .22 LR to the .44 Magnum, via the .30 calibre for the standard M1 service carbine, all attaching to the same frame. It should be noted, however, that this is a one-round pistol which has made it possible to eliminate all the problems associated with recoil springs and clips.

Holsters and transport accessories

When they are to be transported or carried, guns can be put into holsters — rigid or soft, padded or otherwise — or in small cases, where they will be carried, assembled or dismantled. There are countless models to be had. Handguns are carried in holsters. We should remember in passing that the law prohibits the carrying of handguns except under special circumstances as defined by the law. Thanks to their long experience and the unrivalled quality of their leather, the Americans are the undisputed masters where holster-making is concerned. Myres of El Paso, Texas, offers a whole range which clearly reflects the 'Western' influence. His 'Quick Draw' holsters made of tooled leather attached to a 'Buscadero' belt are the dream of many an amateur cowboy.

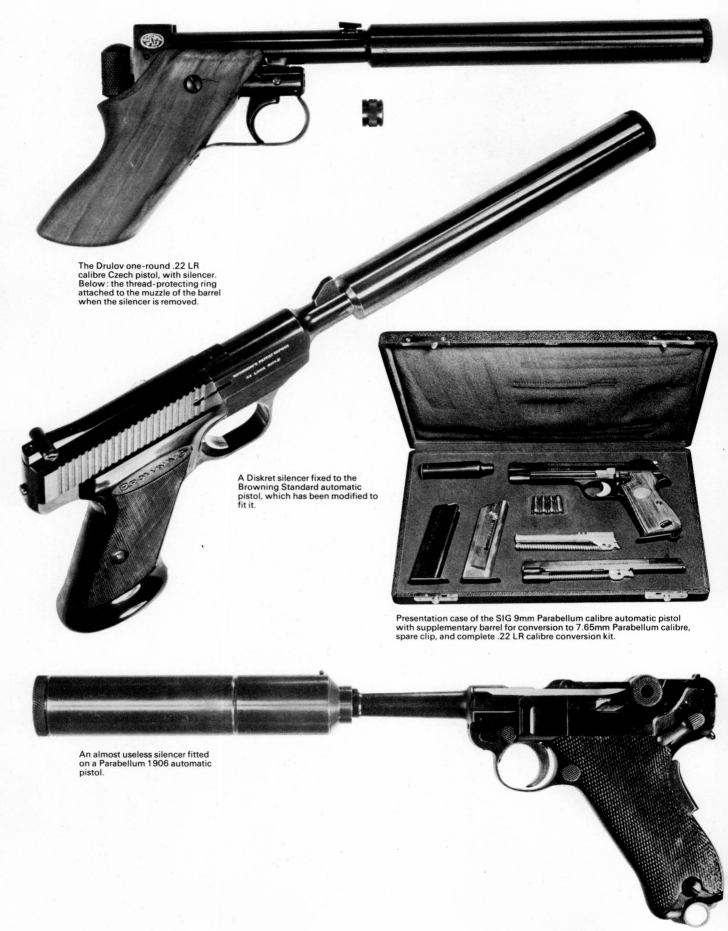

The Drulov one-round .22 LR calibre Czech pistol, with silencer. Below: the thread-protecting ring attached to the muzzle of the barrel when the silencer is removed.

A Diskret silencer fixed to the Browning Standard automatic pistol, which has been modified to fit it.

Presentation case of the SIG 9mm Parabellum calibre automatic pistol with supplementary barrel for conversion to 7.65mm Parabellum calibre, spare clip, and complete .22 LR calibre conversion kit.

An almost useless silencer fitted on a Parabellum 1906 automatic pistol.

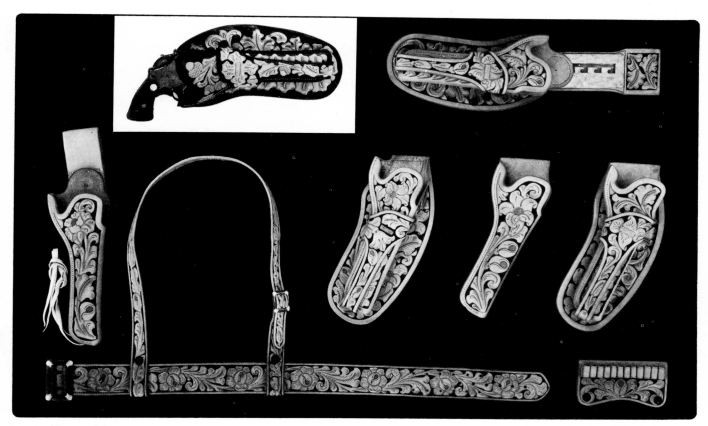

Part of the Myres of El Paso
(Texas) range.

These revolver holsters are made
by Myres Saddle Co., of El Paso.

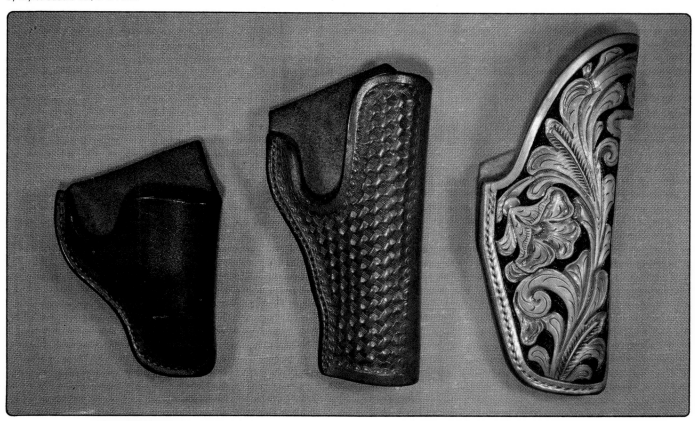

207

Less showy, but just as functional, are the holsters made by Lawrence of Portland (Oregon), aimed at a less folklore-conscious clientele, if one might use the term. Bianchi, in California, a newcomer to the field, offers a very complete range of eminently functional holsters: his M.66, which can take the standard US Army .45 Colt Government Model automatic pistol on either side, left or right, is a novelty in the trade.

Tayra Corporation, with its moulded plastic police models, created a very effective new line allowing the revolver to be drawn extremely quickly, because it was virtually left uncovered. Unfortunately the Tayra Corporation went bankrupt after some business wrangling with a major American arms manufacturer, who produced the holsters under licence for a while.

For some years now Smith and Wesson has also been producing various gun accessories. The excellent quality of its leathers combined with the impeccable workmanship of these accessories are worthy of the fine guns for which they are designed. Accessories sold to civilians are certainly more sophisticated than those supplied with standard military weapons, but the latter are just as well made despite their more utilitarian than decorative purpose.

No army can have an infantry rifle without a bayonet; this goes without saying. But this weapon is outside the scope of this book, and so we shall refer our readers to various excellent books which have quite recently appeared.

As for the automatic pistol, this has received much attention from the various general staffs. In most cases its holster has been designed to hold one or two extra clips, as well as all the necessary stripping and cleaning implements. Some holsters, like the Colt .45 Government Model 1911, are only designed to take the gun, and the extra clips are kept in different canvas holsters attached to the belt.

Miscellaneous accessories

Shotguns, carbines and rifles have slings. To keep the gun firmly in place against the shoulder, marksmen use special slings made by Walther and Gehman in Europe, or Frandbron and Lawrence in the United States. These same marksmen will probably also use vests specially designed for ball-trap and target-shooting.

Firearms are noisy. This is one of their drawbacks. To protect the ears of the competitor, and those of his immediate neighbours, a whole series of ear-protectors or plugs helps to deaden the report.

The firearm needs servicing if it is to give maximum performance. The barrel should receive very close attention to prevent powder residue from ruining it permanently. An extremely full range of cleaning-rods and brushes of all shapes and sizes is currently available from gunsmiths. The names Parker, Outers, Bonanza and so on crop up. In the United States Parker has developed a series of products (Gun-Blue, Birchwood) for retouching blueing, polishes etc. Europeans also have their similar products.

Some objects are especially cunning, and may be likened almost to gadgetry. For example, FFV Sport AB

(Husqvarna), in Sweden, offers a dummy barrel breech bolt which renders the gun unusable unless you have the key. It can only be used on rifles with a Mauser-system bolt, and looks like a short bolt with two locking lugs, which fit into place in the chamber and are held in place by a 'burglar-proof' bolt. It is fitted without removing the gun's bolt. All you need do is open it. By blocking the chamber it renders it unusable and it is impossible to remove it. Of course, you must not lose the key — that would cause different problems.

Reloading accessories

Hunters have always been ones for making their own cartridges. Half a century ago this was in fact the rule — where shot was concerned — and pre-loaded ammunition on sale was not commonly found for shotguns. A whole industry made a range of basically very simple accessories for loading and reloading. And these still exist: fixed or adjustable powder measures, or scales for the more particular, tampers, dies for unpriming and re-gauging, priming, crimping, all produced by often renowned firms.

More elaborate items have since emerged. They often form a kit which can carry out every operation required, including star-crimping plastic shot shells; Récalmorce is well-known in France. In the United States, Ponsness Warren offers the keen enthusiast three models: Du-O-Matic 375, Mult-O-Matic 600 and Size-O-Matic 800 B which, despite their relatively high cost, enable one to make and reload, in large numbers, shot shells in different gauges.

But for various reasons, such as limited time, the lowering cost of ready-made ammunition, and the impossibility of obtaining certain ammunition which is only made on an industrial scale, gun-owners do their own loading and reloading less and less, and in fact so rarely that some accessories are disappearing altogether, because manufacturers are finding it hard to pay their way. On the other hand, rifled-bore enthusiasts, be it with revolver or rifle, are more and more inclined to reload their own ammunition. The high price of this ammunition, and the need for authorization to purchase certain types of cartridge, explain why this is so.

To reload a rifle or handgun cartridge one needs extremely precise, standardized equipment. If good results are to be achieved, the various stages of the operation must all be carried out with great care. And this is only possible with centre-fire bullets which are designed for reloading.

The trade supplies cases, primers, bullets and powder. But in many cases the enthusiast casts his bullets himself. For this he must have a gas or electric oven or melting-pot, and a calibre mould. The bullets obtained are calibrated on the press and greased with a special mixture of tallow and wax. The composition of the bullet is based not only on the calibre, or the shape of the bullet, but is also influenced by the velocity desired. Due quantities of tin or antimony are added to the pure lead. (It is obviously not possible to make jacketed bullets with this equipment.) The case must then be unprimed, cleaned, recalibrated, and the primer replaced. This is done with a press, often of the turret type, on which the dies of the calibre in question are placed. A

Lawrence no 8 saddle holster for rifle fitted with telescopic sight.

Bianchi's (USA) model 66 holster for the Colt .45 model 1911 A1 can be worn at will to left or right.

Lawrence (USA) no 79 Gunslinger II holster and belt.

Typically American, this Lawrence no 7 shoulder holster is one of the classic items of equipment of plain clothes police in the American gangster films.

The Bianchi 104 holster enables an automatic pistol to be carried cocked.

An American Civil War holster with belt and percussion cap pocket. The holster took all the percussion revolvers of the day (and their modern replicas) with 7.5in. barrels.

Bianchi 27 Break Front spring holster.

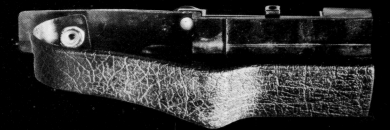

The Tayra Corporation Holster for the Colt Army Special revolver.

The Smith and Wesson rifle ammunition pouch.

The Smith and Wesson B36 swinging holster for the State Patrolman revolver with 4in. barrel, made by S. and W.

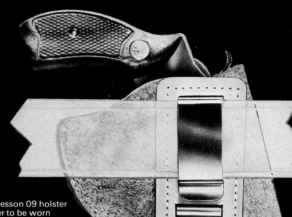

This Smith and Wesson 09 holster allows the revolver to be worn inside the trousers

French holster used by some plain clothes police officers to carry the MAC 50 automatic pistol.

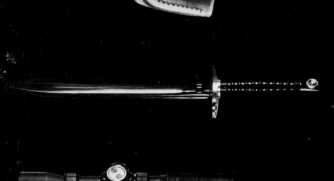

Accessories for the SIG 510–4 assault rifle supplied to the Chilean government.

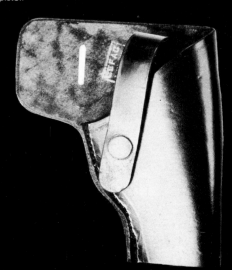

The Swedish Lathi automatic
pistol and service accessories.

The Parabellum 08/14 automatic
pistol with accessories.

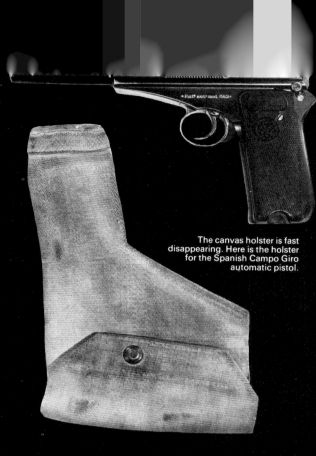

The canvas holster is fast
disappearing. Here is the holster
for the Spanish Campo Giro
automatic pistol.

chamber or cylinder type device, often placed on the turret of the press, enables one to measure the exact amount of powder. Lastly, a final operation will crimp the bullet, already in place in the neck of the case. In the USA there is a whole range of cunning implements suited to various presses, which make it possible to handle practically every calibre and, for example, trim cases which have been stretched by several reloadings.

Reloading charts help the enthusiast to select the right amount of powder on the basis of the weight and shape of the bullet. The Americans are still pastmasters when it comes to this type of equipment. The names of R.C.B.S. and Lyman come naturally to mind, although there are also Pacific and Ohaus, who are equally respected for the quality of their products. European manufacturers, headed by Norma of Sweden, follow the example of the Americans and offer good quality ammunition, which can be reloaded, as well as the necessary cases, primers, and bullets. Gévelot, RWS and DWM are strong in this respect. The Société Nationale des Poudres et Explosifs has drawn up a comparative table of French and American powders enabling the user with access to Lyman or Norma and others' loading tables to choose from the various products of the Société Nationale des Poudres et Explosifs. It is in this same spirit that the French company, Paris Sport, offers cases which are very easy to reload without special equipment as well as matching bullet moulds for making black-powder cartridges, which have not been on the market for many years, such as those used by the standard French 1873 and 1874 service revolvers in 11mm calibre, or relatively expensive ammunition like the .44-40 Winchester or the .45 Colt. If legislation does not harden its restrictive policy, thus prohibiting reloading 'at home', a bright future is in store for this activity.

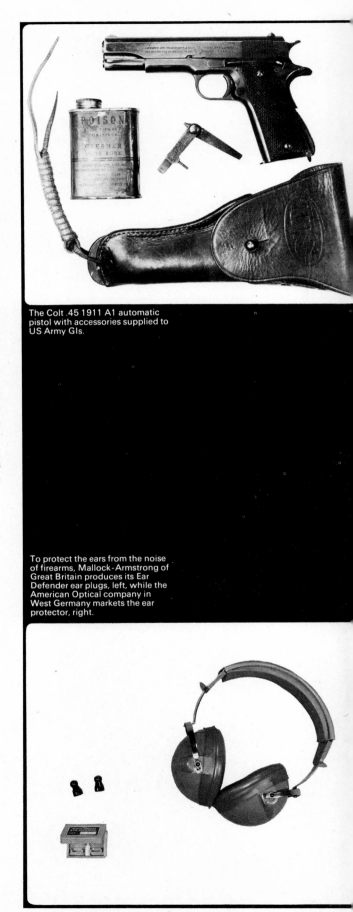

The Colt .45 1911 A1 automatic pistol with accessories supplied to US Army GIs.

To protect the ears from the noise of firearms, Mallock-Armstrong of Great Britain produces its Ear Defender ear plugs, left, while the American Optical company in West Germany markets the ear protector, right.

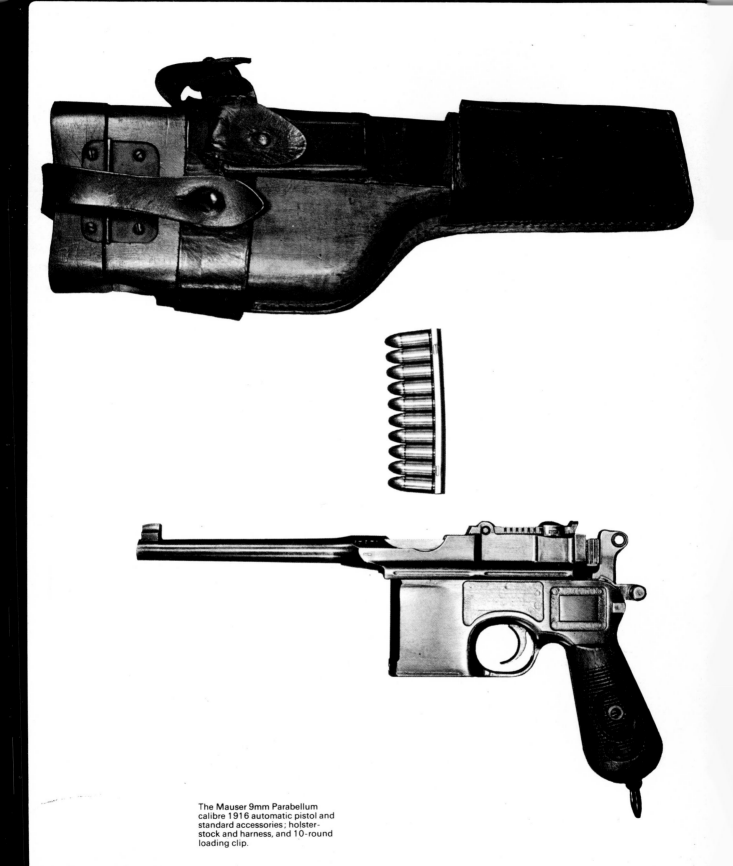

The Mauser 9mm Parabellum
calibre 1916 automatic pistol and
standard accessories; holster-
stock and harness, and 10-round
loading clip.

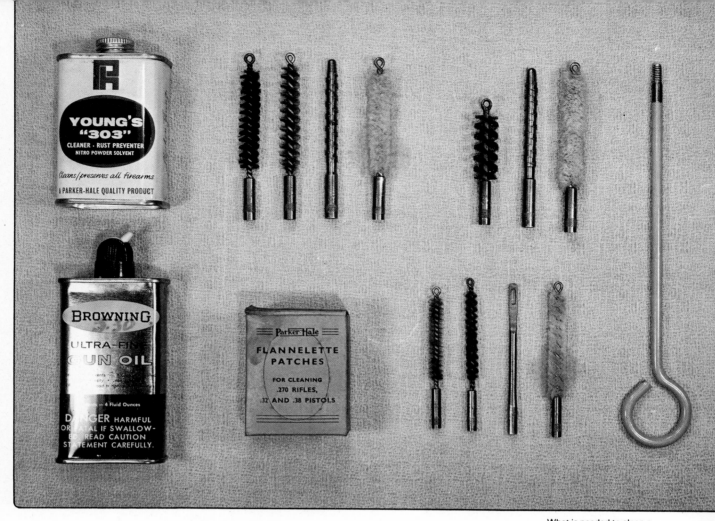

What is needed to clean a handgun, by Parker-Hale. From left to right and top to bottom: cleaning-brushes and extractors for .38 or 9mm calibres, .45 and .22 LR.

Made in Finland by Suomi and marketed in Sweden by Husqvarna, this breech bolt stops anyone using the gun who does not have the key.

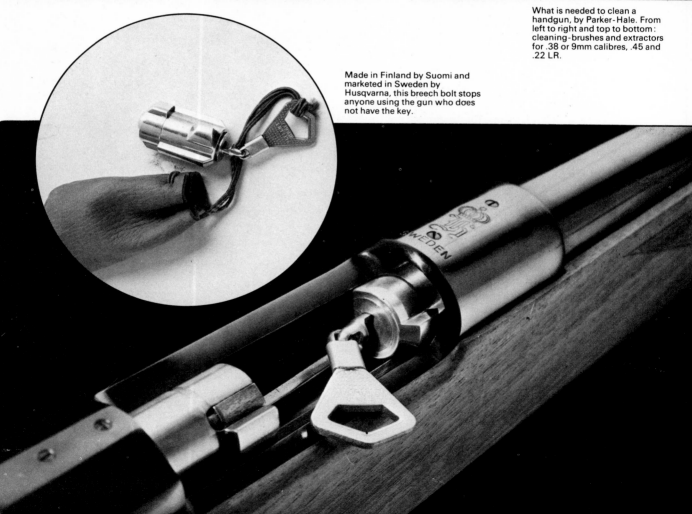

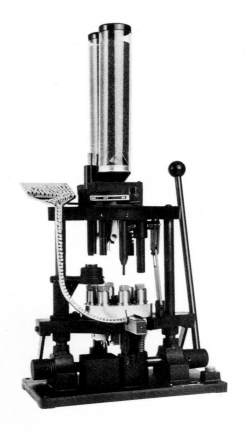

Ponsness-Warren Du-O-Matic 375 reloader for shot shells.

Ponsness-Warren Mult-O-Matic 600 reloader for shot shells.

Ponsness-Warren Size-O-Matic 800 B reloader for shot shells.

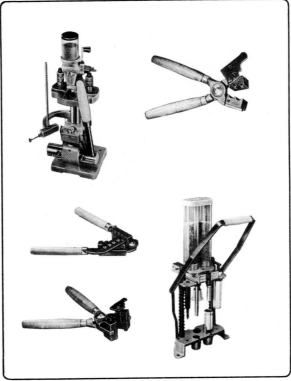

Top: Pacific DI-105 reloader for shot shells. Below: Pacific Deluxe Powder Measure.

Lyman reloading accessories: turret reloading press with interchangeable dies enabling reloading of rifle and revolver cartridges as well as shot shells (top left); bullet moulds enabling simultaneous casting of one, two or four lead bullets; the production of jacketed bullets is not possible with these moulds which exist in virtually every calibre (top right and below left); reloading turret for shot shells only available in 12, 16, 20 and 28 gauge (below right).

Above: Pacific Power C reloading press for metal cartridges; below: Pacific Durachrome dies in .300 Winchester Magnum calibre.

notes

●●

1 **Heckler and Koch VP 70 automatic pistol** (page 29)
This gun, which was to have been put on the market in 1973, embodies nearly all the requirements of modern military authorities, not least because of its cost, which the manufacturers have tried to keep as low as possible, and also because of its double-action lock, 18-round clip and the addition of a holster-stock giving shoulder-fire and 3-round bursts.

2 **7.65mm calibre Parabellum 1900 automatic pistol** (page 42)
3000 such guns were supplied to Switzerland as an initial contract, as evidenced by the Swiss cross against a radiant sun engraved on the top of the chamber.

3 **Parabellum 1900, American Eagle** (page 42)
This was imported to the United States by Steeger and bore the American emblem engraved on top of the chamber.

4 **Smith and Wesson 40 Centennial revolver** (page 56)
This short-barrel gun has double action only. It is the only revolver in the Smith and Wesson range to have a grip safety. It is one of the favourite guns of American plain clothes policemen.

5 **Smith and Wesson Victory revolver** (page 58)
.38 rounds can be used in this 4in. barrel gun (10cm). Some models, destined for the US Department of Justice, have a 2in. barrel (5cm).

6 **W. G. Target revolver** (page 59)
After being put on the market in 1889, it subsequently became the 1892 model, then the 1893 model, and finally the 1896 model (see photo). Pitted against the Colt Target, Colt Bisley and Smith and Wesson no 3 Target, it nevertheless remained one of the best made models in the range of Webley revolvers with its 7.5in. (19cm) barrel and laterally adjustable sight. It used the .455 Webley, standard British ammunition.

7 **Webley-Fosbery 1902 revolver** (page 59)
This revolver uses barrel recoil to rotate the cylinder by means of zigzag slots cut round it. Although this gun never became a standard issue, many of His Majesty's officers carried it at their own expense during World War I.

8 **Enfield no 2 Mark I revolver** (page 59)
The British army adopted this revolver as a standard issue in 1932 in its original form with a single-action lock. It became the no 2 Mark I in 1938, when the hammer spur had been eliminated as well as the full-cock notch, thus giving double-action fire. A second modification to the hammer in 1942 gave rise to the no 2 mark I.

9 **Webley and Scott WS Army revolver** (page 59)
Like earlier Webleys, this had a double-action lock and chambered the standard .455 Webley round.

10 **Mauser 'Schnellfeuer' sub-machine-gun** (page 76)
Only the types of sight used distinguish guns chambering the 7.63mm Mauser round (50–1000m) and those chambering the 9mm Parabellum round (50–500m).

11 **Examples of FN engraving** (page 136)
FN offers fifteen types of engraving for its over-under Browning; they are listed in alpha-numerical order from A2, the most simple, to D5, the most intricate, which is shown in the photo.

12 **Hi-Standard 10B shotgun** (page 142)
Although having a 12 gauge with a 5-round capacity, this extra-short weapon (69cm) is more for police than hunting use. It has an optional adaptor for firing tear-gas grenades and a detachable spotlight, the field of which corresponds to the cone of dispersion.

13 **Falcor over-under model** (page 154)
In its production range, Manufrance offers its Falcor over-under in several variants:
with extractor, double trigger;
with automatic ejector, double trigger;
with automatic ejector, MF double action trigger;
with automatic ejector, single selective trigger.
All these variants are fitted with a 70cm barrel and chambered for 12 gauge. In the same range Manufrance offers its Falcor Sport with interchangeable

barrels: one of 66cm, improved cylinder, and 1/4 choke for skeet and moving target; the other 74cm, full and half-choke for trap and field. The Falcor Sport has an automatic ejector, single selective trigger and extendable butt plate. All these guns are chambered solely for 12 gauge ammunition with a 70mm chamber.

14 **BSA Monarch carbine** (page 154)
This gun is marketed in the following calibres: .222, .243, .308 (7.62mm NATO), .30-06 US Army and 7mm Magnum. The trigger is adjustable.

bibliography

In English:

Belford, J. N. & Dunlap, J.
The Mauser Self-loading Pistol Borden Publishing Co.
Boothroyd, G. *The Handgun Cassell*
Breathed, J. W. & Schroeder, J. J. *System Mauser*
Handgun Press
Chinn, G. M. *The Machine Gun* (USMC)
Haven, C. T. & Belden, F. A.
A History of the Colt Revolver Bonanza
Madis, G. *The Winchester Book*
Art and Reference House
Musgrave, D. D. *The World's Assault Rifles*
T.B.N. Enterprises
Neal, R. J. & Jenks, R. J. *Smith & Wesson 1857–1945*
A. S. Barnes & Co.
Nelson, Thomas B. *The World's Submachine Guns*
T.B.N. Enterprises
Peterson, H. L.
The Remington Historical Treasury of American Guns
Thomas Nelson & Sons
Smith, W. H. B. *The Book of Pistols and Revolvers*
Stackpole
Smith, W. H. B. *Small Arms of the World* Stackpole
Watrous, G. *The History of Winchester Fire Arms*
Winchester Arms Books
Williamson, H. F. *Winchester* A. S. Barnes & Co.

In French

Boudriot, J. & Marquiset, R. *L'arme à feu*
Burnand, T. *La chasse* Denoël
Cadiou, Y. *Monsieur Winchester* Balland
Caranta, R. & Cadiou, Y.
Le guide des collectionneurs d'armes de poing Crépin-Leblond
Caranta, R. *L'arme de défense* Balland
Caranta, R. & Cantegrit, P.
L'aristocratie du pistolet Balland
Josserand, M.
Les pistolets, les revolvers et leurs munitions Crépin-Leblond

In German

Heer, E.
Die Faustfeuerwaffen von 1850 bis zur Gegenwart
Akademische Druk Verlagsanstal
Lockhoven, H. B. *Feuerwaffen von 1300 bis 1967*
International Small Arms Publicat.
Catalogue no 3, 1904, of the Deutsche Waffen und
Munitionsfabriken

In Italian

Simone, G., Belogi, R. & Grimaldi, A. *Il 91*

acknowledgements

We should like to reiterate our thanks to all those people who, by their kind cooperation, have made this book possible, and in particular General Pietro Roggero, Director of the National Artillery Museum of Turin (Italy), Colonel Wemaere, Curator of the Musée de l'Armée in Paris, Captain Jean-Claude Fidel, head of historical information department of the Foreign Legion, Tibor Szecsko, in charge of the Foreign Legion Museum at Aubagne (France), H. J. Woodend, head of the Pattern Room, Enfield (Great Britain), P. F. Hediger of the Hämmerli company (Switzerland), and Hochuli, of the Société Industrielle Suisse (SIG) (Switzerland), all of whom allowed us to consult the magnificent gun collections in their charge, a certain number of models from which appear in this book. We should also like to thank Michel Carrega, silver medallist at the last Olympic Games in Munich, and several times French, European and world trap and skeet champion, who has also given us his assistance. Madame Gisèle Lecourtier, silver medallist in the standard pistol event at the European championships in Belgrade, several times French champion and French women's record-holder, allowed herself to be used as the model for a certain number of action photos; we should like to extend our thanks to her as well.

Our thanks also go to those who have already helped us with our previous publications: Raymond Caranta, co-author of the *Guide des collectionneurs d'armes de poing* (Handgun Collectors' Guide), Jean Jordanoglou, who has been responsible for the drawings, diagrams and photographic retouching, Paul Frache, gunsmith in Marseilles, who allowed us to photograph from his collection, Max Gerin, of the Diacolor company, who carried out the laboratory work for the colour plates, and Messrs Edgard Allouche, André Caspari, Georges Cedou, Antoine Flory, Dr Edmond Gastaud, Madame Maryse Jedrey, Messrs Louis Perrot, Gabriel Jean Sumeire and André Gœury who assisted in various ways with the publication of this book.

We must also mention, in alphabetical order, all the various world experts in the field of firearms who have helped us in our task: the Hon. Richard Beaumont, chairman and managing-director of James Purdey and Sons (Great Britain), Messrs Robert W. Behn of the Marlin Firearms Company (USA), Giancarlo Bernardelli of the Vincenzo Bernardelli company (Italy), John Bianchi, president of the Bianchi Holster Co. (USA), J. J. H. Clowes, of Holland and Holland (Great Britain), Thomas Cotton, of Heckler und Koch (West Germany), Fred Datig, well-known gunsmith and historian (Switzerland), Kristin P. Driscoll of the Ithaca Gun Co. (USA), V. Fresi, of the Mauser Jagdwaffen company (West Germany), Roger Gaussen, of Gévelot (France), Raymond Gérand, Paris importer, Grassdorf, of J. G. Anschütz GmbH (West Germany), Ugo Gussalli, of P. Beretta (Italy), R. Gustafson, of Thompson/Center Arms (USA), Haine, Curator of the Imperial War Museum (Great Britain), Fred Huntington, president of RCBS (USA), Thomas E. Hall, Curator of the Winchester Gun Museum (USA), Eugene Heer, Curator of the Institut suisse d'armes anciennes (Switzerland) (Swiss Institute of Ancient Firearms), Peter Hoffman, of Carl Walther Sportwaffenfabrik (West Germany), Louis Humbert, importer in Saint-Etienne.

Our thanks also to Roy J. Jenks, author of *Smith and Wesson (1857–1945)* and Smith and Wesson historian (USA), Mrs Patricia A. Keegan, of Winchester International (USA), Messrs F. R. Marburger, president of the Tayra Corporation (USA), Burton T. Miller, of Armalite (USA), W. J. Myres, president of the S. D. Myres Saddle Co. (USA), Roll C. Nordholm, of FFV Sport AB (Sweden), Per Olai, of A. B. Gumelius (Sweden), Yves Ragougneau, president of Winchester Europe in Paris, C. M. Rhodes, of Winchester International (USA), Robinson, Master of the Armouries at the Tower of London (Great Britain), N. Ruder, director of the Single Point Company (Great Britain), Friedrich Schober, of Heckler und Koch GmbH (West Germany), Mrs Margareta Sewerin, of the Viking Sports Arms Co. (Sweden), Messrs Austin Sheridan, of the Leisure Group Co. (USA), J. D. Tate, of the Redfield Company (USA), P. Touche, of Gévelot Marseille (France), A. Uria, manager of the Manufacture d'Armes des Pyrénées Françaises (Unique), Nicolo Vital, Curator of the Altes Zeughaus at Solothurn (Switzerland), Stephen K. Vogel, president of Sturm, Ruger and Co. Inc. (USA), Charles E. Warren, president of Ponsness-Warren Inc. (USA), Leni Weirauch, of Hermann Weirauch OHG (West Germany), M. J. Willis of the Imperial War Museum (Great Britain), as well as the head of the publicity division of the Fabrique Nationale de Herstal (Belgium). We are also well aware that it is with the help of the following companies and organizations, who have supplied us with a great deal of technical information as well as numerous photographs, that we have been able to both document and illustrate certain sections of the book so thoroughly; our special thanks to them:

WEST GERMANY

J. G. Anschütz GmbH, Heckler und Koch GmbH, H. Krieghoff OHG, Mauser Jagdwaffen GmbH, Carl Walther Sportwaffenfabrik and Hermann Weirauch GmbH.

EAST GERMANY

Merkel GmbH, and Simson.

BELGIUM

The Fabrique Nationale de Herstal.

SPAIN

Astra Unceta y Compania SA, Llama-Gabilondo y Compania SA, and Star Bonifacio Echeverria SA.

UNITED STATES OF AMERICA

Armalite Inc., Bianchi Holster Co., Hi-Standard Manufacturing Co., Ithaca Gun Co., George Lawrence Co., The Leisure Group, Lyman, Ponsness-Warren Inc., Marling Firearms Co., S. D. Myres Saddle Co., RCBS Co., Redfield, Remington Arms Co., Smith and Wesson, Sturm, Ruger and Co. Inc., Tayra Corporation, Thompson/Center Arms Co., Universal Firearms Corporation, W. R. Weaver Co., Winchester Gun Museum, and Winchester International.

FRANCE

Agédic (Paris), le Comptoir international chasse et de sport (Saint-Etienne) (hunting and sporting guns), Gévelot, Paris, la Manufacture d'Armes des Pyrénées Françaises (Unique, Hendaye), the Manufacture de Machines du Haut-Rhin (Manurhin, Mulhouse), Manufrance (Saint-Etienne), the Musée de l'Armée (Paris), the Musée de la Légion étrangère (Aubagne), the historical information department of the Foreign Legion, Société Raymond Gérand (Paris), and Winchester Europe.

GREAT BRITAIN

Holland and Holland, Imperial War Museum, James Purdey and Sons, Royal Small Arms Factory, Single Point, the Tower of London, and Webley and Scott Ltd.

ITALY

Fabbrica d'armi Pietro Beretta SpA, Fabbrica d'armi Vincenzo Bernardelli SpA, Euroarms, the National Artillery Museum at Turin, and Armi Perazzi SpA.

SWEDEN

A. B. Gumelius, FFV Sport AB, Husqvarna, and Viking Sports Arms Co.

SWITZERLAND

Altes Zeughaus at Solothurn, Hämmerli, the Institut suisse d'armes anciennes, and Société industrielle suisse SIG.

We would ask those omitted from this list to bear with us.

photographic credits

Page 6: Max Mühlberger
Page 93: Keystone Press
Page 126: Reginald Davis-Gamma
(left above); Gamma (right above);
Gilles Caron-Gamma
(left centre); Keystone Press
(right centre); Gamma (bottom)
Page 127: Gamma (left above);
Gilles Caron-Gamma (centre above);
Gamma (right above); Gamma
(left centre); Roger Viollet
(right centre);
Gilles Caron-Gamma (bottom)

index of illustrations